Professional Development Study Guide 2013

Derived from the Professional Development Guide (AFPAM 36-2241)
Effective 1 Oct 2013

Prepare for:
**The Promotion Fitness Examination (PFE) and
The United States Air Force Supervisory Examination (USAFSE)**

Copyright © 2013 Computer and Administrative Solutions, LLC. All Rights Reserved.

All rights reserved. No part of this publication may be reproduced or transmitted in any form or by any means, electronic or mechanical, without prior written consent from the publisher. This includes photocopy, recording, or any information storage and retrieval system.

The views expressed in this book are those of Computer and Administrative Solutions, LLC and do not reflect the official policy or position of the United States Air Force, Defense Department, or the United States Government. No copyrights are claimed on material created by the United States Government.

3nd Edition, 1st Printing 2013

Published by:
MENTOR ENTERPRISES, INC.

121 Castle Dr. STE F
Madison, AL 35758
256.830.8282
info@MentorEnterprisesInc.com

Cover design by Matthew Dail

Disclaimer

This product is designed to provide a source of information concerning the subject matter. It is sold with the understanding that the Computer and Administrative Solutions, LLC and its employees, agents, authors, distributors, officers, publishers, attorneys, assigns, successor parent companies, members, or any other associated entity and/or its affiliates are not providing any legal or any other type of professional service. If legal services/opinions or any other type of professional service is required, the reader should seek guidance from a competent professional. It is also understood that the above mentioned individuals and entities shall in no way be held liable (including, without limitation, any and all compensatory, special, general, punitive, and/or statutory damages of any kind), fees, penalties, cost or expenses arising out of the use or the inability to use the product. Furthermore it is understood that the individuals or entities previously mentioned cannot be held liable for any compensatory, special, direct, indirect, incidental, consequential damages, exemplary damages however caused, whether for negligence, breach of contract, warranty, or otherwise. No individual or entity mentioned above previously assumes or can be held legally liable or responsible for the accuracy or completeness of this product. It is further understood and agreed that the terms and conditions set here in supersede any other agreement or understanding concerning access to any product of Computer and Administrative Solutions, LLC through direct or indirect access.

The content of this product is a compilation of information from public domain information (the formatting of which is copyrighted), and the personal (copyrighted) experience of the numerous contributors, and editors. The samples in this product are suggestions, not exact models. Readers should consult regulatory guides for specifics and staff agencies as required. This product is a guide! It does not in any way take precedence over military regulation or local policies and procedures. In all cases, for the purpose of this product, military regulations, local policies, and orders, are considered the governing sources concerning the subject matter. Readers are encouraged to read all relevant material covering the subject involved.

Every effort was made to ensure that this product was complete and accurate at the time of printing. It is possible that mistakes may be found both in content and typography. This product should be used only as a guide and not as the source or ultimate authority.

The purpose of the product is to educate and entertain only. The authors, agents, editors, or publisher shall have no liability or responsibility to any person or entity concerning loss/damage alleged, to be caused or caused by any means directly or indirectly by the information in this product.

No warranty is made or implied with regard to the completeness, and/or correctness, legal effect, or validity, of this product in any state or jurisdiction. It is further understood that any person or entity that utilizes this product does so at their own risk with full knowledge that they have a legal obligation, duty, and responsibility to ensure the information they provide is in accordance with up to date military law, procedure, regulation, policy, or order. No part of this product shall in anyway substitute for professional guidance or expertise on a subject.

Terms of Use

By using this product you understand that this product is for individual use only, in accordance with the non-exclusive license to use as described herein. It is specifically understood that there shall be no duplication or copying in any medium, redrafting, republishing, or reengineering of the material to create a similar derivative product, unless such product or derivative product is strictly for the individual use of the person or entity who purchased the original license (product) to use.

Note

In this product the term "commander" refers to commanders at all levels. Some commanders have different types of authority. The local policy on the authority of a commander should be checked in your area. In addition, any reference to the term "he" should be understood to include both genders.

We encourage and welcome comments, suggestions, ideas, or questions at: Info@MentorEnterprisesInc.com

All material will be reviewed for possible use in future printings. Please provide your mailing address and phone number with your correspondence.

How to Use This Book

Welcome to the key that fits the lock of your professional future. This book aims to help you prepare for the PFE or the USAFSE. Begin at Chapter 1 and work your way through, or jump to a section that contains material that you are not comfortable with or need some brushing up on. Either way—it is your tool. Use it to succeed.

Example Entry:
Questions are written in bold type. The questions have been generated directly from the PDG.

The answers and references follow directly below in a lighter italic type face. The page numbers correspond with the page on which the answer can be found in the PDG itself.

Contents

Chapter 1
Enlisted History — 1
- Milestones of World War I 1
- Milestones of World War II 1
- The Cold War (1948-1991) 2
- The Berlin Airlift (1948-1949) 2
- The Korean War (1950-1953) 2
- Cuban Missile Crisis (1962) 3
- The War in Southeast Asia (1950-1975) 3
- The Air War Expands (1965-1968) 3
- Vietnamization and Withdrawal (1969-1973) 3
- Humanitarian Airlift 4
- Post-Vietnam Conflicts 4
- Gulf War I (1990) 4
- Operations Provide Comfort and Northern Watch, Iraq (1991-2003) 5
- Operation Southern Watch, Iraq (1992-2003) ... 5
- Operations Provide Relief, Impressive Lift, and Restore Hope - Somalia (1992-1994) 6
- Operation Uphold Democracy, Haiti (1994) 6
- Operation Provide Promise, Sarajevo and Bosnia-Herzegovina (1992-1996) 6
- Operation Deny Flight, Bosnia (1993-1995) 6
- Operation Allied Force, Kosovo (1999) 7
- Operations Noble Eagle and Enduring Freedom .. 7
- Operation Anaconda 7
- Operation Iraqi Freedom 7
- Iraq and Afghanistan 8

Chapter 2
Airman Heritage — 9
- Introduction 9
- Before the Airplane - Military Ballooning ... 9
- Aeronautical Division, US Army Signal Corps (1907-1914) 9
- Aviation Section, US Army Signal Corps (1914-1918) 10
- World War I (WWI) (1917-1918) 10
- Division of Military Aeronautics and the Air Service (1918-1926) 11
- Army Air Corps (1926-1947) 11
- World War II (WWII) (1939-1945) 11
- A Separate Service (1947) 12
- The War in Southeast Asia (1950-1973) 12
- Post Vietnam to Present (1973-Present) 12
- Medal of Honor Recipients 12
- Air Force Cross Recipients 13
- Enlisted Pilot Program 13

Chapter 3
Organization — 15
- Overview 15
- Command Authority, Commander in Chief 15
- Department of Defense (DoD) 15
- Department of Defense (DoD), Secretary of Defense 15
- Department of Defense (DoD), Chairman, Joint Chiefs of Staff 15
- Department of Defense (DoD), Joint Chiefs of Staff 16
- Department of Defense (DoD), Joint Staff 16
- Department of Defense (DoD), Unified Combatant Commands and Combined Commands 16
- Department of Defense (DoD), Combined Commands 16
- Department of Defense (DoD), Military Departments 17
- Department of the Air Force, Secretary of the Air Force (SECAF) 17

Department of the Air Force, Chief of Staff, U.S. Air Force 17
Department of the Air Force, Air National Guard (ANG) 17
Department of the Air Force, Air Staff 17
Department of the Air Force Headquarters U.S. Air Force (HQ USAF) 18
Department of the Air Force, Field Units 18
Department of the Air Force, Lower Levels of Command 20
Wing Organization, Lower Levels of Command 21
Wing Organization, Air Reserve Component (ARC) 22

Chapter 4
Air Force Doctrine, Air and Space Expeditionary Force (AEF), and Joint Doctrine   **23**
Overview 23
Air Force Doctrine 23
Air and Space Expeditionary Force 27
AEF Temp Bands 27
The Joint Force 27
Operational and Administrative Chain of Command 28
Joint and Coalition Capabilities 30
Joint Operation Planning and Execution System (JOPES) 30

Chapter 5
Emergency Management Program   **31**
Overview 31
Emergency Management Program Operation 31
Incident Management 31
Peacetime Airbase Threats 31
CBRNE Enemy Attack and Terrorist Use of CBRNE Material Threats 32

Chapter 6
Standards of Conduct   **35**
Law of Armed Conflict (LOAC) 35
Code of Conduct 37
Everyday Conduct 38
Ethics and Conflict of Interest Prohibitions 39
Political Activities 40

Chapter 7
Enforcing Standards and Legal Issues   **41**
The Air Force Inspection System 41
Inspector General Complaints Program 41
Individual Standards 41
Punitive Actions 42
Legal Issues 46

Chapter 8
Military Customs, Courtesies, and Protocol for Special Events   **49**
Overview 49
Symbols 49
Professional Behavior 50
Drill and Ceremony 52
Honor Guard 53
Protocol 58
Distinguished Visitors (DV) 58
Military Ceremonies 58

Chapter 9
Enlisted Force Development   **59**
Overview 59
The Enlisted Force Structure 59
Enlisted Professional Military Education (EPME) 64

Military Ethics 65
Enlisted Force Development... 65
The Profession of Arms—An Airman's Perspective 66
Personal Professionalism 66

Chapter 10
Leadership   69
Overview.. 69
Leadership 69
Followership.. 71
Mentoring... 72
Development Counseling 72
Full Range Leadership Development 75
Mentorship... 75
Conflict Management 76
Unit Morale 76
Strategic Leadership 77

Chapter 11
The Enlisted Evaluation System (EES)   79
Overview.. 79
Individual Responsibilities 79
Performance Feedback... 79
Enlisted Performance Reports... 81

Chapter 12
Training and Education   91
Overview.. 91
Training Management 91
Community College of the Air Force (CCAF).. 92
Education 92

Chapter 13
Resource Management   95
Managing Organizational Change 95
Traits of a Healthy Team 95
Problem Solving 96
Managing Resources Other than Personnel 97
Planning, Programming, Budgeting, and Execution (PPBE) 98
Government Property and Equipment... 99
Facility Management 99
Energy Conservation Program 100

Chapter 14
Communicating in Today's Air Force   101
Overview.. 101
Communication Basics 101
Seven Steps for Effective Communication 101
Step 1 - Analyze, Purpose and Audience.. 101
Step 2 - Research Your Topic 102
Step 3 - Support Your Ideas 102
Step 4 - Organize and Outline 102
Step 5 - Draft... 103
Step 6 - Edit the Draft 103
Step 7 - Fight for Feedback 103
Writing 103
Face-to-Face: Speaking and Listening.. 104
Electronic Communications and the Internet 107

Conducting an Effective Interview 107
Staff-Level Communication 108
Instruments of Written Communication 108

Chapter 15
Personnel Programs   *111*
Manpower Management 111
Enlisted Assignments 111
Family Care 112
Reenlistment and Retraining Opportunities 112
Benefits and Services 113
Personnel Records and Individual Rights 116
Awards and Decorations 116
Airman Promotion System 116
SNCO Promotion Program 120
Commercial Services Management (CSM) 124
Civilian Personnel Management and Programs 124

Chapter 16
Wing Support   *127*
Air Force Portal 127
Military Pay, Allowances, and Entitlements 127
Leave Management 129
Equal Opportunity (EO) 130
Legal Services 131
Ground Safety 131
Risk Management (RM) 131
Sexual Assault 132

Chapter 17
Dress and Appearance   *135*
Dress and Appearance 135

Chapter 18
Fit Force   *139*
Overview 139
Physical Fitness and Fitness Components 139
Nutrition 141
Nutrients 141
Substance Abuse 141
Tobacco Use 142
Medical Care 142
Suicide Prevention 143
Stress Management 144
Redeployment Support Process 145

Chapter 19
Security   *147*
Information Assurance 147
Installation Security 147
Antiterrorism (AT) Program 149

Abbreviations & Acronyms   *151*
Terms   *159*

Chapter 1
Enlisted History

Milestones of World War I

How many of the 24 squadrons planned in October of 1916 were fully equipped, manned, and organized when the United States declared war on Germany on April 6, 1917?
One
Pg 18, 1.2.2

What was the chief complaint General Staff Officers had about air personnel during World War I?
They refused to wear their cavalry spurs while flying airplanes
Pg 18, 1.2.3

What type of trained enlisted personnel did the Aviation Section realize they needed most of all?
Mechanics
Pg 18, 1.2.4

Where were the two largest special schools and training institutions located during World War I?
St Paul, Minnesota and Kelly Field in Texas
Pg 18, 1.2.4

Which enlisted men were usually the first stationed at overseas locations?
Construction personnel
Pg 18, 1.2.5

Milestones of World War II

How much money did President Franklin D. Roosevelt ask to be appropriated in 1939 for military aviation?
$300 million dollars
Pg 18, 1.3

What happened to training centers from 1939 until 1941?
Private schools
Pg 19, 1.3.1.2

Where did the Army officials turn for help when they could not keep up with expanding training centers during 1939-1941?
Visual, auditory, or tactile/kinesthetic
Pg 19, 1.3.1.2

How many enlisted Airmen served in the Army Air Forces during World War II?
More than 2 million
Pg 19, 1.3.2.1

How many people did it take to support a bomber during World War II?
It is estimated it took approximately 70 people for one airplane
Pg 19, 1.3.2.3

The Women's Army Auxiliary Corps (WAAC) was created in May of what year?
1942
Pg 19, 1.3.2.4

What was the top priority assignment of WAACs?
To serve at aircraft warning stations
Pg 19, 1.3.2.4

Some Commanders were reluctant to accept women into their units. What happened in mid-1943 that changed their mind?
The demand for them far exceeded the numbers available
Pg 19, 1.3.2.4

When did the Air Force become a distinct service?
1947
Pg 19, 1.3.2.5

What was the result of restricting black Airmen to serve in all-black units or in segregated service squads?
It was robbing the Air Force of a major talent pool
Pg 19, 1.3.2.5

Enlisted History 1

What did Air Force Letter 35.3 mandate for black Airmen?
They be screened for reassignment to formerly all-white units
Pg 19, 1.3.2.5

What happened within one year of the integration of the entire Air Force?
It was successful and almost without incident
Pg 19, 1.3.2.5

When the Third Reich surrendered in May 1945 the American forces then turned their full attention against which nation?
Japan
Pg 19, 1.3.2.6

What types of bombs were dropped on Hiroshima and Nagasaki Japan in 1945?
Nuclear
Pg 20, 1.3.2.7

What were the names of the flights that dropped the nuclear bombs in Japan?
Enola Gay and Bock's Car
Pg 20, 1.3.2.7

The Cold War (1948-1991)

Who were known as the Big Three?
Winston Churchill, Josef Stalin, and President Franklin D. Roosevelt
Pg 20, 1.4

Who was responsible for laying the foundation of what became the United Nations (UN)?
The Big Three (Churchill, Stalin, & Roosevelt)
Pg 20, 1.4

What issue did the UN bring up in 1946?
Controlling nuclear weapons
Pg 20, 1.4

What country vetoed the plan to eliminate nuclear weapons?
The Soviet Union
Pg 20, 1.4

How many years of the Cold War resulted from the Soviet Union vetoing the elimination of nuclear weapons?
Almost 50 years
Pg 20, 1.4

The Berlin Airlift (1948-1949)

What did the allies do when the Soviet Union closed off all surface access to Berlin in 1948?
They built a Luftbrucke (an air bridge) into Berlin
Pg 20, 1.5.1

What military air cargo expert did the Air Force get to analyze the US airlift capabilities and requirements during World War II?
Major General William Tunner
Pg 20, 1.5.2

How long did Berlin receive the air bridge support?
For 15 months
Pg 20, 1.5.3

What was air power's single most decisive contribution to the Cold War?
The Berlin Airlift
Pg 20, 1.5.3

The Korean War (1950-1953)

On what date did North Korea invade South Korea igniting the Korean War?
25 June 1950
Pg 21, 1.6.1

What happened over Kimpo on June 27, 1950?
The first aerial combat between the United States and North Korea
Pg 21, 1.6.2

What happened on September 15, 1950 near Seoul South Korea?
US forces landed at Inchon cutting North Korean Army supply lines deep in the south, threatening its rear
Pg 21, 1.6.3

Who shot down the first MiG on November 9, 1950?
Cpl Harry LaVene
Pg 21, 1.6.4

What did Sergeant Billie Beach do on April 12, 1951?
Shot down two MiGs
Pg 21, 1.6.4

Cuban Missile Crisis (1962)

Who overthrew the dictator of Cuba in 1959 by initially promising free elections but instituted a socialist dictatorship instead?
Fidel Castro
Pg 21, 1.7.1

In 1960, President Eisenhower authorized the Central Intelligence Agency (CIA) to plan an invasion of Cuba using what tactic?
Cuban exiles as troops
Pg 21, 1.7.1

Who actually ordered the invasion at the Bay of Pigs?
President John F. Kennedy
Pg 22, 1.7.1

What was the outcome of the invasion at the Bay of Pigs?
The Cuban exiles suffered a crushing defeat
Pg 22, 1.7.1

What did the Soviet Union do after the failed invasion of Cuba in 1961?
Increased economic and military aid to Cuba
Pg 22, 1.7.2

What did the Soviets and Cubans begin constructing in 1962?
Intermediate and medium-range ballistic missile complexes on the island
Pg 22, 1.7.2

What steps did President Kennedy take instead of invading Cuba?
He imposed a naval blockade of the island
Pg 22, 1.7.4

The United States agreed to not invade Cuba in the early 1960s if what demand was met?
Removal of Soviet missiles from the island
Pg 22, 1.7.6

The Cuban Missile Crisis brought the world dangerously close to which event?
A nuclear war
Pg 22, 1.7.7

The War in Southeast Asia (1950-1975)

By 1952 in Vietnam, the United States was supplying one-third of what?
The cost of the French military effort
Pg 23, 1.8.1.2

The Air War Expands (1965-1968)

What happened on February 7, 1965 in Vietnam?
The Viet Cong attacked Camp Holloway killing eight Americans
Pg 23, 1.9.1

In response to the killing of eight Americans, what operation used a series of strikes against military barracks near Dong Hoi in North Vietnam and other targets?
Operation Flaming Dart
Pg 23, 1.9.1

What was the operation where the first sustained bombing campaign began against North Vietnam in 1965 and lasted until 1968?
Operation Rolling Thunder
Pg 23, 1.9.1

What did tail gunner SSgt Samuel Turner do in December 1972?
He shot down an enemy MiG
Pg 23, 1.9.2

Which positions on Gunships did enlisted personnel occupy?
Aerial gunners and loadmasters
Pg 23, 1.9.3

Vietnamization and Withdrawal (1969-1973)

Through 1963 and much of 1964, American forces operated under restrictive rules of engagement in an effort to maintain the U.S. role as air support only. True or false?
False
Pg 24, 1.10.1

In what mission did President Nixon order 11 days of intense bombing of Vietnamese cities?
Linebacker II
Pg 24, 1.10.3

When did the military draft end?
27 January 1973
Pg 24, 1.10.4

When did the last US troop leave Vietnam?
29 March 1973
Pg 24, 1.10.4

Humanitarian Airlift

When did the first known use of a US aircraft for humanitarian assistance occur?
An aircraft dropped food to victims of a Rio Grande flood in 1919
Pg 24, 1.11.1

What was the purpose of Operation Safe Haven I and II?
To airlift 10,000 Hungarian refugees to the United States
Pg 24, 1.11.3

What was the name of the operation where over 1,000 tons of material was airlifted to Chile after earthquakes, volcanic eruptions, avalanches, and tidal waves?
Amigos Airlift
Pg 24, 1.11.3

What four operations were involved in the largest aerial evacuation in history?
Babylift, New Life, Frequent Wind, and New Arrivals.
Pg 25, 1.11.4

Operation Provide Comfort provided more than 7,000 tons of blankets, tents, food, and medical workers to what area?
To Northern Iraq following the Persian Gulf War
Pg 25, 1.11.5

What operation airlifted 3,000 tons of supplies to Bangladesh following a typhoon in 1991?
Operation Sea Angel
Pg 25, 1.11.5

What country or countries did Operation Provide Hope provide 6,000 tons of food, medicine and cargo to?
The republics of the former Soviet Union
Pg 25, 1.11.5

Post-Vietnam Conflicts

What operation was to rescue hundreds of US citizens attending medical school on the island of Grenada?
Operation Urgent Fury
Pg 25, 1.12.1

What country was one of the leading sponsors of worldwide terrorism in the mid-1980s?
Libya
Pg 25, 1.12.2.1

Why did President Ronald Reagan authorize an air strike against Libya on April 9, 1986?
A large bomb gutted a discotheque in Berlin on April 5, 1986
Pg 25, 1.12.2.3

Why did Manuel Noriega order an attack of the US Embassy?
The US Senate issued a resolution for the Panamanians to oust him
Pg 26, 1.12.3.2

What was Manuel Noriega indicted for by a Miami federal grand jury in 1988?
Drug-trafficking and money-laundering
Pg 26, 1.12.3.2

When Manuel Noriega intensified his harassment against his own people and all Americans following an indictment by a Miami Federal Grand Jury, what did President George H.W. Bush do?
He decided to invade Panama
Pg 26, 1.12.3.2

What operation featured the first use of night vision goggles by Air Force personnel?
Operation Just Cause
Pg 26, 1.12.3.3

What happened to Manuel Noriega after Operation Just Cause?
He surrendered on January 3, 1990 and was flown to Miami FL to face trial
Pg 26, 1.12.3.4

Gulf War I (1990)

What nation did Saddam Hussein invade on August 2, 1990?
Kuwait
Pg 26, 1.13.1.1

After invading Kuwait in 1990, Iraq had the fourth largest army in the world and was on the door step of invading which country?
Saudi Arabia
Pg 26, 1.13.1.1

What was one of the main concerns if Saudi Arabia fell to Hussein in the 1990s?
Saddam Hussein would control over 50 percent of the world's oil
Pg 26, 1.13.1.1

The United States sought and received UN sanctions against Iraq and joined 27 other nations to launch what operation?
Operation Desert Shield
Pg 26, 1.13.1.2

What did President George H. W. Bush demand from Iraq in 1990?
The immediate withdrawal of Iraqi forces from Kuwait
Pg 26, 1.13.1.2

What did Saddam believe about the American public and war?
The American public did not have the stomach for war
Pg 26, 1.13.1.2

What date did Operation Desert Storm begin?
15 January 1991
Pg 26, 1.13.2

How long did it take to essentially win the air war of Desert Storm?
Within the first 24 hours
Pg 27, 1.13.2.2

What type of response did Saddam's troops have when the coalition forces began the ground assault in Desert Storm?
They were ready to surrender to the first allied troops they saw
Pg 27, 1.13.2.2

What is tank plinking?
The destruction of tanks on the ground one at a time
Pg 27, 1.13.2.2

What was the key to the air campaign success during Operation Desert Storm?
Maintenance
Pg 27, 1.13.2.3

How long did Desert Storm last?
43 days
Pg 27, 1.13.2.4

What is the significance of September 27, 1991?
The Cold War was officially over
Pg 27, 1.13.2.4

Operations Provide Comfort and Northern Watch, Iraq (1991-2003)

How many Kurds fled to Iran and Turkey in the early 1990s?
More than one million
Pg 27, 1.14.1

What operation did the UN Security Council authorize on April 3, 1991?
Operation Provide Comfort
Pg 27, 1.14.2

What happened in the Iraqi no-fly zone on April 14, 1994?
Two American F-15s accidentally shot down two UH-60 Black Hawk helicopters
Pg 27, 1.14.3

Operation Southern Watch, Iraq (1992-2003)

What operation established a no-fly zone in southern Iraq?
Operation Southern Watch
Pg 28, 1.15.1

What happened on December 27, 1992 in the no fly zone area during Operation Southern Watch?
F-16s shot down one Iraqi MiG-25 and chased a second aircraft back across the border
Pg 28, 1.15.2

The United States launched cruise missiles against Iraq to retaliate for a planned assassination of former US President George H. W. Bush. What was the target of this attack?
The Iraq Intelligence Service Headquarters in Baghdad
Pg 28, 1.15.3

What operation placed thousands of US Armed Forces into the theater due to Iraqi troops and elite Republican Guard units massing at the Kuwaiti border?
Operation Vigilant Warrior
Pg 28, 1.15.4

What concept did the United States Air Force test during Operation Southern Watch?
The Air and Space Expeditionary Force (AEF)
Pg 28, 1.15.4

How long did it take the AEF to begin flying after landing during Operation Southern Watch?
Within 12 hours
Pg 28, 1.15.4

How much of the Iraqi airspace fell into the no-fly zone when President Clinton expanded Southern Watch to the 33rd parallel?
Most of it
Pg 28, 1.15.5

When did Operation Southern Watch officially end?
26 August 2003
Pg 28, 1.15.6

Operations Provide Relief, Impressive Lift, and Restore Hope - Somalia (1992-1994)

What killed approximately 350,000 people in Somalia in 1992?
Famine
Pg 28, 1.16.1

What prevented much of the relief supplies from getting into the hands of those who most needed them during Operation Provide Relief?
Civil war and clan fighting within Somalia
Pg 28, 1.16.1

What operation airlifted hundreds of Pakistani soldiers under the UN banner into Somalia?
Operation Impressive Lift
Pg 28, 1.16.2

What operation was to establish order in the country of Somalia so that food could reach those in need?
Operation Restore Hope
Pg 28, 1.16.2

Operation Uphold Democracy, Haiti (1994)

Who offered a diplomatic proposal that persuaded the military leader in Haiti to relinquish his control in 1994?
Former President Carter
Pg 29, 1.17.1

What type of entry plan did the United States use for Operation Uphold Democracy in Haiti?
A passive-entry plan
Pg 29, 1.17.1

Operation Provide Promise, Sarajevo and Bosnia-Herzegovina (1992-1996)

Where did Operation Provide Promise airlift supplies to?
Sarajevo
Pg 29, 1.18.2

What operation provided 50 tons of toys, children's clothing, and shoes to Sarajevo in December 1993?
Operation Provide Santa
Pg 29, 1.18.4

Why did Operation Provide Promise flights get suspended by the UN for a week?
A United States C-130 suffered damage from an artillery shell at the Sarajevo airport
Pg 29, 1.18.4

Where was the peace accord for Sarajevo signed on December 14, 1995?
At Wright-Patterson AFB, OH
Pg 29, 1.18.5

Operation Deny Flight, Bosnia (1993-1995)

What operation imposed a no-fly zone over Bosnia in an effort to limit the war there?
Operation Deny Flight
Pg 29, 1.19.1

What historic event took place on February 28, 1994 in Bosnia?
NATO aircraft scored the first aerial combat victory in its 45-year history
Pg 29, 1.19.2

What did the Bosnian Serbs do after Operation Deny Flight aircraft struck a munitions depot in May 1995?
They took 370 UN soldiers hostage
Pg 30, 1.19.3

What operation served notice to Bosnian Serb forces that they would be held accountable for their actions?
Operation Deliberate Force
Pg 30, 1.19.4

What was different about the airstrikes during Operation Deliberate Force?
It marked the first campaign in aerial warfare where precision munitions outweighed conventional bombs
Pg 30, 1.19.4

Operation Allied Force, Kosovo (1999)

What did Serbian President Slobodan Milosevic say about the oppressing of ethnic Albanians?
He considered the matter an internal one
Pg 30, 1.20.1

NATO leaders hoped Slobodan Milosevic would give in after a few days of airstrikes. How long did it actually take?
78 days
Pg 30, 1.20.2

Operations Noble Eagle and Enduring Freedom

What was the President of the United States forced to do during the attacks of September 11, 2001?
Board Air Force One and seek a safe haven
Pg 30, 1.21.1

How long did it take the United States to respond with Operation Nobel Eagle after the attacks of September 11, 2001?
It began the same day as the attacks
Pg 30, 1.21.2

How many of the pilots flying Operation Noble Eagle belonged to the Air National Guard (ANG)?
More than 80 percent
Pg 30, 1.21.2

What operation was to provide a humanitarian airlift to the oppressed people of Afghanistan and to conduct military action to root out terrorists and their supporters?
Operation Enduring Freedom
Pg 31, 1.21.3

When did US, British, and French aircraft begin a sustained campaign against terrorist targets in Afghanistan?
7 October 2001
Pg 31, 1.21.3

Operation Anaconda

What other names were given to Operation Anaconda?
The press called it the battle at Shah-I-Kot Mountain
Pg 31, 1.22

What happened on 4 March 2002 at Takur Ghar?
al Qaeda soldiers fired on an MH-47E helicopter which caused a Navy SEAL to fall to the ground
Pg 31, 1.22

What was the death toll at Takur Ghar?
Seven US servicemen and all of the al Qaeda terrorists defending the mountaintop
Pg 31, 1.22

Operation Iraqi Freedom

How long of an ultimatum did President George W. Bush give Saddam Hussein on March 17, 2003?
48 hours
Pg 31, 1.23.1

What date did Operation Iraqi Freedom begin?
20 March 2003
Pg 31, 1.23.1

How devastating were the air strikes during Operation Iraqi Freedom?
So devastating they left Saddam's soldiers unable or unwilling to fight
Pg 31, 1.23.2

What was the name of the concept developed at National Defense University and used during Operation Iraqi Freedom?
Shock and Awe
Pg 31, 1.23.2

What did Shock and Awe focus on?
The psychological destruction of the enemy's will to fight rather than the physical destruction of the opposing military forces
Pg 31, 1.23.2

Who was the first Airman killed in Operation Iraqi Freedom?
SSgt Scott Sather
Pg 32, 1.23.3

What did jubilant crowds do in Baghdad when American commanders declared Saddam's regime was no longer in control?
They toppled a 40-foot statue of Saddam
Pg 32, 1.23.4

Iraq and Afghanistan

What medal did TSgt Kevin Whalen receive for his actions in Afghanistan?
Silver Star
Pg 32, 1.24.3

What is the deployment phase of Basic Military Training now called?
The Beast
Pg 32, 1.24.4

Who received one of the first Combat Action Medals and the Bronze Star with Valor for his actions in suppressing enemy fire?
SMSgt Ramon Colon-Lopez
Pg 33, 1.24.5

What happened to TSgt Bryan Patton and SSgt David Orvosh when they went to help Iraqi Police make an arrest?
They were ambushed
Pg 33, 1.24.7

Who called in a 500-lb laser-guided bomb in Najaf which hit only 100 meters from his location?
SSgt Ryan Wallace
Pg 33, 1.24.7

When was the troop withdrawal from Iraq completed?
18 December 2011
Pg 33, 1.24.9

The war in Afghanistan is the longest running war in the history of the United States. True or false?
True
Pg 34, 1.24.10

Many EOD warriors wounded by IEDs have decided to remain on Active Duty. True or false?
True
Pg 34, 1.24.12

Chapter 2
Airman Heritage

Introduction

In 1907, what were Cpl Edward Ward and Pvt Joseph E. Barrett told by their commanding officer they would learn how to do?
Inflate and repair balloons
Pg 35, 2.1

In a century, what has evolved from a fragile and uncertain curiosity into the most devastating weapon system in the history of humankind?
The airplane
Pg 35, 2.1

Before the Airplane - Military Ballooning

Who rose to a height of 1,400 feet in a balloon and was able to see for a 30 mile radius on July 31, 1861?
John La Mountain
Pg 35, 2.2.1

What was John La Mountain able to tell MG Benjamin Butler about the strength of the Confederate forces when he was in a balloon at 1,400 feet?
It was weaker than originally thought
Pg 35, 2.2.1

How much money did the War Department give Thaddeus Lowe for balloon demonstrations and transmission of a telegraph message from up in the air?
$250
Pg 35, 2.2.1.1

In 1896, William Ivy Baldwin and his wife built a 14,000 cubic foot silk balloon. What was the name of the balloon?
The Santiago
Pg 35, 2.2.1.2

What battle was the balloon Santiago used in during the Spanish-American war?
San Juan Hill
Pg 35, 2.2.1.2

What is believed by some historians concerning the use of the balloon Santiago for The Battle of San Juan Hill?
It was a determining factor in the victory of the battle
Pg 35, 2.2.1.2

When did the Wright brothers fly their heavier than air contraption at Kitty Hawk, North Carolina?
1903
Pg 36, 2.2.2.1

Who won the 1906 Gordon Bennett trophy in the first international balloon race from Paris, France to Flying Dales, England?
Lt Frank P. Lahm and Maj Henry P. Hersey
Pg 36, 2.2.2.1

Aeronautical Division, US Army Signal Corps (1907-1914)

When did the Aeronautical Division, US Army Signal Corps exist?
1907 to 1914
Pg 36, 2.3

How many people were assigned to the newly created US Army Signal Corps Aeronautical Division in August 1907?
Three
Pg 36, 2.3.1

Who was the Army's first enlisted pilot in 1912?
PFC Vernon Burge
Pg 36, 2.3.1

What happened in August 1908 at Fort Myers?
The Wright Brothers arrived with the US Army's first airplane
Pg 36, 2.3.2

Why did it seem to be a miracle that the US government purchased an airplane?
For more than four years after the successful flight at Kitty Hawk, the government refused to accept that man had flown in a heavier-than-air machine
Pg 36, 2.3.2

What was the name of the US Army's first plane?
Aeroplane No. 1
Pg 36, 2.3.3

Who tinkered with the first US airplane during the trial and training period?
The Wright brothers along with their own civilian mechanics
Pg 36, 2.3.3

What happened to Orville Wright and Lieutenant Thomas E. Selfridge on September 17, 1908?
They crashed
Pg 36, 2.3.3

What happened after the 1908 crash involving Orville Wright and Lt Selfridge?
Flying was suspended until the plane could be repaired and Orville could recover
Pg 36, 2.3.3

In what year did the Signal Corps formally accept Aeroplane No. 1?
1909
Pg 36, 2.3.3

Who was in charge of the first plane when part of the Division transferred to Fort Sam Houston in San Antonio, TX?
Lt Benjamin D. Foulois
Pg 36, 2.3.4

What did the US Air Force consist of when it arrived at Fort Sam Houston with Lieutenant Benjamin D. Foulois in 1910?
A pilot who had never taken off, landed, or soloed, one beat up and much patched airplane, a civilian aircraft mechanic, and 10 enlisted mechanics
Pg 36, 2.3.4

How did Lt Benjamin D. Foulois learn to fly?
He taught himself
Pg 36, 2.3.4

What type of system did Pvts Glenn Madole and Vernon Burge (along with a civilian mechanic) build?
A wheeled landing system to ease takeoff and relieve the strain of landing
Pg 36, 2.3.4

Who was the first enlisted person to die in an accident in a military aircraft?
Cpl Frank Scott
Pg 36, 2.3.5

What was named in honor of Cpl Frank Scott?
Scott Field (now Scott Air Force Base)
Pg 37, 2.3.5

Aviation Section, US Army Signal Corps (1914-1918)

When did the Aviation Section, US Army Signal Corps exist?
1914 to 1918
Pg 37, 2.4

US House Resolution 5304 was passed and provided Army aviation with official status. What date did the bill get passed?
18 July 1914
Pg 37, 2.4.1

What did US House Resolution 5304 provide enlisted men who were instructed in the art of flying?
A 50% pay increase while they were on flying status
Pg 37, 2.4.1

What order was given by President Woodrow Wilson to the 1st Aero Squadron in March 1916?
Protect the border and apprehend Pancho Villa
Pg 37, 2.4.2

What valuable lessons were learned about aviation under field conditions during the search for Pancho Villa?
Adequate maintenance was essential
Pg 37, 2.4.3

World War I (WWI) (1917-1918)

When did Americans begin flying in the European war?
1915
Pg 37, 2.5

What was Cpl Eugene Bullard known for?
Being the first African American pilot
Pg 37, 2.5.1

What award did Cpl Eugene Bullard receive as a member of the French Foreign Legion?
The Croix de Guerre
Pg 37, 2.5.1

What was Cpl Eugene Bullard's nickname?
Black Swallow of Death
Pg 38, 2.5.1

What did Sgt Fred C. Graveline receive The Distinguished Service Cross for?
His part in driving off almost two dozen German planes and shooting down two
Pg 38, 2.5.2

Division of Military Aeronautics and the Air Service (1918-1926)

Who was able to score two hits on targets when 10 other aircraft were unable to do so on September 5, 1923?
Sgt Ulysses Sam Nero
Pg 39, 2.6.2

Why did General Mitchell disqualify Sgt Nero from a competition after he had scored two hits on targets?
Sgt Nero used different tactics than General Mitchell had instructed.
Pg 39, 2.6.2

By the end of WWI, both the Army and the Navy planned to experiment with what?
Bombing enemy ships from the air
Pg 39, 2.6.4

What was the name of the German battleship that was sunk on July 21, 1921?
The Ostfriesland
Pg 39, 2.6.4

Where did Master electrician Jack Harding and SFC Jerry Dobias fly a Martin bomber in 1919?
Around the rim of the country
Pg 39, 2.6.5

How long did it take four DH-4Bs to fly 9,000 miles (round-trip) from Mitchell Field to Nome, Alaska in 1929?
3 months
Pg 39, 2.6.5

The safety record for the flight from Mitchell Field to Nome, Alaska in 1929 was largely attributable to which individuals?
MSgt Albert Vierra
Pg 39, 2.6.5

Who were the mechanics on the air service's around-the-world flight in 1924?
SSgts Alva Harvey and Henry Ogden
Pg 39, 2.6.5

Army Air Corps (1926-1947)

When did the Army Air Corps exist?
1926 to 1947
Pg 39, 2.7

What did Sgt Ralph Bottriell test?
The first backpack-style parachute
Pg 39, 2.7

World War II (WWII) (1939-1945)

When did World War II occur?
1939 to 1945
Pg 39, 2.8

What nickname did Cpl John D. Foley earn?
Johnny Zero
Pg 40, 2.8.1

What forced Cpl John Foley to return to the United States in 1943?
Malaria
Pg 40, 2.8.1

Who was the first Chief Master Sergeant of the Air Force?
Paul Airey
Pg 40, 2.8.2

What medal was Paul Airey the first to receive in 1988?
The Air Force POW medal
Pg 40, 2.8.2

What did the Air Wing of the Army do only when forced by Congress and a wartime emergency in 1942?
It began accepting black officers and enlisted men
Pg 40, 2.8.3

Initially, what single, separate base were the training and service of black Airmen and officers mostly confined to?
Tuskegee, Alabama
Pg 40, 2.8.3

What did an all black combat fighter unit form?
The Tuskegee Airmen
Pg 40, 2.8.3

Who was the first woman in the Air Force?
Esther Blake
Pg 41, 2.8.4

What was unique about Esther Blake's enlistment on July 8, 1948?
She enlisted on the first minute of the first hour of the first day regular Air Force duty was authorized for women
Pg 41, 2.8.4

What relatives did Esther Blake have in the Army Air Forces?
Her sons, she was a widow
Pg 41, 2.8.4

Why did Esther Blake join the Air Force?
She hoped to free a soldier from clerical work to fight, thus speeding the end of the war
Pg 41, 2.8.4

Where did Esther Blake go to work in 1954 when she separated from service?
The Veterans Regional Headquarters in Montgomery, Alabama
Pg 41, 2.8.4

What two awards did Staff Sergeant James Nichols earn in 1944?
The Air Medal and Silver Star
Pg 41, 2.8.5

A Separate Service (1947)

What year did the Air Force officially change the name of the lower four ranks?
1952
Pg 41, 2.9.1

The War in Southeast Asia (1950-1973)

What did tail gunner SSgt Samuel Turner do in December 1972?
He shot down an enemy MiG
Pg 42, 2.10

What actions won CMSgt Wayne Fisk his second Silver Star?
He helped recover a ship, the crew and the trapped United States Marines
Pg 42, 2.10.2

Who was recognized as the last American serviceman to engage Communist forces in ground combat in Southeast Asia?
CMSgt Wayne Fisk
Pg 42, 2.10.2

What did CMSgt Wayne Fisk become the first director of in 1986?
The Air Force Enlisted Heritage Hall
Pg 42, 2.10.2

After SSgt William Piazza drove through hails of rocket, mortar, machine-gun and sniper fire to resupply ammunition what was he still able to do?
Rally his men for eight hours in a countering assault
Pg 43, Figure 2.17

Post Vietnam to Present (1973-Present)

Who was the first Airman killed in Operation Iraqi Freedom?
SSgt Scott Sather
Pg 43, 2.11.1

What took the life of A1C Elizabeth Nicole Jacobson?
Her vehicle made contact with an improvised explosive device (IED)
Pg 43, 2.11.2

Medal of Honor Recipients

Who was the first enlisted man to receive the Medal of Honor?
Maynard Snuffy Harrison Smith, 1943
Pg 44, 2.12.1

What earned Sgt Maynard Smith the Medal of Honor?
He battled intense flames while assisting crewmates with first-aid and manning guns to fight off enemy fighter attacks
Pg 44, 2.12.1

What earned TSgt Forrest L. Vosler the Medal of Honor?
After sustaining facial injuries, he managed to repair a damaged radio by touch alone and send out a distress call
Pg 45, 2.12.2

When did SSgt Archibald Mathies receive the Medal of Honor?
It was awarded posthumously
Pg 45, 2.12.3

What did SSgt Archibald Mathies refuse to do?
Abandon an injured pilot
Pg 45, 2.12.3

Who cradled a 1300-degree, prematurely ignited flare and hurled it through the co-pilot's window?
SSgt Henry E. Erwin
Pg 46, 2.12.4

What award did SSgt Henry E. Erwin receive by General Curtis LeMay a week after he was injured?
The Medal of Honor Recipients
Pg 46, 2.12.4

What award did President Richard Nixon present to A1C John Levitow for falling on a flare and heaving it outside the plane?
The Medal of Honor
Pg 46, 2.12.5

Why did A1C William Pitsenbarger receive the Air Force Cross?
He volunteered to ride a hoist more than 100 feet through the jungle because Army personnel were having trouble loading casualties
Pg 46, 2.12.6

What happened to A1C Pitsenbarger's Air Force Cross award 34 years after he received it?
It was upgraded to the Medal of Honor
Pg 47, 2.12.6

What award did CMSgt Richard L. Etchberger receive for defending his comrades while under heavy fire, calling in air strikes, and directing an air rescue?
The Medal of Honor
Pg 47, 2.12.7

Air Force Cross Recipients

Sergeant Steve Northern earned two Silver Stars and a Purple Heart during his tours in Vietnam and was credited with the most combat rescues in Air Force history. How many combat rescues were credited to Northern?
51
Pg 47, 2.13

Who was awarded the Air Force Cross for his actions in the downing of a US UH-60 in Mogadishu on October 3, 1993?
TSgt Timothy A. Wilkinson
Pg 48, 2.13.1

Why was Senior Airman Jason D. Cunningham awarded the Air Force Cross?
He saved 10 lives and made it possible for the remains of 7 others to come home
Pg 48, 2.13.2

Where was Senior Airman Jason D. Cunningham buried?
Arlington National Cemetery
Pg 48, 2.13.2

Who received the Air Force Cross for volunteering to rescue a team member from the enemy stronghold atop Takur Ghar mountain?
TSgt John A. Chapman
Pg 49, 2.13.3

Who was awarded the Air Force Cross for preventing his team from being overrun during a harrowing 6 ½ hour battle by directing close air support strikes and protecting multiple wounded soldiers by providing suppressive fire?
SrA Zachary J. Rhyner
Pg 49, 2.13.4

Who received the Air Force Cross for directing precision strafe runs in Afghanistans' Herat Providence?
SSgt Robert Gutierrez Jr
Pg 50, 2.13.5

Enlisted Pilot Program

In 1912, how many people volunteered for pilot training at Fort William McKinley in the Philippines?
One
Pg 50, 2.14.1

Who was the first enlisted man in the history of United States aviation to train as a pilot?
Cpl Vernon Burge
Pg 50, 2.14.1

Why were there limited enlisted pilots even though the National Defense Act of 1916 authorized the training of enlisted aviators?
An institutional bias against training enlisted aviators
Pg 50, 2.14.2

What did Public Law 99 provide in 1941?
Training for enlisted aviation students who were awarded the rating of pilot and warranted as a staff sergeant
Pg 50, 2.14.3

Who was known as the Father of Blind Flight?
William C. Ocker
Pg 51, 2.14.4

What pilot was hand-picked by General Billy Mitchell to scout land parcels that later became Bolling Field, Washington, DC?
William C. Ocker
Pg 51, 2.14.4

What prevented some enlisted members from qualifying for regular Army commissions?
They lacked the required education
Pg 51, 2.14.5

What percentage of all Air Corps pilots from the enlisted ranks were the Corps directed to train, with the passage of Legislation in 1926?
20%
Pg 51, 2.14.5

What caused the Air Corps to halt enlisted pilot training in 1933?
A shortage of funds
Pg 51, 2.14.5

Sergeant pilots William C. McDonald, John H. Williamson, along with Lieutenant Haywood S. Hansel formed what aerobatics team?
Three Men on a Flying Trapeze
Pg 51, 2.14.6

Why did the Army Air Corps participate in a series of national races during the decades following World War I?
To arouse interest in aviation and to promote favorable public support
Pg 51, 2.14.6

What two enlisted members were the first, last, and only sergeant pilots to wear the Air Force blue uniform?
George Holmes and Tom Rafferty
Pg 52, 2.14.9

What happened to the sergeant pilots produced by the enlisted pilot program when Public Law 658 was passed in 1942?
They were promoted to flight officers
Pg 52, 2.14.10

Chapter 3
Organization

Overview

The Armed Forces of the United States are separate and independent parts of the Government. True or false?
False
Pg 53, 3.1

Who makes national military policy decisions?
Civilians assigned to the military and to the executive and legislative branches of the government
Pg 53, 3.1

Command Authority, Commander in Chief

What establishes the basic principle of civilian control of the Armed Forces?
The US Constitution
Pg 53, 3.2

Who has final command authority of the Armed Forces?
The President as Commander in Chief (CINC)
Pg 53, 3.2

What is the President subject to as the head of the executive branch?
Checks and balances by the legislative and judicial branches
Pg 53, 3.2

Department of Defense (DoD)

What Act established the DoD?
The National Security Act of 1947
Pg 53, 3.3

What agency of the government has the function to maintain and employ the Armed Forces?
The Department of Defense (DoD)
Pg 53, 3.3

Who is the civilian head of the DoD?
The Secretary of Defense (SECDEF)
Pg 53, 3.3

Who does the SECDEF report directly to?
The President
Pg 53, 3.3

Department of Defense (DoD), Secretary of Defense

Who appoints the SECDEF?
The President with the advice and consent of the Senate
Pg 53, 3.4

Who serves as principal defense policy advisor to the President and is responsible for the execution of approved policy
The Secretary of Defense
Pg 53, 3.4

What is the operational chain of command within the DoD?
President to the SECDEF to the combatant commanders
Pg 53, 3.4

What council assists in matters requiring long-range view and in formulation of broad defense policies?
The Armed Forces Policy Council
Pg 53, 3.4.1

How many Under Secretaries of Defense are there?
Five
Pg 53, 3.4.2

Department of Defense (DoD), Chairman, Joint Chiefs of Staff

Who appoints the Chairman, Joint Chiefs of Staff?
The President with the advice and consent of the Senate
Pg 54, 3.5

What pool of individuals is the Chairman, Joint Chiefs of Staff selected from?
Officers of the regular components of the Armed Forces
Pg 54, 3.5

How does the Chairman, Joint Chiefs of Staff compare in rank to all other officers of the Armed Forces?
The Chairman, Joint Chiefs of Staff outranks all other officers
Pg 54, 3.5

The Chairman, Joint Chiefs of Staff can exercise military command over the Joint Chiefs of Staff or any of the Armed Forces. True or false?
False
Pg 54, 3.5

What permits the President to authorize communication through the Chairman, Joint Chiefs of Staff?
A provision of the Goldwater-Nichols DoD Reorganization Act of 1986
Pg 54, 3.5

Who is the Chairman, Joint Chiefs of Staff principal military advisor to?
The President, the National Security Council, and the SECDEF
Pg 54, 3.5

Who is able to assign the Chairman, Joint Chiefs of Staff responsibility for overseeing the activities of the combatant commands?
SECDEF
Pg 54, 3.5

Department of Defense (DoD), Joint Chiefs of Staff

What is required when a member disagrees with an opinion of the Chairman, Joint Chiefs of Staff?
The Chairman, Joint Chiefs of Staff must present this advice in addition to his or her own
Pg 54, 3.6.2

Department of Defense (DoD), Joint Staff

How many personnel make up the Joint Staff?
Over 1,500 military and civilian personnel
Pg 54, 3.7

The percentages of members on the Joint Staff are divided up equally among the services. True or false?
False
Pg 54, 3.7

Department of Defense (DoD), Unified Combatant Commands and Combined Commands

How are the Unified Combatant Commands established?
By the President, assisted by the Chairman, Joint Chiefs of Staff through the SECDEF
Pg 54, 3.8.1

Who assigns the military missions?
The SECDEF
Pg 54, 3.8.1

What is the name of forces combined from two or more military departments called?
A Unified Combatant Command
Pg 54, 3.8.1

How are Unified commands organized?
By geographical and functional basis
Pg 54, 3.8.1

Name the different Unified Combatant Commands.
U.S. European Command (USEUCOM), U.S. Pacific Command (USPACOM), U.S. Northern Command (USNORTHCOM), U.S. Southern Command (USSOUTHCOM), U.S. Central Command (USCENTCOM), U.S. Special Operations Command (USSOCOM), U.S. Transportation Command (USTRANSCOM), and U.S. Strategic Command (USSTRATCOM)
Pg 54, 3.8.1

Once assigned to a unified command, can a force be transferred to another command?
Only with authority of the SECDEF or under special procedures of the SECDEF office with the approval of the President
Pg 54, 3.8.1

Where do all other units not assigned to a unified command belong?
They remain with their respective service
Pg 54, 3.8.1

Department of Defense (DoD), Combined Commands

What is the definition of a combined command?
Forces from more than one allied nation
Pg 54, 3.8.2

Since combined commands are bi-national or multi-nation, what is unique about their missions and responsibilities?
They must establish, assign, and conform with all bi-national and multi-national agreements
Pg 54, 3.8.2

Department of Defense (DoD), Military Departments

What services make up the Military Departments?
The Army, Navy (including the Marine Corps and, in wartime the Coast Guard), and the Air Force
Pg 55, 3.9

What are the responsibilities of the Service secretaries?
To provide efficiently organized, trained, and equipped ready forces to the combatant commanders
Pg 55, 3.9

Who established the functions of each branch of the Armed Forces in the Key West Agreement of 1948?
The SECDEF and the Joint Chiefs of Staff
Pg 55, 3.9.1

What did the SECDEF and Joint Chiefs of Staff establish that states the functions of each branch of the Armed Forces?
The Key West Agreement of 1948
Pg 55, 3.9.1

Department of the Air Force, Secretary of the Air Force (SECAF)

Is the SECAF appointed from military members or from civilians?
From civilian
Pg 56, 3.12

Department of the Air Force, Chief of Staff, U.S. Air Force

How long is the Chief of Staff Air Force appointed for?
4 years
Pg 56, 3.13

Who appoints the Chief of Staff Air Force?
The President with the advice and consent of the Senate
Pg 56, 3.13

Who presides over Air Staff?
The CSAF
Pg 56, 3.13

Department of the Air Force, Air National Guard (ANG)

What departments make up the National Guard Bureau?
It is a joint bureau of the departments of the Army and Air Force
Pg 56, 3.14

Where is the National Guard Bureau located?
In the Pentagon, Washington DC
Pg 56, 3.14

The Air National Guard (ANG) is a MAJCOM. True or false?
False
Pg 56, 3.14

What types of missions does the ANG have?
Both state and federal missions
Pg 56, 3.14.1

Where does an Air National Guard member report when they are not mobilized or under federal control?
To the Governor of their respective state, territory or the commanding general of the District of Columbia National Guard
Pg 56, 3.14.3

What is the state mission of the Air National Guard?
Provide protection of life and property, and preserve peace, order and public safety
Pg 56, 3.14.3

How many Air National Guard members are there?
Over 106,000
Pg 57, 3.14.4

What is the primary source of the full-time support for ANG units?
Dual-status military technicians and guardsmen on active duty
Pg 57, 3.14.4

What are dual-status military technicians?
Civil service employees who must be military members of the unit that employs them
Pg 57, 3.14.4

Department of the Air Force, Air Staff

What office has the function of assisting the Secretary of the Air Force in carrying out his responsibilities?
The Air Staff
Pg 57, 3.15

Organization 17

In addition to non-specific Air Force members and civilian employees assigned to it, what titled individuals compose the Air Staff?
(1) Chief of Staff, (2) Vice Chief of Staff, (3) Deputy Chiefs of Staff, (4) Assistant Chiefs of Staff, (5) Surgeon General of the Air Force, (6) Judge Advocate General of the Air Force, and (7) Chief of the Air Force Reserve
Pg 57, 3.15

Department of the Air Force Headquarters U.S. Air Force (HQ USAF)

How many major entities make up HQ USAF?
Two, the Secretariat and the Air Staff
Pg 57, 3.16

Department of the Air Force, Field Units

How is the Air Force organized?
On a functional basis in the United States and a geographical basis overseas
Pg 57, 3.17.1

What is a major Air Force subdivision with a specific portion of the Air Force mission called?
Major Command (MAJCOM)
Pg 57, 3.17.1

Who is a MAJCOM directly subordinate to?
HQ USAF
Pg 57, 3.17.1

What does an operational command consist of?
It consists (in whole or in part) of strategic, tactical, space, or defense forces, or of flying forces that directly support such forces
Pg 57, 3.17.1

What does ACC stand for?
Air Combat Command
Pg 57, 3.17.1.1

Where is ACC headquartered?
Langley AFB, VA
Pg 57, 3.17.1.1

When was ACC created?
1 June 1992
Pg 57, 3.17.1.1

What does ACC primarily provide?
Prepares assigned forces for air combat in a theater of operation
Pg 57, 3.17.1.1.1

How many active duty and civilians are in the ACCs workforce?
More than 67,000
Pg 57, 3.17.1.1.3

How many ANG and AFR members are assigned to ACC when mobilized?
More than 50,000
Pg 57, 3.17.1.1.3

What resources does ACC have?
Over 1,800 aircraft
Pg 57, 3.17.1.1.3

What does AMC stand for?
Air Mobility Command
Pg 58, 3.17.1.2

Where is AMC headquartered at?
Scott AFB, IL
Pg 58, 3.17.1.2

When was AMC created?
1 June 1992
Pg 58, 3.17.1.2

Approximately how many personnel does AMC have?
More than 134,000
Pg 58, 3.17.1.2.3

What does AFSPC stand for?
Air Force Space Command
Pg 58, 3.17.1.3

When was AFSPC created?
1 September 1992
Pg 58, 3.17.1.3

Where is AFSPC headquartered?
Peterson AFB, CO
Pg 58, 3.17.1.3

What is the AFSPC mission?
Provides resilient and cost-effective Space and Cyberspace capabilities for the Joint Force and the Nation
Pg 58, 3.17.1.3.1

How many personnel does it take to perform the AFSPC mission?
Approximately 41,000
Pg 60, 3.17.1.3.3

Where is Pacific Air Force (PACAF) headquartered?
Joint Base Pearl Harbor-Hickam AFB, HI
Pg 59, 3.17.1.4

What area does PACAF provide ready airspace and cyberspace capabilities to?
Asia-Pacific region
Pg 59, 3.17.1.4.1

How many square miles does PACAF cover?
More than 100 million
Pg 59, 3.17.1.4.2

Approximately how many people and countries does PACAFs responsibility cover?
Nearly 50 percent of the world's population
Pg 59, 3.17.1.4.2

How many personnel serve PACAF?
Approximately 45,000
Pg 59, 3.17.1.4.3

How many aircraft does PACAF have?
Approximately 400 fighter and attack aircraft
Pg 59, 3.17.1.4.3

What does USAFE stand for?
US Air Forces in Europe
Pg 59, 3.17.1.5

Where is the headquarters for USAFE?
Ramstein AB, Germany
Pg 59, 3.17.1.5

How many personnel are assigned to USAFE?
More than 39,000
Pg 59, 3.17.1.5.3

How many aircraft does USAFE have?
About 225
Pg 59, 3.17.1.5.3

What does AETC stand for?
Air Education and Training Command
Pg 60, 3.17.1.6

Where is the headquarters for AETC located?
Randolph AFB, TX
Pg 60, 3.17.1.6

When was AETC established?
1 July 1993
Pg 60, 3.17.1.6

What is the AETC mission?
To recruit, train, and educate professional Airmen to sustain the combat capability of America's Air Force
Pg 60, 3.17.1.6.1

How many aircraft does AETC have?
Approximately 1,500
Pg 60, 3.17.1.6.3

What does AFMC stand for?
Air Force Materiel Command
Pg 62, 3.17.1.7

Where is AFMC headquartered?
Wright-Patterson AFB, OH
Pg 60, 3.17.1.7

When was AFMC created?
1 July 1992
Pg 60, 3.17.1.7

How many personnel are assigned to AFMC?
Approximately 80,000
Pg 60, 3.17.1.7.3

What does AFSOC stand for?
Air Force Special Operations Command
Pg 61, 3.17.1.8

Where is the headquarters for AFSOC located?
Hurlburt Field, FL
Pg 61, 3.17.1.8

When was AFSOC established?
22 May 1990
Pg 61, 3.17.1.8

How many personnel are assigned to AFSOC?
Approximately 18,000
Pg 61, 3.17.1.8.3

What does AFGSC stand for?
Air Force Global Strike Command
Pg 61, 3.17.1.9

When was AFGSC activated?
7 August 2009
Pg 61, 3.17.1.9

Where is AFGSC headquartered?
Barksdale AFB, LA
Pg 61, 3.17.1.9

What is the mission of AFGSC?
To develop and provide safe combat ready forces to conduct deterrence and global strike operations in support of the President of the US and combatant commanders
Pg 63, 3.17.1.9.1

Approximately how many professionals are assigned to AFGSC?
Approximately 23,000
Pg 61, 3.17.1.9.3

What does AFRC stand for?
Air Force Reserve Command
Pg 62, 3.17.1.10

Where is the headquarters for AFRC located?
Robins AFB, GA
Pg 62, 3.17.1.10

When did AFRC become a MAJCOM?
17 February 1997
Pg 62, 3.17.1.10

The mission of AFRC is to be a force held in reserve for possible war or contingency operations. True or false?
False
Pg 62, 3.17.1.10.1

How many personnel are assigned to AFRC?
Approximately 74,000
Pg 62, 3.17.1.10.3

How many mission support units are in AFRC?
More than 620
Pg 62, 3.17.1.10.3

What is a FOA?
Field Operating Agency
Pg 62, 3.17.2

What is a DRU?
Direct Reporting Unit
Pg 62, 3.17.3

What type of mission does a DRU perform?
Missions that do not fit into any of the MAJCOMs
Pg 62, 3.17.3

Department of the Air Force, Lower Levels of Command

Where do Air Force Component Commands and Numbered Air Forces (NAFs) administratively report to?
The MAJCOM
Pg 62, 3.18

Where do wings, groups, squadrons, and flights report?
Either an Air Force Component Command or a Numbered Air Force (NAF), whichever is appropriate
Pg 62, 3.18

How many new Air Force Component Numbered Air Forces (CNAFs) have been established?
13
Pg 62, 3.18.1

What is the nickname for Component Numbered Air Forces (CNAFs)?
Warfighting headquarters
Pg 62, 3.18.1

The Component Numbered Air Forces (CNAF) Commander is required to be prepared to assume responsibilities for The Joint Force Air Component Commander (JFACC). True or false?
True
Pg 62, 3.18.1

What is a NAF?
An administrative level of command directly under a MAJCOM
Pg 62, 3.18.2

What does a NAF provide?
Intermediate-level operational leadership and supervision
Pg 62, 3.18.2

A NAF does not have a complete functional staff; how many manpower authorizations can a NAF have without an approved waiver from HQ USAF/AIM?
99
Pg 62, 3.18.2

Wings, groups, and squadrons are subordinate units to a NAF. True or false?
True
Pg 62, 3.18.2

What is the responsibility of a Wing?
To maintain the installation
Pg 63, 3.18.3

What is the primary mission of an Operational Wing?
Usually to maintain and operate the base
Pg 63, 3.18.3.1

An Operational Wing is capable of self-support. True or false?
True
Pg 63, 3.18.3.1

What type of function does an Air Base Wing perform?
A support function
Pg 63, 3.18.3.2

A Specialized Mission Wing performs a specialized mission and usually has aircraft or missiles assigned. True or false?
False
Pg 63, 3.18.3.3

Wing Organization, Lower Levels of Command

What level of command is a Group?
It is a level below the wing
Pg 63, 3.18.4

How many subordinate units does a Group usually have?
Two or more
Pg 63, 3.18.4

What is the definition of a Squadron?
It is the basic unit in the Air Force
Pg 64, 3.18.5

What is the normal size of a Squadron?
At least 35
Pg 64, 3.18.5

What subdivisions can be in a flight?
Sections and elements
Pg 64, 3.18.6

What level of unit is a Numbered Flight?
It is the lowest level unit in the Air Force
Pg 64, 3.18.6.1

What is an Alpha Flight a part of?
Squadron
Pg 64, 3.18.6.2

An Alpha Flight is subject to unit reporting. True or false?
False
Pg 64, 3.18.6.2

What are Functional Flights normally a part of?
A Squadron
Pg 64, 3.18.6.3

A Functional Flight is subject to unit reporting. True or false?
False
Pg 64, 3.18.6.3

Wing Organization, Air Reserve Component (ARC)

What is an ARC?
An Air Reserve Component.
Pg 64, 3.19.1

When are forces drawn from the ARC?
When circumstances require the active forces to rapidly expand
Pg 64, 3.19.1

ARC forces receive the same staffing and training as active component forces and are supplied with the same equipment True or false?
True
Pg 64, 3.19.2

What equipment can the active force withdraw, divert, or reassign for other commitments?
None without written approval from the SECDEF
Pg 64, 3.19.2

When was the Total Force policy established and by who?
1973 by DoD
Pg 64, 3.19.3

The Total Force policy considers all aspects of active and reserve forces a part of a single US military resource when determining an appropriate force mix. True or false?
True
Pg 64, 3.19.3

Considerations unique to ANG units include what?
Their dual state and federal missions
Pg 64, 3.19.3

Who has command jurisdiction for non-mobilized ANG units?
The Governor of the state
Pg 64, 3.19.5

The gaining MAJCOM is the operational commander of the ARC when it is activated. True or false?
True
Pg 64, 3.19.5

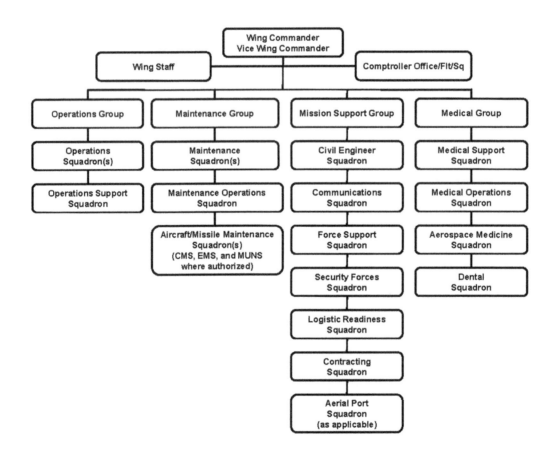

Chapter 4
Air Force Doctrine, Air and Space Expeditionary Force (AEF) and Joint Force

Overview

What must we do to remain dominant in the war on terrorism and overcome future threats and conflicts?
Maintain our air, space, and cyberspace power advantage over potential adversaries
Pg 67, 4.1.1

How will the Air Force meet the challenges of a rapidly changing world?
By understanding and applying Air Force Doctrine
Pg 67, 4.1.2

What is the Air Force methodology for presenting forces to combatant commanders (CCDRs)?
Air and Space Expeditionary Force (AEF)
Pg 67, 4.1.3

What three main principles provide the foundation of how the AEF is structured and executed?
Transparency, predictability, and equitability
Pg 67, 4.1.3

Joint operations are routine in all US military services. True or false?
True
Pg 67, 4.1.4

How must the US Armed Forces be ready to operate?
In a smooth, functioning joint team
Pg 67, 4.1.4

Air Force Doctrine

Air Force doctrine is an official statement of sanctioned beliefs, warfighting principles and terminology that describes and guides the use of air, space, and cyberspace power in military operations. True or false?
True
Pg 67, 4.2.1

What is Air Force doctrine based on?
Our experience to date
Pg 67, 4.2.1

What teaches the best way to prepare and employ Air Force forces?
Air Force doctrine
Pg 67, 4.2.2

Air Force doctrine is designed to be followed exactly. True or false?
False
Pg 67, 4.2.3

Many things remain constant from operation to operation. True or false?
True
Pg 68, 4.2.4 NOTE

What does bad doctrine do?
Overly binds and restricts creativity
Pg 68, 4.2.5

What is the arrangement of military actions in time, space, and purpose to produce maximum combat power at a decisive place and time?
Synchronization
Pg 69, 4.2.11

A joint force requires equal parts of all the Services. True or false?
False
Pg 69, 4.2.13

A senior Air Force officer once said, "Joint war-fighting is like little league baseball, where everybody gets a chance to play." True or false?
False
Pg 69, 4.2.13

What are the three different levels/depths of detail with regard to airpower?
Basic, operational, and tactical
Pg 69, 4.3

What is the basic Airman's doctrine?
AFDD 1
Pg 69, 4.3.1

Basic doctrine changes rapidly. True or false?
False
Pg 69, 4.3.1

Which doctrine describes the elemental properties of airpower?
Basic
Pg 69, 4.3.1

Which doctrine applies the principles of basic doctrine to military actions?
Operational
Pg 69, 4.3.2

Which doctrine may change more rapidly than other levels of doctrine?
Tactical
Pg 69, 4.3.3

What type of force is Airpower?
Strategic
Pg 70, 4.4.1.2

At what level is war and peace decided, organized, planned, supplied, and commanded?
Strategic
Pg 70, 4.4.1.2

Airpower dominates the fourth dimension of time. True or false?
True
Pg 70, 4.4.1.3

What can apply force against any facet of enemy power?
Airpower
Pg 70, 4.4.1.4

Airpower is the most versatile component of military power and can be rapidly employed against what type(s) of objectives?
Strategic, operational and tactical
Pg 70, 4.4.1.6

How should weapons be selected?
Based on their ability to influence an adversary's capability and will
Pg 70, 4.4.1.8

One of the most important characteristics of airpower is the ability to move anywhere quickly and rapidly begin operations. True or false?
True
Pg 70, 4.4.1.9

The principles of war are aspects of warfare that are universally true, relevant and tend to produce military victory. True or false?
True
Pg 71, 4.4.2

What provides focus for defining campaign or theater operations?
A clear state of national objectives
Pg 71, 4.4.2.2

Unity of command ensures concentration of effort for every objective that is under one responsible commander. True or false?
True
Pg 71, 4.4.2.1

What is the purpose of an offensive action?
To seize, retain, and exploit the initiative.
Pg 71, 4.4.2.3

Is success in war generally attained when on the offensive or defensive?
Offensive
Pg 71, 4.4.2.3

Historically speaking, a well-planned and executed air attack is extremely difficult to what?
To stop
Pg 71, 4.4.2.3

From the beginning of an operation, how does airpower seize the initiative?
By flying over enemy lines and around massed defenses to directly attack enemy capabilities.
Pg 71, 4.4.2.3

A maneuver places the enemy in a position of disadvantage. True or false?
True
Pg 72, 4.4.2.5

Airpower plays a critical role in American diplomacy. True or false?
True
Pg 72, 4.4.2.5

What principle of war provides for the allocation of minimum essential resources to secondary efforts?
Economy of forces
Pg 72, 4.4.2.6

What principle of war calls for the rational use of force by selecting the best mix of airpower?
Economy of forces
Pg 72, 4.4.2.6

The purpose of security is to never permit the enemy to acquire an unexpected advantage. True or false?
True
Pg 72, 4.4.2.7

Where is airpower most vulnerable?
On the ground
Pg 72, 4.4.2.7

What principle of war is obtained by staying beyond the enemy's reach?
Security
Pg 72, 4.4.2.7

What principle is used to attack the enemy at a time, place, or in a manner for which they are not prepared?
Surprise
Pg 73, 4.4.2.8

How do air forces achieve surprise on an enemy more readily than using surface forces?
With speed, flexibility, versatility, and range of airpower
Pg 73, 4.4.2.8

What principle calls for avoiding unnecessary complexity in organizing, preparing, planning, and conducting military operations?
Simplicity
Pg 73, 4.4.2.9

What can help overcome complexity?
Understanding of service/joint doctrine, familiarity with procedures, and common equipment
Pg 73, 4.4.2.9

The tenets of airpower compliment the principles of war. True or false?
True
Pg 73, 4.4.3

The principles of war provide general guidance on the application of military forces. True or false?
True
Pg 73, 4.4.3

Commanders have to apply their professional judgment and experience to the principles and tenets as they employ airpower in a given situation. True or false?
True
Pg 73, 4.4.3

Does airpower's unique potential affect the strategic or operational levels of war?
Both
Pg 73, 4.4.3.1

What element(s) are critical to effective employment of airpower?
Centralized control and decentralized execution
Pg 73, 4.4.3.1

Often used interchangeably, flexibility and versatility are basically the same. True or false?
False
Pg 74, 4.4.3.2

Flexibility allows airpower to exploit mass and surprise simultaneously. True or false?
False
Pg 74, 4.4.3.2

The synergistic effects of airpower are the ability to apply a coordinated force that can produce effects that exceed the contributions of forces employed individually. True or false?
True
Pg 74, 4.4.3.3

What allows forces to visit and revisit wide ranges of targets nearly at will?
Airpower's exceptional speed and range
Pg 74, 4.4.3.4

Who is uniquely and best suited to determine the proper theater-wide balance between offensive and defensive operations?
An Airman
Pg 75, 4.4.3.7

Which Air Force task is the broad and enduring purpose established by law?
Role
Pg 75, 4.4.4.1

What are the tasks assigned by the President or SECDEF called?
Missions
Pg 75, 4.4.4.2

What are the specific responsibilities that enable services to fulfill their legally established roles?
Functions
Pg 75, 4.4.4.3

What operates, maintains, and secures nuclear forces to deter an advisory from taking action against US interests?
Nuclear Deterrence Operations
Pg 75, 4.4.4.4.1

What allows rapid and accurate target strikes in a devastating manner?
Nuclear strike
Pg 76, 4.4.4.4.1.2

What ensures the safety, security and effectiveness of nuclear operations?
Nuclear surety
Pg 76, 4.4.4.4.1.3

What is responsible for destroying, degrading, or disrupting enemy air and missile power as close to its source as possible?
Offensive counterair
Pg 76, 4.4.4.4.2.1

Which type of operation is the most preferred method for achieving the appropriate degree of air superiority?
OCA
Pg 76, 4.4.4.2.1

Which mission has both active and passive defense measures?
DCA
Pg 76, 4.4.4.4.2.2

What is the process used to increase operational effectiveness by promoting safe, efficient and flexible use of airspace?
Airspace control
Pg 76, 4.4.4.4.2.3

What is defined as combat operations in, through, and from space to influence the course and outcome of conflict?
Space force application
Pg 77, 4.4.4.4.3.2

Which command and control levels goal is to achieve a commander's intent and desired effects?
Tactical level C2
Pg 78, 4.4.4.4.5.3

Which globally integrated ISR sub-element is the conversion of collected information into forms suitable to the production of intelligence?
Processing and exploitation
Pg 78, 4.4.4.4.6.3

Which globally integrated ISR sub-element is the delivery of intelligence to users in a suitable form?
Dissemination and integration
Pg 78, 4.4.4.4.6.5

Which sub-element of Global Precision attack seeks to weaken the adversary's ability or will to engage in conflict?
Strategic attack
Pg 78, 4.4.4.4.7.1

What type of operation may require covert, clandestine, or low-visibility capabilities?
Special operations
Pg 78, 4.4.4.4.8

What is the exercise of the commander's authority and direction over assigned and attached forces?
Command and control (C2)
Pg 79, 4.4.4.4.8.4

What sub-element of Special Forces is to induce or reinforce foreign attitudes and behavior?
Military information support operations
Pg 79, 4.4.4.4.8.7

What provides joint military forces the capability to move from place to place while retaining ability to fulfill their primary mission?
Rapid global mobility
Pg 79, 4.4.4.4.9

What is considered as a force multiplier because it allows assets to move rapidly and reach any spot around the world?
Air refueling
Pg 80, 4.4.4.4.9.2

Which sub-element of personal recovery is the primary method used by the Air Force?
Combat search and rescue
Pg 80, 4.4.4.4.10.1

Air and Space Expeditionary Force

The AEF establishes a predictable, standardized battle rhythm ensuring rotational forces are organized and ready to respond. True or false?
True
Pg 81, 4.5.2

What is the vulnerability period of the baseline AEF operation?
6-month
Pg 82, 4.5.3.2

AEF forces are considered on-call during the entire 4-month vulnerability period. True or false?
False
Pg 83, 4.5.3.2

AEF Temp Bands

What is normally the smallest independently deployable AETF?
Air Expeditionary Group (AEG)
Pg 83, 4.5.4.3

What is the basic war-fighting organization of the Air Force and is the building block of the AETF?
The AES
Pg 83, 4.5.4.4

If requirements exceed forces available within an AEF vulnerability period, it is designed to handle the increased requirements within its current structure. True or false?
False
Pg 84, 4.6.4.2

What are some surge methods the AEF is designed to use to meet increased requirements?
Reaching forward, reaching deeper, rebanding capability, and mobilization of ARC forces.
Pg 84, 4.6.4.2

An Airman can be assigned to more than one AEF vulnerability period in a Tempo Band. True or false?
False
Pg 85, 4.7.1

The Joint Force

What do the Armed Forces ultimately serve under?
The Commander in Chief, the President of the United States
Pg 86, 4.8.2

What demands that the Armed Forces operate as a fully integrated joint team?
Global challenges
Pg 86, 4.8.3

All forces are equally represented in each operation. True or false?
False, the JFCs may choose the capabilities they need from the forces at their disposal
Pg 86, 4.8.4

Operational and Administrative Chain of Command

In Joint C2, does unity of command or unity of effort require coordination and cooperation among all forces toward a common objective?
Unity of effort
Pg 87, 4.12.1

The Combatant Command Authority (COCOM) can be delegated or transferred by the CCDR (Combatant Commander). True or false?
False
Pg 88, 4.12.2.1

Operational Control (OPCON) authority can be delegated. True or false?
True, within the command
Pg 88, 4.12.2.2

How are National Guard and Reserve forces assigned to the combatant commands?
By the SECDEF
Pg 88, 4.12.4

At what three levels are Joint forces established?
Unified commands, subordinate unified commands, and Joint Task Forces (JTF)
Pg 88, 4.13.1

A commander, Air Force forces (COMAFFOR), provides a single face for all Air Force issues to a Joint Force Commander (JFC). True or false?
True
Pg 89, 4.13.2.1

An AETF is tailored to a mission. Where are the forces drawn from first?
From in-theater resources, if available
Pg 90, 4.13.2.2.1

The AETF requires a command entity responsible for deployment and sustainment of forces. What are these sustainment activities sometimes referred to as?
Beans, bullets, and beds
Pg 90, 4.13.2.2.3

What type of planning is used when the Armed Forces (or part of them) are brought to a state of readiness for war or other national emergencies?
Mobilization planning
Pg 92, 4.14.1.1

What specific portion of the Reserve component may be activated during a mobilization?
All or part
Pg 92, 4.14.1.1

What type of planning is moving forces and their sustainment resources from their original locations to a specific destination to conduct joint operations?
Deployment planning
Pg 92, 4.14.1.2

What type of planning is how to apply military force to attain specified military objectives within an operational area?
Employment planning
Pg 92, 4.14.1.3

What planning activity is the provision of logistics and personnel required to maintain and prolong operations until mission accomplishment?
Sustainment planning
Pg 92, 4.14.1.4

All the developed databases for joint, conventional time-phased force deployment are located in JOPES. True or false?
True
Pg 92, 4.14.2.1

The objective of DCAPES is to enable Air Force-unique operation planning and execution processes. True or false?
True
Pg 93, 4.14.2.2

How many volumes are in the War and Mobilization Plan (WMP)?
Five
Pg 93, 4.14.3

What does the War and Mobilization Plan (WMP) System provide for the Air Staff, Air Force planners, and Air Force commanders?
Current policies, apportioned forces, and planning factors for conducting and supporting operations
Pg 93, 4.14.3

What are commonly used terms for multi-national operations?
Terms include allied, bilateral, combined, coalition, or multilateral, as appropriate.
Pg 93, 4.15.2

What type of operation is conducted with units from two or more allies?
A combined operation
Pg 93, 4.15.2

Are coalitions formed for a single occasion or for longer cooperation of common interests?
Single occasions
Pg 93, 4.15.2

What type of operation is conducted with units from two or more coalition members?
Coalition operation
Pg 93, 4.15.2

Each alliance or coalition is responsible for developing their own OPLANs that guide multinational actions. True or false?
True
Pg 93, 4.15.3

What heavily influences the ultimate shape of the command structure for each alliance or coalition?
Political considerations
Pg 93, 4.15.4

What type of common understanding must there be among all national forces in a multinational operation?
The overall aim
Pg 93, 4.15.5

What is one of the three types of basic structures for multinational operations?
Integrated command
Pg 93, 4.15.6

Which multinational structure has representative members from member nations in the command headquarters?
Integrated command
Pg 93, 4.15.6

What type of structure exists in a multinational operation when all member nations place their forces under the control of one nation?
Lead nation
Pg 94, 4.15.6

Which command structure has no single force commander designated?
Parallel command
Pg 94, 4.15.6

Forces participating in a multinational operation normally have only one chain of command. True or false?
False
Pg 94, 4.15.8

Who has national command authority for the United States Forces?
The President
Pg 94, 4.15.8

The President of the United States is able to relinquish national command authority of US forces. True or false?
False
Pg 94, 4.15.8

What is the cooperation and communication between agencies of the United States Government (USG), including the DoD, to accomplish an objective?
Interagency coordination
Pg 94, 4.16.1

What agency advises and assists the President in integrating all aspects of national security policy?
The National Security Council (NSC)
Pg 94, 4.16.3

Who provides a parallel forum with the National Security Council for matters concerning terrorism within the United States?
Homeland Security Council
Pg 94, 4.16.4

The Constitution, law, and other governmental directives limit the scope and nature of military actions in domestic situations. True or false?
True
Pg 95, 4.16.6

Joint and Coalition Capabilities

What Act provided a statutory basis for change in our military command structure?
Goldwater-Nichols
Pg 95, 4.17.2

What helped ensure Desert Shield/Storm had more military cohesion than any major operation in decades?
Goldwater-Nichols Act
Pg 96, 4.17.3

It is rare to see any one country unilaterally plan, organize, or execute an operation. True or false?
True
Pg 96, 4.17.7

Chapter 4 ends here for those testing to SSgt, TSgt, or MSgt. If testing to SMSgt or CMSgt, continue studying this chapter

Joint Operation Planning and Execution System (JOPES)

What provides the combatant commander with information to determine the best method of accomplishing assigned tasks?
Joint Operation Planning Process
Pg 100, 4.18.2

The use of Joint Operation Planning and Execution System (JOPES) is an optional set of guidance. True or false?
False, its use is directed
Pg 100, 4.18.3

Deliberate and Crisis Action Planning and Execution segments (DCAPES) is the system that provides an Air Force feed to JOPES. True or false?
True
Pg 100, 4.19

Chapter 5
Emergency Management Program

Overview

What is the acronym for chemical, biological, radiological, nuclear, or high-yield explosives?
CBRNE
Pg 103, 5.1

What will Air Force members use to prevent, prepare, respond, and recover from emergency incidents?
The Air Force Emergency Management (EM) Program
Pg 103, 5.1

Emergency Management Program Operation

What does AFIMS stand for?
Air Force Incident Management System
Pg 103, 5.2

Incident Management

What are the response phases for incident management?
Prevention, preparedness, response, recovery, and mitigation
Pg 103, 5.5

During which Air Force Incident Management System (AFIMS) phase does intelligence collection and analysis occur?
The prevention phase
Pg 104, 5.5.1

Identifying augmentation manpower needs and reviewing expeditionary support plans (ESP) are performed during which phase of AFIMS?
The preparedness phase
Pg 104, 5.5.2

The immediate action of the commander to save lives, prevent human suffering, or mitigate great property damage occur during which phase of the AFIMS process?
The response phase
Pg 104, 5.5.3

How soon are actions for the recovery phase of the AFIMS initiated?
As soon as possible in order to restore normal operations and ensure crucial mission sustainment
Pg 104, 5.5.4

The mitigation phase is an ongoing process in AFIMS. True or false?
True
Pg 104, 5.5.5

Peacetime Airbase Threats

What does AFI 10-2501 define a major accident to be?
An accident involving DoD materiel or activities that is serious enough to warrant response by the installation Disaster Response Force (DRF)
Pg 104, 5.6.1

What are the four things personnel should do after an accident has been reported in order to protect themself?
(1) Stay uphill and upwind. Avoid inhaling fumes, smoke, or vapors. (2) Attempt to rescue and care for casualties. (3) Avoid handling any material or component involved in the accident. (4) Evacuate the area if rescue or containment is impractical, or if directed to evacuate.
Pg 104, 5.6.2.1 - 5.6.2.4

If you hear a 3-5 minute steady tone on a siren or similar warning device (or voice announcement), what does it mean?
A disaster/incident affecting the base is imminent or in progress
Pg 105, Figure 5.2

What type of 3-5 minute tone will you hear when an attack or hostile act is imminent or in progress?
It will be a wavering tone
Pg 105, Figure 5.2

When the All Clear announcement is made after an incident, what should each individual prepare to do?
Remain alert for secondary hazards, account for all personnel, report fires, injuries and hazards
Pg 105, Figure 5.2

CBRNE Enemy Attack and Terrorist Use of CBRNE Material Threats

What are two types of attacks against air bases that are a growing concern?
TIM (Toxic industrial materials) and TIC (Toxic industrial chemicals)
Pg 106, 5.12

What are the most effective individual protective equipment (IPE) used during a conventional attack?
A helmet and personal body armor
Pg 106, 5.12.2

Which phase of attack is the period of time from the present until the beginning of hostilities?
Attack preparation
Pg 106, 5.13.2.1

What tool does a commander use to recall people to their duty locations?
A recall roster
Pg 107, 5.13.2.1.1

During which phase of attack are contamination avoidance measures utilized?
They are used during all levels and during all attack conditions
Pg 107, 5.13.2.1.2

Who is responsible for implementing mission-oriented protective postures (MOPP)?
The Commander
Pg 107, 5.13.2.1.3

Which attack phase means an attack is imminent or in progress?
Attack response phase
Pg 107, 5.13.2.2

MOPP levels are always used in conjunction with the alarm conditions to quickly increase or decrease individual protection against CBRNE threats. True or false?
True
Pg 108, 5.13.2.2.1

The purpose of having alarm conditions is to initiate or limit individual and airbase-wide movement and action. True or false?
True
Pg 108, 5.13.2.2.1.1

A mission-oriented protective posture (MOPP) level lets the individual know what to wear for minimum protection. True or false?
True
Pg 108, 5.13.2.2.1.2

Why must work-rest cycles be used as a tool when mission-oriented protective posture (MOPP) levels change?
To help maintain consistent work levels and prevent heat-related casualties
Pg 108, 5.13.2.2.1.2

How must CBRNE reconnaissance be accomplished?
Every Airman must be a detector
Pg 108, 5.13.2.3.1

When can exposure to chemical and biological warfare agents occur?
During and after an attack
Pg 108, 5.13.2.3.2.1

What are the most effective methods of removing chemical agents from the skin?
The reactive skin decontamination lotion (RSDL) and M295 individual decontamination kit
Pg 108, 5.13.2.3.3

What MOPP level is used as the normal wartime level?
MOPP 0
Pg 109, Figure 5.4

What MOPP level is used when the enemy has a CBRN capability?
MOPP 0
Pg 109, Figure 5.4

What MOPP level should you be at when it is determined enemy attacks could occur with little or no warning?
MOPP 1
Pg 109, Figure 5.4

What MOPP level is used to provide additional protection to personnel when crossing or operating in previously contaminated areas?
MOPP 2
Pg 109, Figure 5.4

Which MOPP level is used when a negligible contact or percutaneous vapor hazard is present?
MOPP 3
Pg 109, Figure 5.4

Which MOPP level is used to provide maximum individual protection to personnel?
MOPP 4
Pg 109, Figure 5.4

What is the best immediate protective equipment against chemical agents?
Ground crew ensemble
Pg 110, 5.13.3.2.1.2

When should pyridostigmine bromide tablets (P-tabs) and/or nerve agent antidotes be taken?
Only when directed by the Commander
Pg 110, 5.13.3.2.2

What means will base personnel use to communicate security and provide information to the unit control center (UCC) or the emergency operations center (EOC)?
The most expedient means possible and any means available
Pg 110, 5.13.5

What is defined as the calculated use of unlawful violence, threat of unlawful violence to instill fear, intimidate governments to pursue goals that are generally political, religious, or ideological?
Terrorism
Pg 111, 5.14.1

CONDITION	IF YOU HEAR	THIS INDICATES	INDIVIDUAL ACTIONS
Disaster Warning [1,3]	3-5 minute steady tone on siren or similar warning device (or voice announcement)	A disaster/incident affecting the base is imminent or in progress (tornado, wildfire, flood, etc)	• Be award, ensure all personnel are warned • Follow instructions to take cover, evacuate to a safe location, or shelter-in-place • Conduct personnel accountability
Attack Warning [1,2,3]	3-5 minute wavering tone on siren or similar warning device (or a voice announcement)	An attack/hostile act is imminent or in progress (bomb, release of chemical, biological, or radioactive material)	• Be alert, ensure all personnel are warned • Implement security measures, as appropriate • Follow instructions to take cover, evacuate to a safe location, or shelter-in-place • Conduct personnel accountability
All Clear [3]	Voice announcement	The immediate disaster threat has ended or the attack is over	• Remain alert for secondary hazards • Account for all personnel • Report fires, injuries, and hazards

NOTES:
1. See AFI 10-2501, Air Force Emergency Management (EM) Program Planning and Operations, and AFMAN 10-2504, Air Force Incident Management for Major Accidents and Natural Disasters, for further guidance on warning systems and protective actions.
2. During wartime or combat operations, AFVA 10-2511, USAF Standardized Attack Warning Signals for CBRNE Medium and High Threat Areas, will be used to initiate passive defense actions in accordance with AFMAN 10-2503, Operations in a Chemical, Biological, Radiological, Nuclear, and High-Yield Explosive (CBRNE) Environment, as directed by the installation commander.
3. Monitor commander's channel or local media for information regarding specifications for base populace.
4. Senior ranking person accomplishes personnel accountability and reports as soon as possible using local procedures.

Table 5.1. SALUTE Reporting.

LINE	A Report Area	B Information to Report
1	(S)ize	The number of persons and vehicles seen or the size of an object
2	(A)ctivity	Description of enemy activity (assaulting, fleeing, observing)
3	(L)ocation	Where the enemy was sighted (grid coordinate or reference point)
4	(U)nit	Distinctive signs, symbols, or identification on people, vehicles, aircraft, or weapons (numbers, patches, or clothing type)
5	(T)ime	Time activity is observed
6	(E)quipment	Equipment and vehicles associated with the activity

Figure 5.3. United States Air Force Standardized Attack Warning Signals for CBRNE Medium and High Threat Areas.

ALARM CONDITION	IF YOU	THIS INDICATES	GENERAL ACTIONS
GREEN	Hear: Alarm Green See: Green Flag/ Transition Sign	Attack is not probable	☒ MOPP 0 or as directed[1,3] ☒ Normal wartime condition ☒ Resume operations ☒ Continue recovery actions
YELLOW	Hear: Alarm Yellow See: Yellow Flag/ Transition Sign	Attack is probable in less than 30 minutes	☒ MOPP 2 or as directed[1] ☒ Protect and cover assets ☒ Go to protective shelter or seek best protection with overhead cover[2]
RED	Hear: Alarm Red Siren: Wavering Tone See: Red Flag/ Transition Sign	Attack by in-direct fire, air, or missile is imminent or in progress	☒ Seek immediate protection with overhead cover[2,3] ☒ MOPP 4 or as directed[1] ☒ Report observed attacks
RED	Hear: Ground Attack Bugle: Call-to-Arms See: Red Flag/ Transition Sign	Attack by ground forces is imminent or in progress	☒ Take immediate cover[2,3] ☒ MOPP 4 or as directed[1] ☒ Defend self and position ☒ Report activity
BLACK	Hear: Alarm Black Siren: Steady Tone See: Black Flag/ Transition Sign	Attack is over and CBRN contamination and/or UXO hazards are suspected or present	☒ MOPP 4 or as directed[1,3] ☒ Perform self-aid/buddy care ☒ Remain under overhead cover or within shelter until directed otherwise[4]

Notes:
1. Wear field gear and personal body armor (if issued) when directed.
2. Commanders may direct mission-essential tasks or functions to continue at increased risk.
3. This alarm condition may be applied to an entire installation or assigned to one or more defense sectors or CBRN zones.
4. See AFI 10-2501, *Air Force Emergency Management (EM) Program Planning and Operations*, and AFMAN 10-2503, *Operations in a Chemical, Biological, Radiological, Nuclear, and High-Yield Explosive (CBRNE) Environment*, for further guidance on warning systems and protective actions.

Chapter 6
Standards of Conduct

Law of Armed Conflict (LOAC)

What is the part of international law that regulates the conduct of armed hostilities?
The Law of Armed Conflict
Pg 113, 6.2

What obligates the United States to provide Law of Armed Conflict (LOAC) training?
The provisions of the 1949 Geneva Conventions
Pg 113, 6.3

What document states that treaty obligations of the United States are the supreme law of the land?
Article VI of the US Constitution
Pg 113, 6.4

What group of individuals must observe the United States Law of Armed Conflict (LOAC) obligations?
All persons subject to US law
Pg 113, 6.4

What can happen to individuals who violate the Law of Armed Conflict (LOAC)?
They may be held criminally liable for war crimes and court-martialed under the Uniformed Code of Military Justice (UCMJ)
Pg 113, 6.4

What five important LOAC principles govern armed conflict?
Military necessity, distinction, proportionality, humanity, and chivalry
Pg 113, 6.5

What LOAC principle permits the application of only the degree of force required for partial or complete submission with the least expenditure of life, time, and physical resources?
Military necessity
Pg 113, 6.5.1.1

Under the LOAC, what types of objects are attacks limited to?
Military objectives
Pg 113, 6.5.1.2

What principle under the LOAC requires a determination between military objectives and civilian objects?
Distinction
Pg 114, 6.5.2.1

What are some examples of civilian objects that are protected from attack under the LOAC?
Places of worship, schools, hospitals, and dwellings
Pg 114, 6.5.2.1.1

Civilian objects can lose their protected status under the LOAC. True or false?
True, if the object is being used to make an effective contribution to military action
Pg 114, 6.5.2.1.2

How is the LOAC principle of proportionality applied?
To take into consideration the extent of civilian destruction and probable casualties that will result
Pg 114, 6.5.3.1

Military facilities and forces are legitimate targets anywhere and anytime. True or false?
True
Pg 114, 6.5.3.2

What LOAC principle is also known as the principle of unnecessary suffering?
Humanity
Pg 114, 6.5.4

What prohibits the use of poison, hollow-point bullets, bacterial weapons, or poisoned weapons in combat?
The 1907 Hague Convention
Pg 114, 6.5.4

What forbids treacherous attempts to injure the enemy?
The common law of war
Pg 114, 6.5.5.1

The misuse of the white flag of truce is an example of a treacherous attempt to injure the enemy. True or false?
True, misuse of the white flag of truce is considered a war crime
Pg 114, 6.5.5.1

How is an individual who is hors de combat (outside the fight) required to be treated?
They are required to be treated and protected as one would wish to be treated and protected by the enemy if the roles were reversed
Pg 114, 6.5.5.2

How many separate international treaties make up the Geneva Conventions of 1949?
Four
Pg 114, 6.6

What are identifiable characteristics of a combatant?
In general, any person who engages in violent acts on behalf of a state party to an armed conflict is a combatant. The lawful combatant is commanded by a person responsible for subordinates; wears fixed distinctive emblems recognizable at a distance, such as uniforms; carries arms openly; and conducts his or her combat operations according to LOAC.
Pg 115, 6.6.1.1.1

Under the Geneva Conventions, civilians are protected persons that may not be made the object of direct attack. True or false?
True
Pg 115, 6.6.1.1.3

If you are unable to determine the status of a captured individual what should you do?
Extend the protections of the Geneva Prisoner of War Convention until status is determined
Pg 115, 6.6.2

Military targets should be spared if their destruction may cause collateral damage resulting in unintended death or injury to civilians. True or false?
False
Pg 115, 6.7.1

What happens if a protected object (under LOAC) is used for military purposes?
They lose their protected status
Pg 116, 6.7.2

Enemy military aircraft can be attacked and destroyed wherever found. True or false?
True, unless they are in neutral airspace
Pg 116, 6.8.1

When must an attack on an enemy military aircraft be discontinued?
When it is clearly disabled and has lost its means of combat
Pg 116, 6.8.1

Enemy (public and private) non-military aircraft are subject to attack. True or false?
False, unless they are used for a military purpose
Pg 116, 6.8.2

Where are prosecutions for LOAC violators held?
In a national or international forum
Pg 116, 6.9.1

Individual Airmen are responsible for their actions. True or false?
True, and they must comply with the LOAC
Pg 116, 6.9.1

Who can authorize US Forces to use reprisal?
Only the President of the United States, as Commander in Chief
Pg 117, 6.9.2

What publication includes guidance on handling possible LOAC violations?
AFI 51-401
Pg 117, 6.10

To where is a report made when allegations of a violation of LOAC involves a US Commander?
The next higher US Command authority
Pg 117, 6.10

The purpose of having rules of engagement (ROE) is to set parameters for when, where, how, why, and against whom commanders and their Airmen may use force. True or false?
True
Pg 117, 6.11

What element states that force used must be reasonable in intensity and duration compared to the threat
Proportionality
Pg 117, 6.11.2

Code of Conduct

The Code of Conduct outlines basic responsibilities and obligations of enemy forces. True or false?
False
Pg 117, 6.12

How many articles are in the Code of Conduct?
Six
Pg 117, 6.12

What type of basic information is contained in the Code of Conduct?
Information useful to POWs to help them survive honorably while resisting captors efforts to exploit them
Pg 117, 6.12

How many training levels are there for the Code of Conduct?
Three
Pg 118, 6.13

What is the minimum level of understanding required by all members of the Armed Forces of the Code of Conduct?
Level A - given to all personnel during entry training
Pg 118, 6.13.1

Who published the first Code of Conduct for members of the Armed Forces of the United States?
President Dwight D. Eisenhower
Pg 118, 6.14

Why did President Ronald W. Reagan amend the Code of Conduct in March 1988?
To include gender neutral language
Pg 118, 6.14

Article I of the Code of Conduct applies only while on combat duty. True or false?
False, it applies to all members and at all times whether in active combat participation or captivity
Pg 118, 6.14.1.1

What has past experience of captured Americans revealed about honorable survival in captivity?
That it requires a high degree of dedication and motivation
Pg 118, 6.14.1.2.1

Why must members never surrender voluntarily even if isolated and unable to inflict casualties on the enemy or defend themselves?
It is their duty to evade capture and rejoin the nearest friendly force
Pg 118, 6.14.2.1

Being captured is considered dishonorable. True or false?
False, as long as all reasonable means of avoiding it have been exhausted and the only alternative is death
Pg 119, 6.14.2.2

What must you be aware of concerning the POW compound that is against the 1949 Geneva Conventions?
That the enemy may treat the POW compound as an extension of the battlefield
Pg 119, 6.14.3.1.1

Why is it critical for a POW to continue efforts to escape?
It will divert enemy forces that may otherwise be fighting
Pg 119, 6.14.3.2

What must POWs help prevent the enemy from discovering?
Which fellow POWs may have valuable knowledge
Pg 119, 6.14.4.1

Who assumes command if the senior POW is incapacitated or otherwise unable to act for any reason?
The next senior POW
Pg 119, 6.14.4.1

What do you do if the senior POW is from a different service than you are?
Members must accept leadership from those in command and abide by the decision of the senior POW regardless of military service
Pg 119, 6.14.4.2

Who is required to represent POWs in matters regarding camp administration, health, welfare, and grievances?
The senior POW
Pg 120, 6.14.5.1.1

Why should a POW provide the enemy with as little information as possible?
It allows a POW to keep faith with the United States, fellow POWs, and him/herself
Pg 120, 6.14.5.1.2

Members of the Armed Forces are always responsible for their personal actions. True or false?
True
Pg 120, 6.14.6.1

US military personnel are still required to follow DoD and Air Force policies when isolated from US control. True or false?
True, they are required to do everything in their power to follow them
Pg 120, 6.15.1

What are captors often attempting to do when they detain or capture US military personnel?
Exploit both the individual and the US Government for their own purposes
Pg 121, 6.15.2

What can a US military person have faith in if they are detained or held hostage?
That the US Government will make every effort to obtain their release
Pg 121, 6.15.3.1

What laws are detainees in custody of a hostile government subject to?
The laws of that government
Pg 121, 6.15.5.1

What should detainees ask for immediately and continually?
To see US embassy personnel or a representative of an allied or neutral government
Pg 121, 6.15.5.1

What subjects does DoD policy recommend US personnel talk to terrorists about in order to create a person status rather than a symbol of a country the terrorist may hate?
Your hobbies, family, and sports
Pg 122, 6.15.6.2

Everyday Conduct

Define ethics.
Standards of conduct based on values
Pg 122, 6.18

What are core beliefs such as duty, honor, and integrity which motivate attitudes and actions called?
Values
Pg 122, 6.18

What is the bond that holds the Nation and the US Government together?
Loyalty
Pg 123, 6.18.3

When do personal relationships between Air Force members become matters of official concern?
When they adversely affect the Air Force or have the potential to
Pg 123, 6.19

What AFI establishes responsibilities for maintaining professional relationships?
AFI 36-2909, Professional and Unprofessional Relationships
Pg 123, 6.19

Why does the Air Force encourage personnel to communicate freely with their superiors regarding their careers, performance, duties, and missions?
Because this type of communication enhances morale and discipline and improves the operational environment
Pg 123, 6.19.1

Fraternization between members of different services is permitted. True or false?
False
Pg 124, 6.20.1

A military member can be subject to prosecution under the UCMJ for violating an order to cease an unprofessional relationship. True or false?
True
Pg 125, 6.21

Which individual bears primary responsibility for maintaining professionalism in a relationship?
The senior member (officer or enlisted)
Pg 125, 6.22.1

What can happen to a commander who fails to maintain good order, discipline, and morale within their units?
They may be held accountable for failing to act in appropriate cases
Pg 125, 6.22.2

What is often an effective first step in curtailing unprofessional relationships?
Counseling
Pg 125, 6.23

Who is responsible for receiving a complaint concerning financial obligation of a military member?
The individual's Commander
Pg 126, 6.24.2

How long does the individual's Commander have to respond to a complaint concerning financial obligations of a military member?
15 days
Pg 126, 6.24.2

What must a Commander do to ensure a complaint concerning financial obligation against a military member is resolved?
The Commander must actively monitor the complaint until it is resolved
Pg 126, 6.24.2

What is the cost of personal financial management program (PFMP)?
It is free of charge
Pg 126, 6.24.3

Ethics and Conflict of Interest Prohibitions

A civilian DoD employee can hold two distinctly different Federal Government positions and receive salaries if both duties of each job are performed. True or false?
True, subject to certain limitations
Pg 127, 6.28

Can the spouse or another household member of a senior-ranking person (military or DoD) solicit sales to a junior person?
It is not specifically prohibited but may give the appearance that the DoD employee or military member is using public office for personal gain
Pg 127, 6.29

Air Force military and civilian personnel (and their dependents) are required to report gifts, or combination of gifts at one presentation, from foreign governments exceeding what US retail value?
$305
Pg 127, 6.30

When does a gift or gift report valued over $305.00 have to be submitted?
Within 60 days of receiving the gift
Pg 127, 6.30

What is the penalty for not reporting gifts from Foreign Governments with a retail value in excess of $305?
It could result in a penalty in any amount, not to exceed the retail value of the gift plus $5,000
Pg 127, 6.30

When a gift is given to a supervisor (regardless of how many contribute) what is the limit of the market value the gift can be?
$300
Pg 127, 6.31.2

What is the maximum contribution any one DoD employee may solicit from another for a gift to a supervisor?
$10
Pg 127, 6.31.2

Agencies can permit employees or military members to make limited personal use of resources other than personnel. True or false?
True, for items such as computers, calculators, libraries, etc. as long as the use meets established criteria
Pg 128, 6.32

DoD personnel away from home (on official DoD business) are authorized to use Federal Government communication systems and equipment. True or false?
True, if approved by the commander in the interest of morale and welfare.
Pg 128, 6.33

Checking on minor children, scheduling doctor, auto, appointments, and brief Internet searches are considered as authorized purposes for using Federal Government communications systems. True or false?
True, when it is reasonable that they are made at the workplace
Pg 128, 6.33

Private wagers among DoD personnel may be transacted. True or false?
True, if based on a personal relationship and transacted entirely within assigned Government living quarters and subject to local laws
Pg 128, 6.34.2

Political Activities

An Armed Forces member can attend a partisan or nonpartisan political meeting or rally. True or false?
True, they can attend as spectators but not in uniform
Pg 128, 6.36

An enlisted member can seek and hold a nonpartisan civil office such as a notary public, school board member, neighborhood planning commission, or similar local agency. True or false?
True, as long as it is held in a private capacity and does not interfere with the performance of their military duties
Pg 129, 6.37.1

A member can perform clerical duties or other duties for a partisan political committee during a campaign or on Election Day. True or false?
False
Pg 129, 6.37.2.5

A member can march or ride in a partisan political parade. True or false?
False
Pg 129, 6.37.2.6

What does an Air Force member have to do prior to releasing any proposed statement, text, or imagery publicly?
Obtain the necessary review and clearance which begins with public affairs
Pg 130, 6.40.1

Chapter 7
Enforcing Standards and Legal Issues

The Air Force Inspection System

Who develops applicable guidelines, procedures and criteria for conducting inspections?
MAJCOM IG
Pg 131, 7.3

How long after being rated overall unsatisfactory on a NSI will a unit be re-inspected?
Within 90 days
Pg 132, 7.4.3

What is the web-based program Airmen use to self assess program management and compliance with higher headquarters?
Management internal control toolset
Pg 132, 7.5.2

Inspector General Complaints Program

Which leadership tool indicates where command involvement is needed to correct weaknesses and ensures proper use of resources?
IG Complaints Program
Pg 133, 7.8

Who investigates allegations of reprisal under the Military Whistleblower's Protection Act?
The Inspector General
Pg 133, 7.8

Who does the installation IG report to?
Installation Commander
Pg 133, 7.9

What role does the IG play for the commander?
The eyes and ears
Pg 133, 7.9.1

Commander-directed inquiries and investigations are covered under the IG complaint resolution program. True or false?
False
Pg 134, 7.9.2.1.1

Complaints should be resolved at the lowest possible level using command channels before addressing them to a higher level or to the IG. True or false?
True
Pg 134, 7.9.3

Complaints cannot be submitted anonymously. True or false?
False
Pg 134, 7.9.4

A complaint may be filed at any level without following the chain of command. True or false?
True
Pg 135, 7.9.5.1

How long after learning of an alleged wrong does a complaint have to be filed?
60 days
Pg 136, 7.9.6

When can the IG release the name of a complainant?
Only on an official need-to-know basis
Pg 136, 7.9.7

Individual Standards

What type of file contains information about an individual's performance, responsibility, and behavior?
Unfavorable Information File (UIF)
Pg 136, 7.11

How long after assuming a command must a Commander review the unit's Unfavorable Information Files (UIFs)?
Within 90 days
Pg 137, 7.11.3

When are Unfavorable Information Files (UIFs) reviewed?
Commanders review unit UIFs within 90 days of assuming command; UIFs are also reviewed when individuals are considered for promotion, reenlistment, permanent change of station (PCS), permanent change of assignment (PCA), and voluntary or mandatory reclassification or retraining.
Pg 137, 7.11.3

Who maintains the Unfavorable Information Files (UIFs) and its documents for the disposition period?
Commanders
Pg 137, 7.11.4

What tool can be used to establish a 6-month observation period for individuals who fail to meet or maintain Air Force standards of conduct?
A control roster
Pg 137, 7.12

Being on a control roster shields an individual from receiving other actions. True or false?
False
Pg 137, 7.12.1

How long can an individual stay on the control roster before Commander initiates more severe action?
6 months
Pg 137, 7.12.1

How long does an individual have to submit a statement before a control roster action is finalized?
3 duty days
Pg 137, 7.12.2

A Letter of Admonishment (LOA) is more severe than a Letter of Counseling (LOC) or a Record of Individual Counseling (RIC). True or false?
True
Pg 137, 7.13.2

The Group Commander or equivalent-level Commander can demote a Master Sergeant and below. True or false?
True
Pg 138, 7.14

What must the Commander do when an Airman is informed he/she is being demoted?
It must be done in writing
Pg 138, 7.14.2

How long does the Airman have to agree or disagree with the intent to be demoted and to present written or oral statements to the Commander?
3 duty days
Pg 138, 7.14.2

How long is most first-term Airman's Mandatory Service Obligation (MSO)?
8 years
Pg 138, 7.15.1

If an Airman does not qualify for re-enlistment what type of discharge does he/she receive?
Honorable
Pg 138, 7.15.2

An Airman may request an administrative discharge instead of trial by court-martial if their punishment authorizes a punitive discharge. True or false?
True
Pg 139, 7.15.3.4

Punitive Actions

What is the primary source of our military law?
The Constitution
Pg 139, 7.16.1

What year was the Uniform Code of Military Justice (UCMJ) enacted by Congress?
1950
Pg 140, 7.16.2.1

Which president created the Manual for Courts-Martial (MCM)?
Truman
Pg 140, 7.16.2.2

How often is the Manual for Courts-Martial (MCM) revised?
Annually
Pg 140, 7.16.2.2

Which Amendment to the Constitution states no person shall be compelled to be a witness against him or herself?
The Fifth Amendment
Pg 140, 7.16.3.1.1

What is the cost for the accused to be represented by a military attorney?
It is free
Pg 140, 7.16.3.2.1

Who does an Area Defense Counsel (ADC) report to in order to insure undivided loyalty to the client?
Senior defense attorneys
Pg 141, 7.16.3.2.2

The officer's Commander is the only individual that can order pretrial restraints of an officer. This authority can be delegated. True or false?
False
Pg 141, 7.17.1.2

Any commissioned officer may order pretrial restraint of any enlisted person. This authority can be delegated. True or false?
True
Pg 141, 7.17.1.2

Is an arrest in military terms a moral or physical one?
Moral
Pg 141, 7.17.1.2.3

What amendment of the Constitution protects against unreasonable searches and seizures?
The Fourth Amendment
Pg 141, 7.17.2.1

The authorization to search only has to describe the place to be searched. True or false?
False
Pg 141, 7.17.2.1

What is nonjudicial punishment often referred to as?
Article 15
Pg 141, 7.18

What types of punishment can be given under an Article 15?
Reduction in grade, forfeiture of pay, restrictions, extra duties, and/or correctional custody
Pg 142, 7.18.2

Who makes the decision to impose nonjudicial punishment?
The Commander
Pg 142, 7.18.3.1

If a member accepts the Article 15, it is considered an automatic admission of guilt. True or false?
False
Pg 142, 7.18.3.3

An oral statement is acceptable as an appeal to a nonjudicial punishment. True or false?
False
Pg 142, 7.18.3.6

What happens if an offender has no further misconduct after a suspension for an Article 15?
It is cancelled
Pg 143, 7.18.4.1

How long can a probationary period imposed by an Article 15 last?
It cannot exceed 6 months
Pg 143, 7.18.4.1

What does the Manual for Courts Martial (MCM) and Air Force policy encourage the use of for first-time offenders?
A suspended sentence
Pg 143, 7.18.4.1

What action cancels any portion of the unexecuted punishment as a reward for good behavior or when it is determined the punishment imposed was too severe for the offense?
Remission
Pg 143, 7.18.4.2

What action is a reduction in either the quantity or quality of a punishment?
Mitigation
Pg 143, 7.18.4.3

What action can the Commander use only when they believe the punishment resulted in clear injustice?
Set Aside
Pg 143, 7.18.4.4

Who can be tried in the Summary Court-Martial?
Only enlisted members
Pg 143, 7.19.1

Who can be tried by the Special Court-Martial (SPCM)?
Any service member
Pg 144, 7.19.2

An enlisted accused can request the panel (jury) in a Special Court Martial (SPCM) consist of at least 1/3 enlisted members. True or false?
True
Pg 144, 7.19.2

What type of court martial can impose any punishment authorized by the UCMJ except death, dishonorable discharge, dismissal, or confinement in excess of one year?
Special Court Martial (SPCM)
Pg 144, 7.19.2

What type of court martial tries the most serious offenses?
General Court-Martial (GCM)
Pg 144, 7.19.3

What court-martial can impose the maximum allowable punishment under the UCMJ for the offenses charged which may include death?
The General Court-Martial (GCM)
Pg 144, 7.19.3

What grade must a panel member in a trial be in relationship to the accused?
Senior
Pg 144, 7.20.1

What has to happen in order for an accused to be found guilty in a court-martial?
Guilt has to be proven beyond a reasonable doubt
Pg 144, 7.20.2

Table 7.2. Permissible NJPs on Enlisted Members. (Notes 1, 2, 3, and 4)

RULE	A		B	C	D
	Punishment		Imposed by Lieutenant or Captain	Imposed by Major	Imposed by Lt Colonel or Above
1	Additional restrictions		May not impose NJP on CMSgt or SMSgt	May not impose NJP on CMSgt or SMSgt	See note 2 for reduction of CMSgt or SMSgt
2	Correctional custody		Up to 7 days	30 days	30 days
3	Reduction in grade (note 2)	CMSgt	No	No	Note 2
4		SMSgt	No	No	Note 2
5		MSgt	No	No	One grade
6		TSgt	No	One grade	One grade
7		SSgt	One grade	One grade	One grade
8		SrA	One grade	To AB	To AB
9		A1C	One grade	To AB	To AB
10		Amn	One grade	To AB	To AB
12	Reprimand		Yes	Yes	Yes
13	Restriction		14 days	60 days	60 days
14	Extra duties		14 days	45 days	45 days

Notes:
1. See MCM, part V, paragraph 5d, for further limitations on combinations of punishments.
2. CMSgt or SMSgt may be reduced one grade only by MAJCOM commanders, commanders of unified or specified commands, or commanders to whom promotion authority to theses grades has been delegated. See AFI 36-2502, *Airman Promotion Program*. 51-202, *Nonjudicial Punishment*, Table 3.1, note 2.
3. Bread and water and diminished rations punishments are not authorized.
4. Frocked commanders may exercise only that authority associated with their actual pay grade. No authority is conferred by the frocked grade.

Table 7.3. Composition, Appointment, and Jurisdiction of Courts-Martial.

LINE	A Court	B Required Membership	C Convening Authority	D Persons Triable	E Offenses Triable	F Maximum Punishment
1	Summary	One commissioned officer (RCM 1301(a), Art. 16, UCMJ)	The officer exercising GCM or SPCM convening authority over the accused, or the commander of a detached squadron or other detachment (RCM 1302, Art. 24, UCMJ)	Enlisted members. If an accused objects to trial by SCM, the convening authority may order trial by SPCM or GCM (RCM 1301(c) and 1303, Art. 20, UCMJ)	Any noncapital offense punishable under UCMJ. SCM normally used to try minor offenses for which the accused was first offered NJP (RCM 1301(c), Art. 20, UCMJ)	1 month's confinement, hard labor without confinement for 45 days, restriction for 2 months, forfeiture of 2/3 of 1 month's pay, reduction to AB, reprimand, and a fine (RCM 1301 (d)(1), Art. 20, UCMJ). If the accused is SSgt or above, an SCM may not impose a sentence of confinement, hard labor without confinement, or reduction except to the next pay grade (RCM 1301 (d)(2), UCMJ)
2	Special	Three or more members and a military judge or, if requested, a military judge only (RCM 501 (a)(2), Art. 16, UCMJ)	The officer exercising GCM convening authority over the accused; the commander of a base, wing, group, or separate squadron when expressly authorized by the MAJCOM commander or designated SECAF; or any commander designated by the SECAF (RCM 504 (b)(2), Art. 23a, UCMJ)	Any person subject to the UCMJ (RCM 201 (b)(4), Art. 19, UCMJ)	Any noncapital offense punishable under the UCMJ (RCM 201(b)(5), Art. 19, UCMJ)	**Upon enlisted members:** Bad conduct discharge, confinement for 1 year, hard labor without confinement for 3 months, restriction for 2 months, forfeiture of 2/3 pay per month for 1 year, reduction to AB, reprimand, and a fine (RCM 201 (f)(2)(B)(i), Art. 19, UCMJ)
3	General	A military judge and at least five members, or a military judge only in noncapital cases (RCM 501(a)(1), Art. 16, UCMJ)	The President, SECAF, the commander of an air command, an air force, an air division or a separate wing of the Air Force, or any commander when designated by the President or SECAF (RCM 504 (b)(1), Art. 22, UCMJ)	Any person subject to the UCMJ (RCM 201 (b)(4), Art. 18, UCMJ)	Any offense punishable under the UCMJ (RCM 201(b)(5), Art. 18, UCMJ)	The maximum punishment authorized by the UCMJ, which may include death, a punitive separation (dismissal, dishonorable discharge, or bad conduct discharge), confinement for life or a specified period, hard labor without confinement for 3 months (enlisted members only), restriction for 2 months, forfeiture of all pay and allowances, reduction to AB (enlisted members only), reprimand, and a fine (RCM 201 (f)(1)(A)(ii), Art. 18, UCMJ)

In a court-martial, to give a sentence of death, what portion of the panel has to agree?
It must to be unanimous
Pg 144, 7.20.2

What percentage of votes is required by a panel in a court-martial in order to sentence a member to confinement in excess of 10 years?
A three-fourths vote
Pg 144, 7.20.2

Who reviews records of trials that include a death sentence, dismissal of a commissioned officer, a punitive discharge, or confinement of 1 year or more?
The US Air Force Court of Criminal Appeals (AFCCA)
Pg 146, 7.22.2

What is the highest appellate court in the military justice system?
The US Court of Appeals for the Armed Forces (USCAAF)
Pg 146, 7.22.3

An NCO must get involved when breaches of discipline occur in their presence. True or false?
True
Pg 146, 7.23.2

Chapter 7 ends here for those testing to SSgt, TSgt, or MSgt. If testing to SMSgt or CMSgt, continue studying this chapter

Legal Issues

The military justice system is separate from the civilian system. True or false?
True
Pg 148, 7.24.1

What was the average number of general court-martial convictions per day during WWII?
More than 60
Pg 148, 7.24.4

Most American citizens approved of the way the criminal laws were being applied in the military during WWII. True or false?
False
Pg 148, 7.24.5

Who decided there should not be separate criminal law rules for the different branches of service?
Secretary James V. Forrestal, the first Secretary of Defense
Pg 148, 7.24.6

What year did the Unified Code of Military Justice (UCMJ) become effective?
1951
Pg 148, 7.24.7

What type of judges does the US Court of Appeals for the Armed Forces (USCAAF) have?
Civilian
Pg 148, 7.24.7

An individual can be tried by a military and a civilian court if the offense violates both the UCMJ and a civilian code. True or false?
True
Pg 150, 7.26.2.2

The Commander ultimately decides how to dispose of a members' alleged misconduct. True or false?
True
Pg 150, 7.27.1

A military judge of a court-martial can consult with the members of the court. True or false?
True, only in the presence of the accused, trial counsel, and defense counsel
Pg 151, 7.28.3

If an enlisted accused makes a timely request for enlisted members to be included on the court, how many must it consist of?
At least 1/3 enlisted personnel
Pg 151, 7.28.4.2

What is the review authority in a General Court-Martial case where the sentence does not include death, dismissal, punitive discharge or confinement for 1 year or more?
The Judge Advocate General (TJAG)
Pg 152, 7.29.2.1

The US Air Force Court of Criminal Appeals (AFCCA) can change a finding of not guilty to guilty. True or false?
False
Pg 152, 7.29.2.3

Who automatically reviews cases involving dismissal of an officer or cadet?
SECAF
Pg 152, 7.29.2.5

Who has to approve sentences involving death?
The President
Pg 153, 7.29.2.6

The President can suspend the part of the sentence that provides for death. True or false?
False
Pg 153, 7.29.2.6

What is the most common type of desertion?
Absence with the intent to remain away permanently
Pg 153, 7.30.1.1.2

What is the maximum punishment for Absence Without Official Leave (AWOL)?
It varies depending of the duration of the absence
Pg 153, 7.30.1.2.3

What General Article addresses unspecified offenses punishable because of their effect on the US Armed Forces?
Article 134
Pg 154, 7.30.3

Running away before the enemy and cowardly conduct is punishable by death. True or false?
True
Pg 154, 7.30.4.1

Which Article prohibits insubordination toward a warrant officer, NCO, or petty officer specifically in the execution of duties?
Article 91
Pg 155, 7.30.5.3

What does Article 90(2) prohibit?
The intentional or willful disobedience of the lawful orders of a superior officer
Pg 155, 7.30.6.1

Chapter 8
Military Customs, Courtesies and Protocol for Special Events

Overview

What are the the four sections of military customs and courtesies?
Symbols, Professional Behavior, Drill and Ceremony, and Honor Guard
Pg 157, 8.1

What are military customs and courtesies?
They are proven traditions that explain what should and should not be done in many situations. They are acts of respect and courtesy when dealing with other people and have evolved as a result of the need for order, as well as the mutual respect and sense of fraternity that exists among military personnel.
Pg 157, 8.1

Symbols

What is the name of the typical flag that is displayed (only in fair weather) from the installation flagstaff?
The Installation Flag
Pg 157, 8.2.2.1

What flag is used as an alternate for the installation flag during inclement weather?
All-weather (Storm) flag
Pg 157, 8.2.2.3

What flag is commonly used as the flag presented at retirements?
All-purpose flag
Pg 157, 8.2.2.4

What is the Ceremonial Flag trimmed with on three sides?
A 2-inch wide yellow rayon fringe
Pg 157, 8.2.2.5

What flag is used to drape over closed caskets for deceased military personnel and for deceased veterans?
Interment flag
Pg 158, 8.2.2.7

Organizational and maintenance (O&M) funds can be used to purchase Retirement Flags. True or false?
True
Pg 158, 8.2.2.8

How many sizes of automobile flags are there?
Two
Pg 158, 8.2.2.9

What size flag is displayed on the automobile of the President and Vice President of the United States?
12 in x 18 in
Pg 158, 8.2.2.10

What times are appropriate to display the flag?
Only from sunrise to sunset on buildings and on stationary flagstaffs in the open
Pg 158, 8.2.3

What should you do when displaying a flag in the hours of darkness?
Properly illuminate it
Pg 158, 8.2.3

What is the normal location of the installation flag that is flown from reveille to retreat?
On a flagstaff placed in front of the installation headquarters
Pg 158, 8.2.3.1

What is the proper way to hoist and lower a flag?
Hoist it briskly and lower it ceremoniously
Pg 158, 8.2.3.2

What is the proper way to display the United States Flag and another flag against the wall when the staffs are crossed?
The United States Flag should be on the right (observer's left) and its staff should be in front of the staff of the other flag
Pg 158, 8.2.4.2

When a number of flags are grouped and displayed from staffs radiating from a central point with no foreign flags, the flag of the United States should be in the center and at the highest point in the group. True or false?
True
Pg 158, 8.2.4.3.1

When flags of two or more nations are displayed and flown from separate staffs of the same height, what order are they placed in?
Alphabetically, using the English alphabet, with the flag of the United States at its own right (the observer's left)
Pg 160, 8.2.4.3.3

When in NATO countries, how are NATO member country flags displayed?
Alphabetically, using the French alphabet
Pg 160, 8.2.4.3.3

When the United States Flag is displayed horizontally or vertically against a wall, where should the union (blue field) be located?
It should be uppermost and to the flags own right (observer's left)
Pg 160, 8.2.4.3.5

When a flag is displayed in a church or public auditorium, it should be in the position of honor at the clergyman's or speaker's left as he/she faces the audience. True or false?
False, it should be on the clergyman's or speaker's right
Pg 161, 8.2.4.3.7

When a flag is placed on a closed casket, the union is at the head and over the right shoulder of the deceased. True or false?
False
Pg 161, 8.2.4.3.10

When the flag is folded to a triangular shape and placed in an open casket, which shoulder should it be placed by?
The left shoulder
Pg 161, 8.2.4.3.10

When placing the flag on a half opened casket, which shoulder should the union be positioned by?
The left shoulder
Pg 161, 8.2.4.3.10

At the conclusion of the funeral service, what happens to the flag?
It may be given to the next of kin
Pg 161, 8.2.4.3.10

How is the flag displayed when painted on an aircraft or vehicle?
The union is toward the front and the stripes trail
Pg 162, 8.2.4.3.12

Regimental colors, state flags, and organizational or institutional flags are always dipped as a mark of respect to the flag of the United States. True or false?
True
Pg 162, 8.2.5

When can the flag of the United States be displayed with the union down?
Only as a signal of dire distress in instances of extreme danger to life or property
Pg 162, 8.2.5.1

What is the recommended way to destroy the flag when it is no longer in a condition that it is a fitting emblem of display?
Preferably by burning it
Pg 164, 8.2.7

What are the names of the blue and yellow used in the Air Force seal?
Ultramarine blue and Air Force yellow
Pg 164, 8.3.1

What does the American bald eagle on the Air Force seal represent?
The United States and its air power
Pg 164, 8.3.1.1

What do the white clouds behind the eagle on the Air Force seal represent?
The start of a new sky
Pg 164, 8.3.1.1

What do the upper half (stylized wings) of the Air Force Symbol represent?
Strength
Pg 165, 8.4.2

Professional Behavior

What should you do if you are in a vehicle when you hear the music for the flag raising/lowering?
Stop the vehicle and sit quietly until the music ends
Pg 166, 8.5.2

You are required to stand or salute if the national anthem is played on the radio or television. True or false?
False
Pg 166, 8.5.4

You will salute a flag that is folded. True or false?
False, it is considered as cased
Pg 166, 8.5.4

Who renders a salute first, the junior or senior member?
The junior member
Pg 166, 8.6

If a junior member is carrying articles in both hands when a salute should be rendered, what should he/she do?
Exchange a verbal greeting
Pg 166, 8.6.1

Members are required to salute while in a formation. True or false?
False, unless given the command to do so
Pg 166, 8.6.1.1

In a group where a salute is rendered to a senior officer and the officer addresses an individual or a group, what is the proper protocol to the officer from the group?
All remain at attention, at the end of the conversation, they salute
Pg 166, 8.6.1.2

Saluting is required at public gatherings such as meetings or sporting events. True or false?
False
Pg 166, 8.6.1.3

As a pedestrian, you are required to salute officers in a properly marked staff car. True or false?
True
Pg 166, 8.6.1.4

Who is responsible for saluting when in a work detail situation?
The person in charge salutes for the entire detail, the individual workers do not salute
Pg 166, 8.6.1.6

When are salutes required indoors?
During formal reporting
Pg 167, 8.6.2

What is one of the most valuable habits of etiquette an individual can develop?
Being on time
Pg 167, 8.7.2

It is permissible to address a civil service employee by their first name. True or false?
False
Pg 167, 8.7.3

Figure 8.16 Terms of Address (pg 166)

Grade	Abbreviations	Terms of Address
SNCO Tier		
Chief Master Sergeant of the Air Force	CMSAF	Chief Master Sergeant of the Air Force or Chief
Chief Master Sergeant	CMSgt	Chief Master Sergeant or Chief
Senior Master Sergeant	SMSgt	Senior Master Sergeant or Sergeant
Master Sergeant	MSgt	Master Sergeant or Sergeant
NCO Tier		
Technical Sergeant	TSgt	Technical Sergeant or Sergeant
Staff Sergeant	SSgt	Staff Sergeant or Sergeant
	Airman Tier	
Senior Airman	SrA	Senior Airman or Airman
Airman First Class	A1C	Airman First Class or Airman
Airman	Amn	Airman
Airman Basic	AB	Airman Basic or Airman

What position should the junior person take when walking, riding, or sitting with a senior member?
The position to the senior's left
Pg 167, 8.9.1.1

In what order do military personnel enter automobiles and small boats?
Reverse order according to their rank with the senior officer last to enter and the first to leave
Pg 168, 8.9.1.4

Drill and Ceremony

Does reveille signal the start or the end of the official duty day?
The start of the official duty day
Pg 168, 8.10.1

The retreat ceremony signals the beginning of the official duty day. True or false?
False
Pg 169, 8.10.3.1

When lowering the installation flag, how many Airmen should accompany an NCO?
Five
Pg 170, 8.10.4.1

When or where do many units present awards?
During Commander's call
Pg 170, 8.11.1

How should awards be presented?
The commander/supervisor must ensure the presentation method reflects the significance of the award
Pg 170, 8.11.1

When should award presentations be held?
At the earliest possible date after approval of the decoration
Pg 170, 8.11.2.1

What should military participants and attendees wear to award ceremonies?
The uniform specified by the host. If in doubt, the Service Dress rather than the airman battle uniform (ABU) is recommended.
Pg 170, 8.11.2.1

According to the flag folding ceremony, when did the Second Continental Congress determine what the United States flag would be?
14 June 1777
Pg 172, Figure 8.18

According to the flag folding ceremony, what do the red stripes in the flag of the United States symbolize?
Hardiness and valor
Pg 172, Figure 8.18

According to the flag folding ceremony, what do the white stripes in the flag of the United States symbolize?
Purity and innocence
Pg 172, Figure 8.18

According to the flag folding ceremony, what does the blue in the flag of the United States symbolize?
Vigilance, perseverance and justice
Pg 172, Figure 8.18

Promotions are significant events in the lives of military people. Who is responsible for ensuring personnel receive proper recognition?
Commanders and supervisors
Pg 172, 8.11.3.1

The Airman can invite guests to his/her reenlistment ceremony. True or false?
True
Pg 172, 8.11.4.1

Who is responsible for performing reenlistment ceremonies?
The Airman may request any commissioned officer to perform the ceremony
Pg 172, 8.11.4.1

Who is responsible for ensuring members have a retirement ceremony?
Commanders
Pg 173, 8.11.5.1.1

The member's spouse is customarily presented an award during a retirement ceremony. True or false?
True, a Certificate of Appreciation for the support and sacrifices made during the member's career
Pg 173, 8.11.5.1.2

The retirement certificate can be mailed to the receiving member. True or false?
True, if there is no other choice
Pg 173, 8.11.5.1.3

What event is formal and for military members only?
A Dining-In
Pg 173, 8.12.1.1

Who had famous wingdings and is credited with the current day Dining-In format?
General Henry H. Hap Arnold
Pg 173, 8.12.1.1

What is the appropriate dress for a Dining-In/Outs?
Mess dress or semi-formal uniform for military and whatever dress is specified on the invitation for civilians
Pg 173, 8.12.1.2

The Order of the Sword Induction ceremony is the highest recognition enlisted people can bestow on anyone. True or false?
True
Pg 173, 8.12.2

When planning a retirement ceremony, how far in advance should personal invitations have to be mailed?
They are optional
Pg 174, Figure 8.19

At a retirement ceremony, who is responsible for welcoming everyone and introducing the special guests?
The Emcee
Pg 174, Figure 8.19

What types of standards were established to ensure movements are executed with order and precision during a drill?
The 24-inch step and cadence of 100 to 120 steps per minute
Pg 174, 8.13.1

What are the two oral orders of a drill command?
Preparatory command and the command of execution
Pg 175, 8.13.3.1

What does the preparatory command of a drill explain?
What the movements will be
Pg 175, 8.13.3.1

What does the command of execution in a drill explain?
When the movement will be carried out
Pg 175, 8.13.3.1

What type of angle are your heels in when you come to attention?
A 45 degree angle
Pg 175, 8.13.5.1

What is the proper way to hold your hands when standing at attention?
Hands are cupped but not clenched with palms facing the leg
Pg 175, 8.13.5.1

What are the four positions of rest?
Parade rest, at ease, rest, and fall out.
Pg 175, 8.13.5.2

What are the commands to align the flight in a line formation?
Dress Right, Dress and Ready, Front
Pg 176, 8.13.7.4

Honor Guard

What is the primary mission of the base honor guard program?
To employ, equip, and train Air Force members to provide professional military funeral honors for active duty, retired members, and veterans of the United States Air Force.
Pg 177, 8.14.1

Who is responsible for the base honor guard program?
The Installation Commander
Pg 177, 8.14.1

How are honor guard members selected?
Volunteers are generally selected from the ranks of Airman basic to Technical Sergeant
Pg 177, 8.14.1

When did Headquarters Command, United States Air Force, direct the creation of an elite ceremonial unit comparable to those of the other Services, the result being the base honor guard?
May 1948
Pg 177, 8.14.2

Where was the first base honor guard activated?
The 1100th Air Police Squadron, Bolling Field, Washington DC
Pg 177, 8.14.2

In January of 2000, public law was implemented, providing for all veterans to receive, at a minimum, a funeral ceremony that includes what?
The folding of a United States flag, presentation of the flag to the veteran's family, and the playing of "Taps."
Pg 177, 8.14.3

Figure 8.21 Flight in Column Formation (Pg 175)

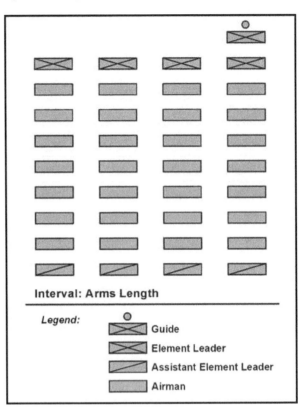

Figure 8.20 Flight in Line Formation (Pg 175)

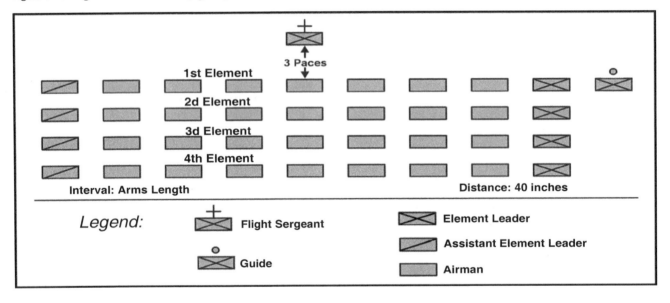

Figure 8.17. Folding the United States Flag.

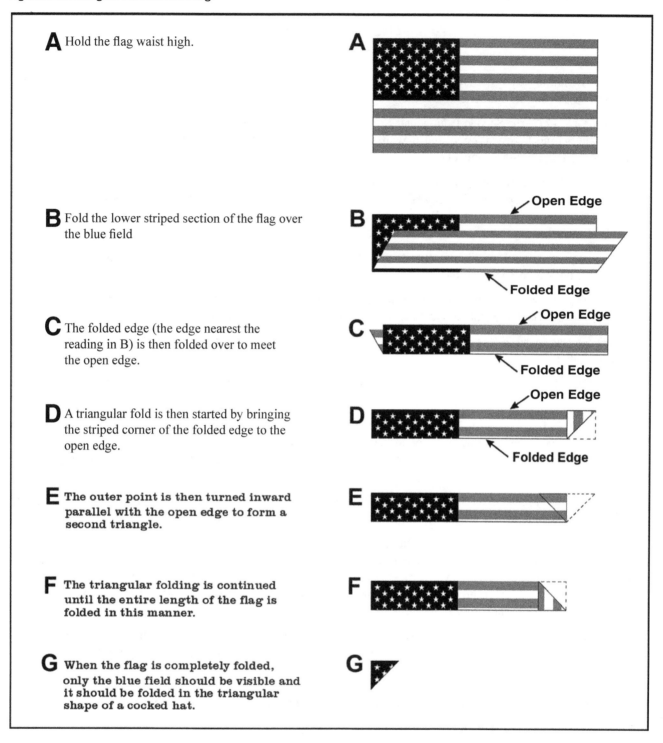

A Hold the flag waist high.

B Fold the lower striped section of the flag over the blue field

C The folded edge (the edge nearest the reading in B) is then folded over to meet the open edge.

D A triangular fold is then started by bringing the striped corner of the folded edge to the open edge.

E The outer point is then turned inward parallel with the open edge to form a second triangle.

F The triangular folding is continued until the entire length of the flag is folded in this manner.

G When the flag is completely folded, only the blue field should be visible and it should be folded in the triangular shape of a cocked hat.

Figure 8.18. Flag Folding Ceremony.

Flag Folding Ceremony

Air Force Script

For more than 230 years, the American flag has been the symbol of our nation's unity, as well as a source of pride and inspiration for millions of citizens.

Born June 14, 1777, the Second Continental Congress determined that the flag of the United States would be 13 stripes, alternating between 7 red and 6 white, and that the union would be 13 stars, white in a blue field representing a new constellation. (1)

Between 1777 and 1960, the shape and design of the flag evolved into the flag presented before you today. The 13 horizontal stripes represent the original 13 colonies, while the stars represent the 50 states of the Union. The colors of the flag are symbolic as well: red symbolizes hardiness and valor; white signifies purity and innocence; and blue represents vigilance, perseverance and justice. (1)

Traditionally, a symbol of liberty, the American flag has carried the message of freedom, and inspired Americans, both at home and abroad.

In 1814, Francis Scott Key was so moved at seeing the Stars and Stripes waving after the British shelling of Baltimore's Fort McHenry that he wrote the words to The Star Spangled Banner. (3)

In 1892 the flag inspired Francis Bellamy to write the "Pledge of Allegiance," our most famous flag salute and patriotic oath. (3)

In July 1969 the American flag was "flown" in space when Neil Armstrong planted it on the surface of the moon. (3)

Today, our flag flies on constellations of Air Force satellites that circle our globe, and on the fin flash of our aircraft that serve in harm's way in every corner of the world. Indeed, it flies in the heart of every Airman who serves our great Nation. The sun never sets on our United States Air Force, nor on the flag we so proudly cherish. (3)

Since 1776, no generation of Americans has been spared the responsibility of defending freedom. Today's Airmen remain committed to preserving the freedom that others won for us for the generations to come.

By displaying the flag and giving it a distinctive fold we show respect to the flag, and express our gratitude to those individuals who fought, and continue to fight for freedom at home and abroad. Since the dawn of the 20th century, Airmen have proudly flown the flag in every major conflict on lands and skies around the world. It is their responsibility - our responsibility - to continue to protect and preserve the rights, privileges and freedoms that we, as Americans, enjoy today.

The United States flag represents who we are. It stands for the freedom we all share and the pride and patriotism we feel for our country. We cherish its legacy, as a beacon of hope to one and all. Long may it wave.

Notes:

1. From a report Secretary of Congress Robert Thompson wrote to define the seal of our nation (1777).
2. Text from President Woodrow Wilson's Flag Day message (1917).
3. Based on historical facts.

Figure 8.19 A General Guideline for Planning a Retirement Ceremony (Pg 172)

- Appoint someone to set up the ceremony.
- Notify the honoree to ensure the date and times are good. Select and reserve a location for the ceremony.
- Determine whom the honoree would like to assist with the ceremony honors and have the honoree extend the invitation.
- Mail personal invitations to guests (optional).
- Ensure all award elements and certificates are ready. Select an emcee and individuals to act as escorts to any special guests as required.
- Request photographic support from the multimedia center.
- Ensure media equipment, if appropriate, is available. Recommend a "walk through" of the actual ceremony.
- Order refreshments.
- Print programs and make or obtain signs for seating and parking for special guests. Verify guest list with honoree and obtain special guest information (relationship, title, and correct spelling of name). Provide guest information, agenda, proposed remarks, applicable biographies or personnel records, and honoree's personal data to officiating officer and emcee.
- Dry run the ceremony with all key players.
- Set up the location at least 2 hours before the ceremony. Meet with honoree to go over last-minute details.
- Honoree and special guests often meet with the officiating officer just before the ceremony. The ceremony begins with the emcee announcing their arrival at the ceremony location.
- Emcee welcomes everyone and introduces the special guests.
- The emcee or officiating officer provides career highlights of the honoree.
- The emcee reads the special order of the honoree and the officiating officer performs ceremony procedures.
- Photos are taken throughout the ceremony.
- Honoree provides remarks.
- The emcee thanks everyone for coming and invites participants to congratulate the honoree and enjoy the refreshments.

Chapter 8 ends here for those testing to SSgt, TSgt, or MSgt. If testing to SMSgt or CMSgt, continue studying this chapter

Protocol

Protocol is an internationally recognized system of courtesy and respect. True or false?
True
Pg 179, 8.15

Distinguished Visitors (DV)

What item is NOT a suggested item to be included in the guest quarters of a distinguished visitor (DV)?
A fully stocked mini bar
Pg 179, 8.16.3

What is a customary timeframe to leave between the end-of-the-day activities and the start of evening functions when scheduling an itinerary for a distinguished visitor (DV)?
Two hours
Pg 179, 8.16.4

Military Ceremonies

When was the rank of NCO established?
In the 12th century
Pg 180, 8.18.1.1

How did ancient NCOs honor their leader and pledge their loyalty?
By ceremoniously presenting him with a sword which was a symbol of truth, justice, and power
Pg 180, 8.18.1.2

When was the first recorded Royal Order of the Sword in the United States?
In the 1860's when General Robert E. Lee was presented a sword by his command
Pg 180, 8.18.1.2

What year was the Royal Order of the Sword revised, updated, and adopted by Air Force NCOs?
1967
Pg 180, 8.18.2

Who is responsible for planning, executing, and paying for the Order of the Sword ceremony?
Host NCO's
Pg 181, 8.18.5

The Order of the Sword list of recipients is maintained by the CMSAF. True or false?
True
Pg 181, 8.18.7

Chapter 9
Enlisted Force Development

Overview

What is considered the backbone of the Air Force?
Their NCOs
Pg 183, 9.1

The Enlisted Force Structure

How many tiers make up the enlisted force?
Three
Pg 184, 9.4

At what rank does an Airman begin to exercise limited supervision and leader skills?
Senior Airman (SrA)
Pg 184, 9.4.1

At what rank does an enlisted member become an expert hands-on tech?
NCO - SSgt and TSgt
Pg 184, 9.4.2

The three Air Force leadership and development levels in the Air Force are Tactical, Operational, and Management. True or false?
False
Pg 184, 9.5

Who does the tactical level of leadership normally apply to?
Airman Basic (AB) through Technical Sergeant (TSgt)
Pg 184, 9.5.1

Where do enlisted members at the operational level of leadership normally work?
At a Numbered Air Force (NAF) and below
Pg 184, 9.5.2

Who does the strategic level of leadership normally apply to?
Chief Master Sergeants (CMSgts) and a few other NCOs who are assigned to higher headquarters
Pg 184, 9.5.3

Where are Airmen expected to seek assistance when having issues that can prevent them from focusing on the mission?
Their supervisory chain
Pg 186, 9.6.2.3.1

Does being spiritually ready include religious activities?
It may or may not
Pg 186, 9.6.2.4

An Airman Basic (AB) performs basic tasks under close supervision. True or false?
True
Pg 186, 9.7.1

What level of leadership and development does an Airman Basic (AB) operate at?
The tactical level
Pg 186, 9.7.1

An Airman is expected to begin to show job proficiency at basic tasks and still require significant supervision and support. True or false?
True
Pg 184, 9.7.2

What level of leadership and development does an Airman operate at?
The tactical level
Pg 186, 9.7.2

What are Airmen First Class (A1C) expected to devote their efforts toward?
Mastery of skills required in their career fields
Pg 186, 9.7.3

What level of leadership and development does an Airman First Class (A1C) operate at?
The tactical level
Pg 186, 9.7.3

Senior Airmen (SrA) serve as reporting officials upon completion of Airman Leadership School (ALS). True or false?
True
Pg 186, 9.7.4

What level of leadership and development does a Senior Airman (SrA) operate at?
The tactical level
Pg 186, 9.7.4

NCOs have authority to issue lawful orders appropriate for completion of their assigned tasks. True or false?
True
Pg 186, 9.8.1

An NCO is responsible for training and developing subordinates to ensure they are technically ready to accomplish the mission. True or false?
True
Pg 187, 9.8.2.1

What must supervisors do in order to support their subordinates as they struggle to resolve their problems?
Stay involved
Pg 187, 9.8.2.3.2

If an NCO notices an individual exhibiting behavior indicating he/she may be suicidal, would the NCO be responsible for immediately seeking assistance until relieved by the proper authority? True or false?
True
Pg 187, 9.8.2.3.4

Why must NCOs frequently visit dining facilities, chapel centers, recreation facilities, and enlisted clubs?
To familiarize themselves with off-duty opportunities and living conditions
Pg 187, 9.8.2.3.5

What determines seniority among NCOs of the same grade?
Date of rank, total active federal military service date, pay date, and date of birth
Pg 188, 9.8.3

What type of leadership and supervisory role must an NCO mentor take with his/her personnel?
An active one
Pg 188, 9.8.5

NCOs need to support voluntary off-duty education opportunities. True or false?
True
Pg 188, 9.8.9

SSgts should be primarily highly skilled technicians with supervisory and training responsibilities. True or false?
True
Pg 188, 9.9.1

What level of leadership and development do Staff Sergeants (SSgts) operate at?
The tactical level
Pg 189, 9.9.1

What do Technical Sergeants (TSgts) usually provide within their specialty for their organization?
Usually they are technical experts
Pg 189, 9.9.2

What level of leadership and development do Technical Sergeants (TSgts) operate at?
The tactical level
Pg 189, 9.9.2

The primary purpose of a SNCO is to lead and manage teams to accomplish the mission. True or false?
True
Pg 189, 9.10.1

SNCOs are at a level to help leadership make informed decisions by drawing upon their knowledge and experience. True or false?
True
Pg 189, 9.10.4

At what rank does an individual go from being technical experts and first-line supervisors to operational leaders?
Master Sergeant (MSgt)
Pg 189, 9.11.1

What level of leadership and development do Master Sergeants (MSgts) normally operate at?
Operational
Pg 189, 9.11.1

What level of leadership and development do Senior Master Sergeants (SMSgts) operate at?
Operational
Pg 190, 9.11.2

What level(s) of leadership and development do Chief Master Sergeants (CMSgts) serve at?
Operational and strategic
Pg 190, 9.11.3

How many subordinate work centers must a Section Chief have?
Two
Pg 190, 9.12.3

What position is critical to providing the Commander a mission-ready force?
First Sergeant
Pg 191, 9.13.1.1

How long is the first sergeant initial duty assignment for?
3 years
Pg 191, 9.13.1.2

What rank is a group superintendent?
Chief Master Sergeant (CMSgt)
Pg 191, 9.13.2

Enlisted academy commandants implement and enforce policies, procedures, and directives directly related to the academies' courses of instruction. True or false?
True
Pg 192, 9.13.3

Who coordinates with AFPC to distribute personnel throughout the MAJCOM?
Enlisted MAJCOM Functional Manager (MFM)
Pg 192, 9.13.4

Who is responsible for organizing and managing one or more enlisted career fields?
Air Force Career Field Manager (AFCFM)
Pg 192, 9.13.5

Why did Air Force leadership initially reject the proposal of having a Chief Master Sergeant of the Air Force?
They feared it might undermined the formal chain of command
Pg 193, 9.13.7

When was the CMSAF created?
24 October 1966
Pg 193, 9.13.7

Who was the first CMSAF?
Paul W. Airey
Pg 193, 9.13.7

What position did CMSAF Paul Wesley Airey occupy when he enlisted on 16 Nov 1942?
A radio operator
Pg 193, 9.13.7.1.1

What was CMSAF Airey awarded for creating equipment from salvaged parts that improved corrosion control of sensitive radio and radar components?
The Legion of Merit
Pg 193, 9.13.7.1.1

What did CMSAF Airey consider as one of his greatest challenges?
Personnel retention
Pg 193, 9.13.7.1.2

What program did CMSAF Airey help produce?
The Weighted Airman Promotion System (WAPS)
Pg 193, 9.13.7.1.2

What did CMSAF Donald L. Harlow serve as when he was drafted into the Army Air Corp?
Armament and gunnery instructor
Pg 193, 9.13.7.2.1

Which CMSAF was known for his no-nonsense approach and keen ability to listen?
CMSAF Donald Harlow
Pg 194, 9.13.7.2.2

What CMSAF was raised on a farm in Iowa during the Great Depression?
CMSAF Richard D. Kisling
Pg 194, 9.13.7.3.1

What position was CMSAF Kisling drafted in to?
The Army's combat infantry
Pg 194, 9.13.7.3.1

What did CMSAF Kisling miss about being in the military during his separation?
The camaraderie
Pg 194, 9.13.7.3.1

What was CMSAF Kisling's first assignment in the Army Air Forces?
Clerk
Pg 194, 9.13.7.3.1

Which CMSAF was one of the first to wear the ranks of SMSgt and CMSgt?
Richard D. Kisling
Pg 194, 9.13.7.3.1

What did CMSAF Kisling's persistence help get approved by Congress in 1972?
The first Senior NCO Academy
Pg 194, 9.13.7.3.2

What nickname did CMSAF Kisling earn from his peers due to his concern for enlisted issues?
The GI's man in Washington
Pg 194, 9.13.7.3.2

What was CMSAF Thomas N. Barnes' first position in the USAF?
Aircraft maintainer
Pg 194, 9.13.7.4.1

What was CMSAF Barnes the first African-American to do?
Serve in the highest enlisted post of any of the military services
Pg 194, 9.13.7.4.1

What program did CMSAF Barnes help establish?
The Air Force Social Actions Program
Pg 194, 9.13.7.4.2

Which CMSAF believed that no one should advance in rank without Professional Military Training (PME)?
Thomas N. Barnes
Pg 194, 9.13.7.4.2

What was the first duty role for CMSAF Gaylor?
Military policeman
Pg 195, 9.13.7.5.1

Which CMSAF made the rank of MSgt in just 7 years and 7 months?
Robert D. Gaylor
Pg 195, 9.13.7.5.1

Which CMSAF was credited with securing a policy allowing SrAs to transport their families at government expense during a PCS move?
Robert D. Gaylor
Pg 195, 9.13.7.5.2

What career did CMSAF James M. McCoy seriously consider prior to enlisting in the USAF?
Priesthood
Pg 195, 9.13.7.6.1

Which CMSAF was selected as one of the USAF's 12 outstanding Airmen of the Year in 1974?
James M. McCoy
Pg 195, 9.13.7.6.1

Which CMSAF became the first senior enlisted advisor (SEA) at Strategic Air Command (SAC)?
James M. McCoy
Pg 195, 9.13.7.6.1

What was CMSAF McCoy's first challenge in office?
To improve the low recruiting and retention numbers
Pg 195, 9.13.7.6.2

What program was instituted during CMSAF McCoy's term?
The Stripes for Exceptional Performers Program (STEP)
Pg 195, 9.13.7.6.2

Which CMSAF volunteered for a position he thought was Air Police and had to pick up cigarette butts for three months because it actually was an Area Policeman position?
Arthur L. Andrews
Pg 196, 9.13.7.7.1

CMSAF Andrews never had the opportunity to enter the military police force. True or false?
False
Pg 196, 9.13.7.7.1

How long did CMSAF Andrews spend as a first sergeant?
A decade
Pg 196, 9.13.7.7.1

Which CMSAF believed Airman needed to begin thinking about "we" instead of "me, me, me"?
Arthur L. Andrews
Pg 196, 9.13.7.7.2

What position did CMSAF Parish hold when he joined the Air Force?
Ground weather equipment operator
Pg 196, 9.13.7.8.1

Which CMSAF trained in the experimental program of weather observation?
Sam E. Parish
Pg 196, 9.13.7.8.1

Which CMSAF was the first in his career field to become the youngest 7-level?
Sam E. Parish
Pg 196, 9.13.7.8.1

What age was CMSAF Parish when he became a SMSgt?
31
Pg 196, 9.13.7.8.1

Which CMSAF obtained approval to allow flight-line personnel to wear a functional badge on their uniform?
Sam E. Parish
Pg 196, 9.13.7.8.2

Which CMSAF established the John Levitow Award for each level of Professional Military Education (PME)?
Sam E. Parish
Pg 196, 9.13.7.8.2

Which CMSAF joined the Civil Air Patrol (CAP) in high school with the aspiration of becoming a pilot?
James C. Binniker
Pg 197, 9.13.7.9.1

Which CMSAF earned Cadet of the year and a scholarship to attend flight school and the right to represent his state as a foreign exchange cadet in Great Britain?
James C. Binniker
Pg 197, 9.13.7.9.1

Which CMSAF did doctors detect a high frequency hearing loss which disqualified him from being in the flight school program?
James C. Binniker
Pg 197, 9.13.7.9.1

Which CMSAF cross-trained into air operations where he planned flights for missions going to Vietnam?
James C. Binniker
Pg 197, 9.13.7.9.1

What was CMSAF Binnicker's first order of business?
Tackling the Airman Performance Report (APR)
Pg 197, 9.13.7.9.2

What did CMSAF Gary R. Pfingston do prior to enlisting in the Air Force as an aircraft mechanic?
He was a minor league baseball player
Pg 197, 9.13.7.10.1

What happened to CMSAF Pfingston during an assignment to Anderson AFB, Guam?
He broke his back
Pg 197, 9.13.7.10.1

What was the toughest challenge CMSAF Pfingston faced?
The Air Force downsizing
Pg 197, 9.13.7.10.2

Which CMSAF worked to prevent involuntary separations by getting the Voluntary Separation Incentive (VSP) and Special Separation Bonus (SSB) implemented?
Gary R. Pfingston
Pg 197, 9.13.7.10.2

Which CMSAF's idea led to the CFETP three-level and seven-level technical schools for all career fields and mandatory in-resident PME schools?
Gary R. Pfingston
Pg 197, 9.13.7.10.2

Which CMSAF fought Congress when they wanted to change the retirement system to "High One" which would have reduced retirement pay?
David J. Campanale
Pg 198, 9.13.7.11.2

Which CMSAF advised anyone wanting to follow in his footsteps to be honest and keep your promise?
David J. Campanale
Pg 198, 9.13.7.11.2

What was the first position CMSAF Eric W. Benken served in?
Administrative specialist
Pg 198, 9.13.7.12.1

Which CMSAF played a major role in developing Warrior Week at Basic Training and changing the curriculum at the First Sergeant Academy to focus on deployments?
Eric W. Benken
Pg 198, 9.13.7.12.2

Which CMSAF was the first co-chair of The Air Force Retiree Council?
Eric W. Benken
Pg 198, 9.13.7.12.2

What position did CMSAF Jim Finch perform prior to becoming a Professional Military Education (PME) instructor?
Missile maintenance crew chief
Pg 199, 9.13.7.13.1

What did CMSAF Gerald R. Murray work as prior to entering the Air Force as a fighter aircraft crew chief in 1977?
He worked in a textile mill and in construction
Pg 199, 9.13.7.14.1

Which CMSAF initiated changes to the management of CMSgts including alignment under the Air Force Senior Leaders Management Office?
Gerald R. Murray
Pg 199, 9.13.7.14.2

During his first tour, CMSAF Rodney J. McKinley was a medical technician. What position did he serve in when he returned to the Air Force?
Aircraft maintenance specialist
Pg 200, 9.13.7.15.1

Which CMSAF was a strong advocate for the American Airman spirit and opened the door for the creation of The Airman's Creed?
Rodney J. McKinley
Pg 200, 9.13.7.15.2

What position did CMSAF James A. Roy enter the Air Force as?
Heavy equipment operator
Pg 200, 9.13.7.16.1

Which CMSAF continued to stress the importance of updating and expanding distance learning opportunities in PME following Airman Leadership School (ALS)?
James A. Roy
Pg 200, 9.13.7.16.2

What position did CMSAF Cody enter the Air Force as
Air Traffic Controller
Pg 201, 9.13.7.17.1

What is a mindset, evident in our behaviors, that causes us to proudly exhibit the highest levels of professional service to our country?
Airmanship
Pg 201, 9.14.1

What does the We Are All Recruiters (WEAR) program grant individuals if they are participating in an event that will help Air Force Recruiting Service efforts?
Permissive TDY status
Pg 201, 9.15.1

Who must approve a request for participation in the WEAR program?
The individual's commander
Pg 202, 9.15.1

How many days of permissive TDY may be granted to a member to attend approved We Are All Recruiters (WEAR) events?
Up to 12 days
Pg 202, 9.15.1

What program grants up to 12 days of non-chargeable leave (including one weekend) to members who positively impact recruiting?
Recruiters Assistance Program (RAP)
Pg 202, 9.15.2

Enlisted Professional Military Education (EPME)

Approximately how many students complete Enlisted Professional Military Education (EPME) a year?
Approximately 40,000 enlisted Airmen
Pg 202, 9.16

Table 9.1 - Airmanship Behaviors (Pg 199)

	Airmanship	Mindset Behaviors
1	Promise keeping	Carrying out the oath of enlistment or commissioning oath
2	Believing and embracing Air Force core values	Living Air Force core values; using them to guide decisionmaking and behavior
3	Willingness to fulfill all mandated responsibilities	Fulfilling all mandated responsibilities

Where is the Educational Programs Cadre (EPC) of the Thomas N. Barnes Center for Enlisted Education (BCEE) located?
Maxwell AFB-Gunter Annex, AL
Pg 202, 9.16.1

What program has the vision to develop Airmen with a warrior ethos and a passion for leading in the cause of freedom?
Academic Affairs (AA)
Pg 202, 9.16.1.1

What is the first of the three programs enlisted professionals attend as they progress through their Air Force Career?
Airman Leadership School (ALS)
Pg 202, 9.16.2.1

Completion of Airman Leadership School (ALS) is required to perform duties as a reporting official and to be eligible for promotion to SSgt. True or false?
True
Pg 203, 9.16.2.1.1

How long is the Airman Leadership School (ALS) program?
5 weeks
Pg 203, 9.16.2.1.2

What rank can be obtained after completing NCOA?
MSgt
Pg 203, 9.16.2.2.1

How long is the NCOA course?
6 weeks
Pg 203, 9.16.2.2.2

What is required before an individual can be promoted to SMSgt?
Completion of Air Force Senior NCO Academy (AFSNCOA)
Pg 203, 9.16.2.3.1

How long is the Air Force Senior NCO Academy (AFSNCOA)?
7 weeks
Pg 203, 9.16.2.3.2

What course is voluntary but highly encouraged for active duty and required for a senior rated endorsement on SNCO performance reports?
SNCO (Course 14)
Pg 203, 9.16.3.3

Which course educates senior enlisted leaders slated to or assigned to joint organizations?
SEJPME
Pg 204, 9.17.1

Military Ethics

According to Dr James H. Toner, former Professor of International Relations and Military Ethics, Air War College, what are ethics rooted in?
The three O's - owing, ordering, and oughting
Pg 204, 9.18.1

Enlisted Force Development

What is the life-cycle approach for Airmen preparing to accomplish the Air Force mission while meeting personal and professional needs?
EFD
Pg 205, 9.19

What provides oversight for enlisted force development efforts?
EFDP
Pg 205, 9.20.1

What is used for planning personnel eligible for critical leadership and development positions?
EDTs
Pg 205, 9.21.1

What web-based resource enables enlisted Airmen to manage their professional development?
My Enlisted Development Plan (MyEDP)
Pg 206, 9.21.2

What tool will help various stakeholders make informed decisions impacting the future of the enlisted force?
Strategic Visual Mapping Tool
Pg 206, 9.21.3

What competencies do leaders use to set the organizational climate:
People/Team
Pg 208, 9.22.2

Which competencies is most in demand at the strategic level?
Organizational
Pg 208, 9.22.3

Chapter 9 ends here for those testing to SSgt, TSgt, or MSgt. If testing to SMSgt or CMSgt, continue studying this chapter

The Profession of Arms—An Airman's Perspective

According to General Ronald Fogleman, former CSAF, what responsibility do we have as guardians of America's future?
To place the needs of our service and our country before personal concerns
Pg 212, 9.24

What goal do all Airmen share?
To accomplish their organizational mission
Pg 213, 9.25.2

What is the mindset designed to build confidence and commitment necessary to shape professional Airmen able to work as a team to accomplish the mission?
The Warrior Ethos
Pg 213, 9.26.1

What is the ability to face danger or hardship in a determined and resolute manner and to have the willingness to step outside of one's comfort zone to deal with an unexpected situation?
Valor
Pg 213, 9.27

According to General Curtis E. LeMay, former Air Force Chief of Staff, what is the most extraordinary kind of heroism?
Saving the lives of your fellow Airman
Pg 214, 9.27

What three forms does courage primarily come in?
Personal, physical, and moral
Pg 214, 9.28

What is defined by doing what's right even at risk to your career?
Personal courage
Pg 214, 9.28

What type of courage is the ability to overcome fears of bodily harm to get the job done?
Physical courage
Pg 214, 9.28

What type of courage is defined by the ability to stand by the core values when it may not be the popular thing to do?
Moral courage
Pg 214, 9.28

What is a willingness to give up one's life, time, or comfort to meet others' needs?
Sacrifice
Pg 215, 9.29.2

Personal Professionalism

What award was Senior Airman Jason D. Cunningham posthumously awarded?
The Air Force Cross
Pg 216, 9.31

Preparedness is one sure way to know someone is a military professional. True or false?
True
Pg 216, 9.31.1

When is most experience gained?
When accepting opportunities as they come, even when conditions are not perfect
Pg 217, 9.31.3

Who created the CSAF Professional Reading Program?
General Fogleman
Pg 217, 9.32.1

Who is responsible for the day-to-day management of the CSAF Professional Reading Program's reading list?
The Air Force Historian
Pg 217, 9.31.3

What is at the heart and soul of the military profession?
Core values
Pg 217, 9.33.1

Upon entering the Air Force, who do Airmen accept a sacred trust from?
The American people
Pg 217, 9.33.2

Chapter 10
Leadership

Overview

What word is defined as to act or to guide?
Lead
Pg 219, 10.1

Leadership

What two elements must leadership support?
The mission and the people who accomplish it
Pg 219, 10.2

What did General Ronald R. Fogleman say about people?
People are the assets that determine our success or failure
Pg 219, 10.2

How does a good leader help with their subordinates' careers?
They get involved
Pg 219, 10.2.1

People may obey commands and orders but what causes them to respond quickly and usually give extra effort?
When they feel their leaders genuinely care about them
Pg 219, 10.2.1

What is sometimes the toughest part of being a leader?
Setting the example
Pg 220, 10.2.3

In addition to being expected to accomplish the mission, what else is a leader expected to do?
To do so with the minimum cost in people, materiel, and money
Pg 220, 10.2.3

What type of style does every leader develop?
A unique one
Pg 220, 10.4

Figure 10.1 Managers and Leaders: A Comparison
Bennis's (an author) Behavioral Characteristics Comparison

Managers	Leaders
Administer	Motivate
Maintain	Develop
Control	Inspire

White's (Professor – Indiana University) Personal Characteristics Comparison

Managers	Leaders
Problem solvers	Analyze purposes and causes
Statistics driven	Values driven
Seek conflict avoidance	Accept and invite conflict
Thrive on predictability	Ambiguous
Ensure organizational objectives are achieved (even if they disagree with them)	Ensure their objectives and those of the organization become one and the same

What did General Louis L. Wilson, Jr. suggest a leader do that will make many of their problems go away?
Get out from behind their desk
Pg 220, 10.4.2

What did General Louis L. Wilson, Jr. say about putting off hard decisions?
It won't be any easier tomorrow
Pg 221, 10.4.8

What should leaders insist their people do with questions they have?
Encourage them to come to you if they have questions
Pg 221, 10.4.10

In addition to knowing the Air Force standards, what must Air Force leaders do?
Enforce them
Pg 221, 10.5

Air Force members are subject to duty 24 hours a day, 365 days a year. True or false?
True
Pg 222, 10.5.3

What is the limit to the number of hours an Air Force member can work?
They must report for duty at any hour and must remain there as long as needed to get the job done
Pg 222, 10.5.3

Standards of conduct apply only while on duty. True or false?
False
Pg 222, 10.5.5

What did Warren G. Bennis (author) say about leaders and managers?
Leaders are people who do the right thing, managers are people who do things right
Pg 222, 10.6

What must wartime forces have at all levels?
Competent leadership
Pg 224, 10.6.2.3.2

The degree to which trust, loyalty, and integrity are present in the leadership directly relates to an organization's effectiveness. True or false?
True
Pg 224, 10.7.2

The right decision is usually the easiest decision. True or false?
False
Pg 224, 10.7.2

How will a subordinate reward a leader they trust?
With trustworthiness and loyalty
Pg 224, 10.7.2

What most often prevents individuals from becoming great leaders?
Lack of character
Pg 224, 10.7.3

What can provide the stimulus to a subordinate to open up and discuss their inner feelings?
Compassion
Pg 224, 10.7.3.2

What must a leader be able to draw out of each organizational member?
Their unique strengths
Pg 224, 10.7.4

Successful leaders earn credibility by leading by example and taking responsibility. True or false?
True
Pg 225, 10.7.4

How does a leader become a positive role model?
Leading by example
Pg 225, 10.7.4.1

A mere vision can be infectious enough to help people accomplish a goal. True or false?
True
Pg 225, 10.8.1.1

What is a common leadership error?
To become preoccupied with the present at the expense of the future
Pg 225, 10.8.1.2

John C. Maxwell said a great leader's courage to fulfill his vision comes from his position. True or false?
False
Pg 225, 10.8.2

What happens when a vision becomes an obsession?
It can adversely affect leader and follower judgment
Pg 226, 10.8.3

What is defined as a force that energizes people and provides responsibility, ownership, and control over the work they perform?
Empowerment
Pg 226, 10.9.1

How does the adage it's lonely at the top apply to leaders?
When the leader does not recognize the strengths of his/her own people
Pg 226, 10.9.2.2

What is the cornerstone of the mutually dependent relationship shared by leaders and followers?
Trust
Pg 226, 10.9.3

A consensus of an organization can divert it from its true goal or vision. True or false?
True
Pg 227, 10.9.4

What should be an integral part of every job?
Adventure
Pg 227, 10.10.2.1

How do leaders encourage the learning process?
By formally recognizing individual and unit successes, no matter how large or small
Pg 227, 10.10.2.2

What is the first step in developing people for leadership positions?
Identify leadership potential early in their careers then determine appropriate developmental challenges for them
Pg 228, 10.10.3.2

A late bloomer is someone whose leadership potential was not evident early on and whose combination of maturity, experience, and untapped potential is a valuable asset to any organization. True or false?
True
Pg 228, 10.10.3.2

Being over confident can prevent capable individuals from pursuing their creativity and innovation. True or false?
False
Pg 228, 10.10.4.1

What is a leader trying to do by explaining the limitations and shortfalls of the present process and the possibilities and benefits of the proposed change?
Create an organizational climate conducive to change
Pg 228, 10.11.2

What is the single most important part of character?
Integrity
Pg 229, 10.12.1

What is the most precious Air Force resource?
People
Pg 230, 10.12.3.2

Followership

Are leaders or their personnel the most technically skilled people in the unit?
Their personnel
Pg 230, 10.14

What skills are crucial for a follower when working in a team environment?
Communication skills
Pg 231, 10.15.3

What must a leader devote to their subordinates in order to be successful?
Attention to what their subordinates want and expect
Pg 231, 10.16

When do followers perform their best?
When they want to be in a unit, not trapped in it
Pg 231, 10.16

Mentoring

What is defined as a person with greater experience and wisdom guiding another person to develop both personally and professionally?
A mentor
Pg 232, 10.18

What does the long-term health of the Air Force depend on?
The experienced member developing the next in line
Pg 232, 10.18

What does mentoring prepare a person for?
Increased responsibilities
Pg 232, 10.19.1

What does mentoring foster between subordinates and supervisors?
Communication
Pg 232, 10.19.1

Who is designated as the primary mentor for each subordinate?
The immediate supervisor or rater
Pg 232, 10.20.1

What must supervisors and commanders do for subordinates who seek career guidance and counsel?
Make time for the subordinate
Pg 232, 10.20.1

What is the key to the mentoring process?
Direct involvement of the commander and supervisor
Pg 232, 10.20.2

It is the responsibility of the supervisor to take an active role in the development of their subordinates. True or false?
True
Pg 232, 10.21

What must a mentor be able to distinguish about an individual?
Individual goals, career aspirations, and realistic expectations
Pg 232, 10.21

PMEs prepare an individual to take on increased responsibilities appropriate to their grade and to enhance their contribution to the Air Force. True or false?
True
Pg 233, 10.22

What is designed to accurately appraise individual performance?
The Air Force evaluation system
Pg 233, 10.24

What is defined as a realistic assessment of performance, career standing, future potential, and actions required to assist the ratee in reaching the next level of professional development?
Performance feedback
Pg 233, 10.24

Is the Weighted Airman Promotion System (WAPS) for SSgt through MSgt or SMSgt and CMSgt?
SSgt through MSgt
Pg 233, 10.25

Which ranks use the whole person concept in the promotion selection process?
SMSgt through CMSgt
Pg 233, 10.25

What happens with the weighted and board scores during the promotion selection process?
They are added together
Pg 233, 10.25

Development Counseling

What is one of the most important responsibilities of every Air Force leader?
Subordinate leadership development
Pg 234, 10.28

A leader coaches subordinates by identifying weaknesses, setting goals, developing and implementing plans of action, and providing oversight and motivation throughout the process. True or false?
True
Pg 234, 10.30

Effective coaches or leaders must thoroughly understand the strengths, weaknesses, and professional goals of their subordinates. True or false?
True
Pg 234, 10.30

What characteristic of effective counseling encourages subordinates through actions while guiding them through the problem?
Support
Pg 234, Fig 10.2

Prior to counseling subordinates, you need to be fully aware of your own values, needs, and biases so you are less likely to project those biases on the subordinate. True or false?
True
Pg 234, 10.31.2

What action allows an individual the ability to understand and be sensitive to the feelings, thoughts, and experiences of another person to the point that you can almost feel or experience them yourself?
Empathy
Pg 234, 10.31.4

What is achieved by a leader when being honest and consistent in their statements and actions?
Credibility
Pg 235, 10.31.5

What general skills are needed in almost every counseling session?
Active listening, responding, and questioning
Pg 235, 10.32

What type of questions should be asked during a counseling session?
Open-ended questions
Pg 235, 10.32.3

What is the key to a successful counseling for a specific performance?
To conduct the counseling as close to the event as possible
Pg 235, 10.33.1.1

A performance and professional growth counseling should focus on the subordinate's strengths and areas needing improvement. True or false?
True
Pg 235, 10.33.2

How does an effective leader approach each subordinate in a counseling session?
As an individual
Pg 236, 10.34

Which counseling approach is normally preferred for most counseling sessions?
Non-directive
Pg 236, 10.34.1

Which type of counseling session should avoid providing solutions or opinions?
Non-directive
Pg 236, 10.34.1

What type of counseling session should be used to correct simple problems, make on-the-spot corrections, and correct aspects of duty performance?
Directive
Pg 236, 10.34.2

What type of counseling session is used to tell the subordinate what to do and when to do it?
Directive
Pg 236, 10.34.2

Which type of counseling session encourages the subordinate to decide on the best solution?
Combined
Pg 236, 10.34.3

When selecting a suitable place for counseling, the subordinates' work area is the preferred place. True or false?
False
Pg 237, 10.35.2.1

Figure 10.2 Characteristics of Effective Counseling (pg 229)

Purpose	Clearly define the purpose of the counseling
Flexibility	Fit the counseling style to the character of each subordinate and to the relationship desired
Respect	View subordinates as unique, complex individuals, each with a distinct set of values, beliefs, and attitudes
Communication	Establish open, two-way communication with subordinates using spoken language, non-verbal actions, gestures, and body language. Effective counselors listen more than they speak
Support	Encourage subordinates through actions while guiding them through their problems

Leadership

Figure 10.3 Counseling Approach Summary Chart (pg 231)

Approach	Advantages	Disadvantages
Non-directive	• Encourages maturity • Encourages open communication • Develops personal responsibility	• Is more time consuming • Requires greater counselor skills
Directive	• Is the quickest method • Is good for people who need clear, concise direction • Allows counselors to actively use their experience	• Doesn't encourage subordinates to be part of the solution • Tends to treat symptoms not problems • Tends to discourage subordinates from talking freely • The counselor provides the solution, not the subordinate
Combined	• Is moderately quick • Encourages maturity • Encourages open communication • Allows counselors to actively use their experience	• May take too much time for some situations

How long should a counseling session normally last?
Less than 1 hour
Pg 237, 10.35.2.2

What type of strategy should you use in the counseling session?
One that suits your subordinate and the situation
Pg 237, 10.35.2.5

What is the best way to open a counseling session?
To clearly state its purpose
Pg 237, 10.35.3.1

The best way to develop a mutual understanding is to let the subordinate do most of the talking and responding/questioning without dominating the conversation. True or false?
True
Pg 237, 10.35.3.2

If the issue of a counseling session is for substandard performance, what should you make clear?
How the performance did not meet the standard and then develop a plan of action
Pg 237, 10.35.3.2

What part of a counseling session identifies a method for achieving a desired result and specifies what the subordinate must do to reach the goals set during the counseling session?
Plan of action
Pg 237, 10.35.3.3

By the end of the counseling session, you should assume your subordinate understands all that was discussed. True or false?
False
Pg 237, 10.35.3.4

You should schedule any future meetings, even if tentative, prior to the dismissing the subordinate. True or false?
True
Pg 237, 10.35.3.4

The counseling process ends with the counseling session. True or false?
False, follow-up continues through implementation of the plan of action and evaluation of results
Pg 237, 10.35.4

It is your responsibility to support the subordinate following a counseling session. True or false?
True
Pg 237, 10.35.4

What is the challenge in today's work environment?
The diversity
Pg 238, 10.36

What improves communication, reduces confusion, provides purpose, and defines end points?
Clear guidelines
Pg 238, 10.36.2

Having a diversity of experience and background provides different ways of looking at problems. True or false?
True
Pg 238, 10.36.5

Sensitivity, mutual respect, and common trust coupled with communication are prime ingredients for what?
Integrating our Airman
Pg 238, 10.36.5

Air Force leaders are expected to challenge any policy, practice, or process that limits the growth and development of potential leaders from all groups. True or false?
True
Pg 238, 10.36.6

Full Range Leadership Development

What did the Air Force adopt because it combines the best parts of past leadership theories?
FRLD
Pg 238, 10.37

How many core elements make up FRLD
Three
Pg 238, 10.37.1

Which leadership behavior is hesitant to make decisions and usually are absent from their place of work?
Laissez-Faire
Pg 239, 10.37.2.1

Which leadership behavior believes "if it ain't broke, don't fix it?"
Management by exception-passive
Pg 239, 10.37.2.2

Which leadership behavior reduces the temptation for employees to avoid their duties or act unethically?
Management by exception-active
Pg 239, 10.37.2.3

Which leadership behavior empathizes and supports each follower while maintaining healthy communication?
Individualized consideration
Pg 240, 10.37.2.5.1

Chapter 10 ends here for those testing to SSgt, TSgt, or MSgt. If testing to SMSgt or CMSgt, continue studying this chapter

Mentorship

What is the process called when wisdom and experience of the senior member are passed on to the junior member?
Mentoring
Pg 242, 10.38.1

What is one of the most powerful means by which we can shape the future?
Mentoring
Pg 242, 10.38.1

What is the individual being assisted by a mentor usually called?
A Protégé
Pg 242, 10.38.1

What helps form a bond which fosters the kind of mutual commitment that characterizes mentoring at its best?
Empathy
Pg 242, 10.39.2

What mentoring component encompasses a caring attitude?
Nurturing
Pg 242, 10.39.3

What type of action must an effective mentor be on the alert for from the student?
Non-verbal
Pg 243, 10.39.6

What should a mentor introduce the student to that would normally take years to build?
A network
Pg 243, 10.39.8

Figure 10.5 The Mentoring Process (pg 236)

Model
Empathize
Nurture
Teach
Organize
Respond
Inspire
Network
Goal-set

Conflict Management

Conflict can be constructive or destructive. True or false?
True
Pg 243, 10.40.1

Constructive conflict can lead to a solution of a problem or a higher level of understanding between individuals or groups. True or false?
True
Pg 237, 10.40.1

Communication is usually a very small part of the communication problem. What is normally the true problem?
Miscommunication
Pg 243, 10.40.2.1

What are three differences that particularly may facilitate behaviors that cause conflict?
Values, perception, and personality
Pg 244, 10.40.3

Religious and political values can bring out the worst arguments and sometimes lead to fights. True or false?
True
Pg 244, 10.40.3.1

What two types of personalities are especially conflict-prone?
Highly authoritarian and low self-esteem
Pg 245, 10.40.3.3

What refers to how willing a person or group is to satisfy the others' needs?
Cooperation
Pg 245, 10.41.1

What conflict management style attempts to overwhelm an opponent with formal authority, threats, or the use of power?
Competing or forcing
Pg 245, 10.41.2.1

What conflict management style involves an attempt to satisfy the concerns of both sides through honest discussions?
Collaborating
Pg 245, 10.41.2.2

What conflict management style combines low assertiveness and high cooperation?
Accommodating
Pg 245, 10.41.2.3

A manager who avoids difficult issues can be resented by his/her subordinates. True or false?
True
Pg 245, 10.41.2.4.1

Unit Morale

A desired and acceptable behavior which influences individual effectiveness and job satisfaction are called norms. True or false?
True
Pg 246, 10.44.2

Norms (behavioral) can be both positive and negative. True or false?
True
Pg 246, 10.44.2

Is the every man for himself attitude a positive or negative norm?
A negative norm
Pg 247, 10.45.2

When group norms change, behavioral change should follow. True or false?
True
Pg 248, 10.46.2

Strategic Leadership

What types of leadership skills are predominately direct and face-to-face?
Tactical
Pg 248, 10.48.1

What type of leadership skill emphasizes people/team leadership development and introduces institutional leadership competencies?
Operational
Pg 248, 10.48.3

What type of leader focuses most of their time on looking forward and positioning the organization for long-term success?
Strategic leader
Pg 249, 10.49.2

Chapter 11
The Enlisted Evaluation System (EES)

Overview

What is the most precious resource the Air Force has?
People
Pg 251, 11.1.1

Individual Responsibilities

What should a ratee do when a required or requested feedback session does not take place?
Notify the rater and other evaluators in the chain
Pg 251, 11.2

How does the rater help the ratee improve performance?
By providing realistic feedback
Pg 251, 11.3.1

It is okay for a ratee to write some of their own performance report. True or false?
False, but the ratee should be encouraged to provide the rater input on his/her specific accomplishments
Pg 252, 11.3.2.2

Who is responsible for concurring or non-concurring with the rater and making comments in Section VI of the EPR?
The additional rater
Pg 252, 11.4

Who manages the performance report program for the organization?
The Unit Commander
Pg 252, 11.6

Who reviews all EPRs before the commander?
The First Sergeant
Pg 252, 11.7

Performance Feedback

What is performance feedback?
A private, formal communication tool a rater uses to tell a ratee what is expected regarding duty performance and how well the ratee is meeting expectations.
Pg 252, 11.8

Who provides performance feedback?
The rater
Pg 252, 11.9

Who is normally the rater for an individuals' performance feedback?
The ratee's immediate supervisor
Pg 252, 11.9

Performance feedbacks are mandatory for all enlisted personnel. True or false?
True
Pg 253, 11.9

How long after a rater initially begins supervising is the initial feedback session held?
Within 60 days
Pg 253, 11.10

What happens when a change of reporting official (CRO) takes place?
A new initial feedback session is due
Pg 253, 11.10

Midterm feedback sessions for ABs through SMSgt are held midway between the date supervision began and the projected EPR close date. True or false?
True
Pg 253, 11.10.1

Midterm feedbacks are required for CMSgts. True or false?
False
Pg 253, 11.10.1

When is the midterm session due for Airmen who do not receive EPRs?
Approximately 180 days after the initial session
Pg 253, 11.10.2

How long does the cycle of initial and midterm sessions continue for Airmen who do not receive EPRs?
Until there is a change of reporting official or the Airman begins to receive EPRs
Pg 253, 11.10.2

The Performance Feedback Worksheet (PFW) is used as a guide for conducting feedback sessions. True or false?
True
Pg 253, 11.11

Are comments typed or hand-written on the PFW?
They can be either
Pg 253, 11.11

What is the rater's feedback generally based on?
The situations that occur in the work environment
Pg 247, 11.12.4

Primary duties and general military factors are used to determine overall duty performance. True or false?
True
Pg 254, 11.12.4

What is the most important objective during a feedback session?
For the ratee to clearly understand the rater's position regarding performance and direction to take
Pg 254, 11.12.4

How is job excellence measured?
Quality of work
Pg 254, 11.12.4.1.1

What does the rater measure performance results against?
The minimum quality standards for the ratee's job
Pg 254, 11.12.4.1.1

A mission can suffer when a job is not completed on time. True or false?
True
Pg 254, 11.12.4.1.2

Who is responsible for knowing the available Professional Military Education (PME) courses for the ratee?
It is the rater's responsibility
Pg 255, 11.12.4.4.2

What are the most common resources SNCOs are involved with?
People, equipment, and money
Pg 259, 11.13.2.4.1

The primary purpose of feedback is to improve performance and professionally develop personnel to their highest potential. True or false?
True
Pg 262, 11.14

What type of environment should the rater hold the feedback session in?
One that is private and free of distractions
Pg 262, 11.14.2

What problems can arise during a feedback session?
They are as varied as the people who are involved in the process, and they can happen at any time
Pg 262, 11.14.5.1

When should the supporting notes be gathered for the performance feedback?
Over a period of time
Pg 263, 11.14.5.2.1

What area should feedback focus on?
Areas the person can exercise some control over
Pg 263, 11.16.4

What type of feedback should be avoided?
Negative comments that do not aid performance
Pg 264, 11.16.6

What should the rater do prior to closing the feedback session?
Review and summarize the key items discussed and reinforce the goals for the next observation period
Pg 264, 11.17.1

What is the most important way to end a feedback session?
On a positive, encouraging, and forward-looking note
Pg 264, 11.17.1

What helps keep a ratee on the road to improvement between feedback sessions?
For the rater to provide informal feedback on a regular basis
Pg 264, 11.17.2

Enlisted Performance Reports

The ratee's Unfavorable Information File (UIF) must be reviewed prior to preparing the Enlisted Performance Report (EPR). True or false?
True
Pg 265, 11.20.1

What should be avoided in the key duties, tasks, and responsibilities section of the Enlisted Performance Report (EPR)?
Jargon and acronyms
Pg 266, 11.22.2.3

What does the additional evaluator do when they disagree with specific comments on the EPR?
Mark the non-concur block and make specific comments regarding the reason for the non-concurrence
Pg 266, 11.22.3

If unable to digitally sign the form, what color ink must be used when manually signing the report?
Reproducible blue or black ink
Pg 266, 11.22.4

Who should the additional rater be?
It must be the rater's rater unless the additional rater does not meet grade requirements
Pg 267, 11.22.7

How many times does the Commander have to sign the EPR if they are part of the rating chain?
Twice (as the Commander's review and the appropriate evaluator's section
Pg 272, 11.22.11

What must a rater ensure regarding information used to document derogatory information relating to unsatisfactory behavior or conduct on an EPR?
That the information is reliable and can be supported by substantial evidence
Pg 273, 11.23.6

What decorations (medal worn on the uniform) can be referred to in an EPR?
Only those that were actually approved or presented during the reporting period
Pg 273, 11.23.10

WAPS scores, SNCO promotion scores, and board scores can be referenced in the EPR report. True or false?
False
Pg 273, 11.23.14

Positive information concerning volunteer service activities (on or off the military installation) of the member's family member can be addressed in the EPR report. True or false?
False
Pg 273, 11.23.15

Can physical fitness or body composition concerns be addressed in the performance evaluation?
Only if the reasons and/or behavior that resulted in the poor physical assessments are used
Pg 273, 11.23.17

What is an EPR called that contains a "Does Not Meet Standards" in any block in Section III or if the ratee receives a "Poor" or "Needs Improvement" in Section V?
A referral report
Pg 274, 11.24.1

What must the rater do prior sending a referral report?
Give the ratee a chance to comment on the report
Pg 274, 11.24.2

What covers periods of ratee performance too short to require a performance report?
A Letter of Evaluation (LOE)
Pg 274, 11.25

Figure 11.1. AF Form 931, *Performance Feedback Worksheet (AB thru TSgt)*.

PERFORMANCE FEEDBACK WORKSHEET (AB thru TSgt)

I. PERSONAL INFORMATION

NAME	GRADE	UNIT
FLORES, RICHARDO M.	SSgt	AFSES/CM

II. TYPES OF FEEDBACK:
☐ INITIAL ☐ MID-TERM ☐ RATEE REQUESTED ☐ RATER DIRECTED

III. PRIMARY DUTIES
- Outline specific duties completed to meet mission requirements
- The entries should include the most important duties and correspond to the job reflected in the EPR

IV. PERFORMANCE FEEDBACK

1. PRIMARY/ADDITIONAL DUTIES. Consider Adapting, Learning, Quality, Timeliness, Professional Growth, Communication Skills. (For SSgt/TSgt also consider Supervisory, Leadership and Technical Ability.)

☐ N/A Initial Feedback ☐ Does Not Meet ☐ Meets ☐ Above Average ☐ Clearly Exceeds

The following are some examples. Does the ratee: (1) display an ability to learn rapidly and adapt quickly to changing situations; (2) demonstrate accuracy, thoroughness, and orderliness in performing work assignments; (3) use systematic methods to accomplish more in less time; (4) actively support professional organizations; and (5) effectively communicate management decisions to achieve understanding and acceptance?

2. STANDARDS, CONDUCT, CHARACTER & MILITARY BEARING. Consider Dress & Appearance, Personal/Professional Conduct On/Off Duty. (For SSgt/TSgt also consider Enforcement of Standards and Customs & Courtesies.)

☐ N/A Initial Feedback ☐ Does Not Meet ☐ Meets ☐ Above Average ☐ Clearly Exceeds

The following are some examples. Does the ratee: (1) meet or exceed AF standards for dress and appearance; (2) project a positive military image according to AFI 36-2903; (3) achieve success when confronted with limited resources; (4) effectively overcome personal and organizational blocks to achieve results; and (5) support organizational, base and (or) community activities (duty or off-duty hours)?

3. FITNESS. Maintains Air Force Physical Fitness Standards.

☐ Does Not Meet ☐ Meets ☐ Exempt

Does the ratee participate in the AF physical training program and meet standards?

4. TRAINING REQUIREMENTS. Consider Upgrade, Ancillary, OJT, & Readiness. (For SSgt/TSgt also consider PME, Off-duty Education, Technical Growth, and Upgrade Training.)

☐ N/A Initial Feedback ☐ Does Not Meet ☐ Meets ☐ Above Average ☐ Clearly Exceeds

The following are some examples. Does the ratee: (1) complete training in the minimum time allowed; (2) accomplish readiness requirements in a timely manner; (3) have required PME for current grade completed; (4) translate innovative or better ways to do "things" into a plan of action; and (5) display a high level of technical competence?

5. TEAMWORK/FOLLOWERSHIP. Consider Team Building, Support of Team & Followership. (For SSgt/TSgt also consider Leadership, Team Accomplishments, Recognition/Reward Others.)

☐ N/A Initial Feedback ☐ Does Not Meet ☐ Meets ☐ Above Average ☐ Clearly Exceeds

The following are some examples. Is the ratee easy to work with? Does the ratee have a positive attitude? Does the ratee complain or foster team work to accomplish the task? Do the other unit, flight, or section personnel enjoy working with the ratee? Does the ratee display leadership traits appropriate to the situation? Does the ratee display the ability to simulate others?

6. OTHER COMMENTS. Consider Promotion, Future Duty/Assignment/Education Recommendations and Safety, Security & Human Relations.

☐ N/A Initial Feedback ☐ Does Not Meet ☐ Meets ☐ Above Average ☐ Clearly Exceeds

Consider future assignments that help the ratee achieve breadth of experience within their career field. Identify educational requirements needed to complete CCAF or higher degree. Ensure ratee exhibits safety and security practices daily to accomplish the mission. Also determine if the ratee works harmoniously and effectively with others.

AF FORM 931, 20080618 PREVIOUS EDITIONS ARE OBSOLETE PRIVACY ACT INFORMATION: The information in this form is FOR OFFICIAL USE ONLY. Protect IAW the Privacy Act of 1974.

V. STRENGTHS, SUGGESTED GOALS, AND ADDITIONAL COMMENTS *(Enlisted Professional Development: EES, Assignments, PME, Mentoring, Career Advice, etc.)*

The comments within this section should help explain the rater's thoughts and use of the performance assessment blocks and serve as a vehicle for the ratee to remember those areas of strength and those needing improvement.

1. When providing performance feedback, consider the following types of feedback to ensure the effective development of your ratee: Encourage and advice.

    a. Encouragement is intended to motivate people by letting them know what they've done well and recognizing or rewarding them for it. Its purpose is to encourage the person to continue or even increase the performance.
    b. Advice lets people know what to improve and how to make the improvement. Its purpose is to advise people about how to perform better the next time.

2. Properly given, encouragement and advice can be very powerful tools for maintaining and strengthening performance. Separation or "splitting" these two forms of feedback can be very important:

    a. If you give only encouragement immediately following performance, you help people gain confidence to feel good about their job or role.
    b. If you then provide advice separately, before the next performance opportunity, you help them do better the next time, increasing competence.

3. Giving both encouragement and advice at the same time sends a mixed message, with often less-than-effective results. People react in unpredictable ways to mixed feedback (also known as the "good job, but..." technique).

    a. They may:
        (1) Respond to both the encouragement and the advice.
        (2) Hear only the encouragement, discounting the advice as "less important."
        (3) Hear only the advice, missing the confidence-building or motivational value of the encouragement.
    b. Separating the two kinds of feedback gives you greater confidence that both messages are getting through.

PRIVACY ACT STATEMENT

AUTHORITY: Title 10, United States Code, Section 8013 and Executive Order 9397, 22 November 1943.
PURPOSE: Information is needed for verification of the individual's name and Social Security Number (SSN) as captured on the form at the time of the rating.
ROUTINE USES: May specifically be disclosed outside the DoD as a routine use pursuant to 5 U.S.C. 552a(b)(3).
DISCLOSURE: Disclosure is mandatory; SSN is used for positive identification.

RATEE SIGNATURE	RATER SIGNATURE	DATE
Click here to sign	Click here to sign	1 Jul 2012

AF FORM 931, 20080618   PREVIOUS EDITIONS ARE OBSOLETE   PRIVACY ACT INFORMATION: The information in this form is FOR OFFICIAL USE ONLY. Protect IAW the Privacy Act of 1974.

Figure 11.2. AF Form 932, *Performance Feedback Worksheet (MSgt thru CMSgt).*

PERFORMANCE FEEDBACK WORKSHEET (MSgt thru CMSgt)

I. PERSONAL INFORMATION

NAME	GRADE	UNIT
SMITH, JOHNNY B.	CMSgt	AFSES/CM

II. TYPES OF FEEDBACK: [ ] INITIAL [ ] MID-TERM [ ] RATEE REQUESTED [ ] RATER DIRECTED

III. PRIMARY DUTIES
- Outline specific duties completed to meet mission requirements.
- The entries should include the most important duties and correspond to the job reflected in the EPR.

IV. PERFORMANCE FEEDBACK

1. PRIMARY DUTIES. Consider Quality, Quantity, Timeliness, Technical Knowledge, Leading, Managing & Supervising

[ ] N/A Initial Feedback [ ] Does Not Meet [ ] Meets [ ] Above Average [ ] Clearly Exceeds

The following are some examples. Does the ratee: (1) show professional concern for quality work; (2) constantly produce more than expected; (3) identify and eliminate timewasters; (4) possess the knowledge to handle work of the most complex nature; (5) inspire the cooperation and confidence of others; (6) stimulate management efficiency and effectiveness; (7) recognize the important relationship between rewards, reinforcement & results?

2. STANDARDS: ENFORCEMENT AND PERSONAL ADHERENCE, CONDUCT, CHARACTER, MILITARY BEARING, CUSTOMS AND COURTESIES. Consider Dress & Appearance and Personal/Professional Conduct On/Off Duty

[ ] N/A Initial Feedback [ ] Does Not Meet [ ] Meets [ ] Above Average [ ] Clearly Exceeds

The following are some examples. Does the ratee: (1) respond positively on inconsequential issues; (2) exceed and enforce a positive military image IAW AFI 36-2903; (3) achieve success when confronted with limited resources; (4) effectively overcome personal and organizational blocks to achieve results; and (5) support organizational, base and/or community activities (duty or off-duty hours)?

3. FITNESS. Maintains Air Force Physical Fitness Standards.

[ ] Does Not Meet [ ] Meets [ ] Exempt

Does the ratee participate in the AF physical training program and meet standards?

4. RESOURCE MANAGEMENT AND DECISION MAKING. Consider Efficiency, Judgment, Setting and Meeting Goals

[ ] N/A Initial Feedback [ ] Does Not Meet [ ] Meets [ ] Above Average [ ] Clearly Exceeds

The following are some examples. Does the ratee: (1) achieve consistent effectiveness; (2) display a practical approach to solving problems; (3) display excellent intuitive judgment; (4) set goals that are compatible with those of the organization; and (5) establish methods for attainment of goals?

5. TRAINING, EDUCATION, OFF-DUTY EDUCATION, PME, PROFESSIONAL ENHANCEMENT AND COMMUNICATION. Consider Providing, Supporting and Personal Growth

[ ] N/A Initial Feedback [ ] Does Not Meet [ ] Meets [ ] Above Average [ ] Clearly Exceeds

The following are some examples. Does the ratee: (1) assist subordinates in reaching new levels of skills, knowledge and attitudes; (2) encourage subordinates to improve abilities for greater responsibility; (3) develop a climate providing motivation, participation and opportunities for subordinate initiative; (4) have required PME for current grade completed?

6. LEADERSHIP/TEAM BUILDING/FOLLOWERSHIP. Consider Team Accomplishments, Leveraging Personal Experiences, Community Support and Recognition/Reward for Others

[ ] N/A Initial Feedback [ ] Does Not Meet [ ] Meets [ ] Above Average [ ] Clearly Exceeds

The following are some examples. Does the ratee have a positive attitude? Does the ratee complain or foster team work to accomplish the task? Do the other unit, flight, or section personnel enjoy working with the ratee. Does the ratee display leadership traits appropriate to the situation? Does the ratee display the ability to stimulate others? Does the ratee use the award programs to recognize subordinate's outstanding accomplishments?

7. OTHER COMMENTS. Consider Promotion, Future Duty/Assignment/Education Recommendations and Safety, Security & Human Relations.

[ ] N/A Initial Feedback [ ] Does Not Meet [ ] Meets [ ] Above Average [ ] Clearly Exceeds

Consider future assignments that help the ratee achieve breadth of experience within their career field. Identify educational requirements needed to complete CCAF or higher degree. Ensure ratee exhibits safety and security practices daily to accomplish the mission. Also determine if the ratee works harmoniously and effectively with others.

AF FORM 932, 20070625   PREVIOUS EDITIONS ARE OBSOLETE   PRIVACY ACT INFORMATION: The information in this form is FOR OFFICIAL USE ONLY. Protect IAW the Privacy Act of 1974.

V. STRENGTHS, SUGGESTED GOALS, AND ADDITIONAL COMMENTS *(Enlisted Professional Development: EES, Assignments, PME, Mentoring, Career Advice, etc.)*

The comments within this section should help explain the rater's thoughts and use of the performance assessment blocks and serve as a vehicle for the ratee to use in remembering those areas of strength and those needing improvement.

1. When providing performance feedback, consider the following types of feedback to ensure the effective development of your ratee: Encouragement and advice.

    a. Encouragement is intended to motivate people by letting them know what they've done well and recognizing or rewarding them for it. Its purpose is to encourage people to continue or even increase their performance.
    b. Advice lets people know what to improve and how to make the improvement. Its purpose is to advise the people how to perform better the next time.

2. Properly given, encouragement and advice can be very powerful tools for maintaining and strengthening performance. Separation or "splitting" these two forms of feedback can be very important:

    a. If you give only encouragement immediately following performance, you help people gain confidence to feel good about their job or role.
    b. If you then provide advice separately, before the next performance opportunity, you help them do better the next time, increasing competence.

3. Giving both encouragement and advice at the same time sends a mixed message, with often less-than-effective results. People react in unpredictable ways to mixed feedback (also known as the "good job, but..." technique).

    a. They may:
        (1) Respond to both the encouragement and the advice.
        (2) Hear only the encouragement, discounting the advice as "less important."
        (3) Hear only the advice, missing the confidence-building or motivational value of the encouragement.
    b. Separating the two kinds of feedback gives you greater confidence that both messages are getting through.

PRIVACY ACT STATEMENT

AUTHORITY: Title 10, United States Code, Section 8013 and Executive Order 9397, 22 November 1943.
PURPOSE: Information is needed for verification of the individual's name and Social Security Number (SSN) as captured on the form at the time of the rating.
ROUTINE USES: None. RATIONALE: This information will not be disclosed outside DoD channels.
DISCLOSURE: Disclosure is mandatory; SSN is used for positive identification.

RATEE SIGNATURE	RATER SIGNATURE	DATE
		1 Jul 2011

AF FORM 932, 20070625 — PREVIOUS EDITIONS ARE OBSOLETE

PRIVACY ACT INFORMATION: The information in this form is FOR OFFICIAL USE ONLY. Protect IAW the Privacy Act of 1974.

Figure 11.3. Sample AF Form 910, *Enlisted Performance Report (AB thru TSgt)*.

ENLISTED PERFORMANCE REPORT *(AB thru TSgt)*

I. RATEE IDENTIFICATION DATA *(Refer to AFI 36-2406 for instructions on completing this form)*

1. NAME *(Last, First, Middle Initial)*	2. SSN	3. GRADE	4. DAFSC
JOHNSTON, MARK E.	123-45-6789	SrA	3D051

5. ORGANIZATION, COMMAND, LOCATION, AND COMPONENT	6. PAS CODE	7. SRID
AF Specialized Equipment Sq (AFSES), HQ Air Education and Training Command (AETC), Randolph AFB TX (AD)	RYOJFCDR	OJIGF

8. PERIOD OF REPORT	9. NO. DAYS SUPERVISION	10. REASON FOR REPORT
From: 31 Jan 2010 Thru: 30 Jan 2011	365	Annual

II. JOB DESCRIPTION

1. DUTY TITLE	2. SIGNIFICANT ADDITIONAL DUTY(S)
Equipment Custodian	Enter any significant additional duties the ratee may hold. If none, then enter "N/A."

3. KEY DUTIES, TASKS, AND RESPONSIBILITIES *(Limit text to 4 lines)*

Enter clear description of ratee's duties. Avoid jargon or acronyms. Describe tasks performed, how selective ratee's assignment is, and scope or level of responsibility. Include dollar value of projects managed and number of people supervised. You may include earlier duties or additional duties held during reporting period if they influence ratings and comments.

III. PERFORMANCE ASSESSMENT

1. PRIMARY/ADDITIONAL DUTIES *(For SSgt/TSgt also consider Supervisory, Leadership and Technical Abilities)*
Consider Adapting, Learning, Quality, Timeliness, Professional Growth and Communication Skills *(Limit text to 4 lines)*

☐ Does Not Meet ☐ Meets ☐ Above Average ☐ Clearly Exceeds

- Place an "X" in block that accurately describes ratee's performance
- Use bullet statements that describe the action, impact, and result of the performance within this criteria

2. STANDARDS, CONDUCT, CHARACTER & MILITARY BEARING *(For SSgt/TSgt also consider Enforcement of Standards and Customs & Courtesies)*
Consider Dress & Appearance, Personal/Professional Conduct On/Off Duty *(Limit text to 2 lines)*

☐ Does Not Meet ☐ Meets ☐ Above Average ☐ Clearly Exceeds

- Place an "X" in block that accurately describes ratee's performance
- Use bullet statements that describe the action, impact, and result of the performance within this criteria

3. FITNESS *(Maintains Air Force Physical Fitness Standards)* *(For referrals, limit text to 1 line)*

☐ Does Not Meet ☐ Meets ☐ Exempt - Place an "X" in block that accurately describes ratee's fitness

4. TRAINING REQUIREMENTS *(For SSgt/TSgt also consider PME, Off-duty Education, Technical Growth, Upgrade Training)*
Consider Upgrade, Ancillary, OJT and Readiness *(Limit text to 2 lines)*

☐ Does Not Meet ☐ Meets ☐ Above Average ☐ Clearly Exceeds

- Place an "X" in block that accurately describes ratee's performance
- Use bullet statements that describe the action, impact, and result of the performance within this criteria

5. TEAMWORK/FOLLOWERSHIP *(For SSgt/TSgt also consider Leadership, Team Accomplishments, Recognition/Reward Others)*
Consider Team Building, Support of Team, Followership *(Limit text to 2 lines)*

☐ Does Not Meet ☐ Meets ☐ Above Average ☐ Clearly Exceeds

- Place an "X" in block that accurately describes ratee's performance
- Use bullet statements that describe the action, impact, and result of the performance within this criteria

6. OTHER COMMENTS
Consider Promotion, Future Duty/Assignment/Education Recommendations and Safety, Security & Human Relations *(Limit text to 2 lines)*

- Place an "X" in block that accurately describes ratee's performance
- Use bullet statements that describe the action, impact, and result of the performance within this criteria

IV. RATER INFORMATION

NAME, GRADE, BR OF SVC, ORGN, COMMAND AND LOCATION	DUTY TITLE	DATE
MANNY Z. BRIGHT, MSgt, USAF AF Specialized Equipment Squadron (AETC) Randolph AFB, TX	Training Manager, EC Flight	
	SSN: 9876 SIGNATURE: Click here to sign	

AF FORM 910, 20080618   PREVIOUS EDITIONS ARE OBSOLETE   PRIVACY ACT INFORMATION: The information in this form is FOR OFFICIAL USE ONLY. Protect IAW the Privacy Act of 1974.

V. OVERALL PERFORMANCE ASSESSMENT Overall Performance During Reporting Period		RATEE NAME:	JOHNSTON, MARK E.		
ASSESSMENT	POOR (1)	NEEDS IMPROVEMENT (2)	AVERAGE (3)	ABOVE AVERAGE (4)	TRULY AMONG THE BEST (5)
RATER'S ASSESSMENT	☐	☐	☐	☐	☐
ADDITIONAL RATER'S ASSESSMENT	☐	☐	☐	☐	☐

Last feedback was performed on: 30 Jul 2010   If feedback was not accomplished in accordance with AFI 36-2406, state the reason.

If feedback was not accomplished, list the reason why in this area.

VI. ADDITIONAL RATER'S COMMENTS (Limit text to 3 lines)	☐ CONCUR	☐ NON-CONCUR

- Use this section to support rating decisions and allow evaluators to comment on overall performance
- Additional rater must be the rater's rater unless additional rater does not meet grade requirements
- Use bullet statements that describe the action, impact and result of the ratee's performance

NAME, GRADE, BR OF SVC, ORGN, COMMAND AND LOCATION	DUTY TITLE		DATE
RODNEY P. SMITH, CMSgt, USAF AF Specialized Equipment Squadron (AETC) Randolph AFB, TX	Chief, Professional Equipment Flight		
	SSN 0123	SIGNATURE Click here to sign	

VII. FUNCTIONAL EXAMINER/AIR FORCE ADVISOR
(Indicate applicable review by marking the appropriate box.)   ☐ FUNCTIONAL EXAMINER   ☐ AIR FORCE ADVISOR

NAME, GRADE, BR OF SVC, ORGN, COMMAND AND LOCATION	DUTY TITLE		DATE
See AFI 36-2406 for applicability.			
	SSN	SIGNATURE Click here to sign	

VIII. UNIT COMMANDER/CIVILIAN DIRECTOR/OTHER AUTHORIZED REVIEWER	☐ CONCUR	☐ NON-CONCUR

NAME, GRADE, BR OF SVC, ORGN, COMMAND AND LOCATION	DUTY TITLE		DATE
JULES A. PARKER, Lt Col, USAF AF Specialized Equipment Squadron (AETC) Randolph AFB, TX	Commander, AFSES		
	SSN 5678	SIGNATURE Click here to sign	

IX. RATEE'S ACKNOWLEDGEMENT

I understand my signature does not constitute agreement or disagreement. I acknowledge all required feedback was accomplished during the reporting period and upon receipt of this report.   ☐ Yes   ☐ No

SIGNATURE Click here to sign	DATE

INSTRUCTIONS

Complete this report IAW AFI 36-2406. Reports written by Colonels or civilians (GS-15 or higher, or Supervisory Pay Band 3), do not require an additional rater; however, endorsement by the rater's rater is permitted unless the report is written by a senior rater or the Chief Master Sergeant of the Air Force. When the rater's rater is not at least a MSgt or civilian (GS-07 or higher, or Supervisory Pay Band 1), the additional rater is the next official in the rating chain meeting grade requirements. An overall rating of 2 or negative comments require the EPR to be referred IAW AFI 36-2406. Rationale for any additional evaluator nonconcurring with an overall rating must be included. Section VIII Reviewer nonconcurrence must be included on an AF Form 77, Letter of Evaluation. If ratee is deployed, provide copy and feedback via e-mail/telecon.

PRIVACY ACT STATEMENT

AUTHORITY: Title 10 United States Code, Section 8013 and Executive Order 9397, 22 November 1943.

PURPOSE: Information is needed for verification of the individual's name and Social Security Number (SSN) as captured on the form at the time of rating.

ROUTINE USES: May specifically be disclosed outside the DoD as a routine use pursuant to 5 U.S.C. 552a(b)(3).

DISCLOSURE: Disclosure is mandatory; SSN is used for positive identification.

AF FORM 910, 20080618   PREVIOUS EDITIONS ARE OBSOLETE   PRIVACY ACT INFORMATION: The information in this form is FOR OFFICIAL USE ONLY. Protect IAW the Privacy Act of 1974.

Figure 11.4. Sample AF Form 911, *Enlisted Performance Report (MSgt thru CMSgt).*

ENLISTED PERFORMANCE REPORT *(MSgt thru CMSgt)*				
I. RATEE IDENTIFICATION DATA *(Refer to AFI 36-2406 for instructions on completing this form)*				
1. NAME *(Last, First, Middle Initial)* JAMES, ROBERTA M.	2. SSN 123-45-6789	3. GRADE MSgt	4. DAFSC 3S271	
5. ORGANIZATION, COMMAND, LOCATION, AND COMPONENT AF Specialized Equipment Sq (AFSES), HQ Air Education and Training Command (AETC), Randolph AFB TX (AD)		6. PAS CODE RYOJFCDR	7. SRID OJIGF	
8. PERIOD OF REPORT From: 31 Jan 2010 Thru: 30 Jan 2011		9. NO. DAYS SUPERVISION 365	10. REASON FOR REPORT Annual	

II. JOB DESCRIPTION

1. DUTY TITLE Heavy Equipment Manager	2. SIGNIFICANT ADDITIONAL DUTY(S) Enter any significant additional duties the ratee may hold. If none, then enter "N/A."

3. KEY DUTIES, TASKS, AND RESPONSIBILITIES *(Limit text to 4 lines)*
Enter clear description of ratee's duties. Avoid jargon or acronyms. Describe tasks performed, how selective ratee's assignment is, and scope or level of responsibility. Include dollar value of projects managed and number of people supervised. You may include earlier duties or additional duties held during reporting period if they influence ratings and comments.

III. PERFORMANCE ASSESSMENT

1. PRIMARY DUTIES
Consider Quality, Quantity, Timeliness, Technical Knowledge, Leading, Managing and Supervising *(Limit text to 4 lines)*
☐ Does Not Meet   ☐ Meets   ☐ Above Average   ☐ Clearly Exceeds
- Place an "X" in block that accurately describes ratee's performance
- Use bullet statements that describe the action, impact, and result of the performance within this criteria

2. STANDARDS: ENFORCEMENT AND PERSONAL ADHERENCE, CONDUCT, CHARACTER, MILITARY BEARING & CUSTOMS AND COURTESIES
Consider Dress & Appearance, Personal/Professional Conduct On/Off Duty *(Limit text to 2 lines)*
☐ Does Not Meet   ☐ Meets   ☐ Above Average   ☐ Clearly Exceeds
- Place an "X" in block that accurately describes ratee's performance
- Use bullet statements that describe the action, impact, and result of the performance within this criteria

3. FITNESS (Maintains Air Force Physical Fitness Standards) *(For referrals, limit text to 1 line)*
☐ Does Not Meet   ☐ Meets   ☐ Exempt

4. RESOURCE MANAGEMENT AND DECISION MAKING
Consider Efficiency, Judgment, Setting and Meeting Goals *(Limit text to 2 lines)*
☐ Does Not Meet   ☐ Meets   ☐ Above Average   ☐ Clearly Exceeds
- Place an "X" in block that accurately describes ratee's performance
- Use bullet statements that describe the action, impact, and result of the performance within this criteria

5. TRAINING, EDUCATION, OFF-DUTY EDUCATION, PME, PROFESSIONAL ENHANCEMENT AND COMMUNICATION
Consider Providing, Supporting and Personal Growth *(Limit text to 2 lines)*
☐ Does Not Meet   ☐ Meets   ☐ Above Average   ☐ Clearly Exceeds
- Place an "X" in block that accurately describes ratee's performance
- Use bullet statements that describe the action, impact, and result of the performance within this criteria

6. LEADERSHIP/TEAM BUILDING/FOLLOWERSHIP/MENTORSHIP
Consider Team Accomplishments, Leveraging Personal Experiences and Community Support, Recognition/Reward for Others *(Limit text to 2 lines)*
☐ Does Not Meet   ☐ Meets   ☐ Above Average   ☐ Clearly Exceeds
- Place an "X" in block that accurately describes ratee's performance
- Use bullet statements that describe the action, impact, and result of the performance within this criteria

7. OTHER COMMENTS (Consider Promotion, Future Duty/Assignment/Education Recommendations, Safety, Security & Human Relations) *(Limit text to 2 lines)*
- Place an "X" in block that accurately describes ratee's performance
- Use bullet statements that describe the action, impact, and result of the performance within this criteria

IV. RATER INFORMATION

NAME, GRADE, BR OF SVC, ORGN, COMMAND AND LOCATION JOAN E. SMITH, CMSgt, USAF AF Specialized Equipment Squadron (AETC) Randolph AFB, TX	DUTY TITLE Chief, Professional Equipment Flight		DATE
	SSN 0123	SIGNATURE Click here to sign	

AF FORM 911, 20070625   PREVIOUS EDITIONS ARE OBSOLETE   PRIVACY ACT INFORMATION: The information in this form is FOR OFFICIAL USE ONLY. Protect IAW the Privacy Act of 1974.

V. OVERALL PERFORMANCE ASSESSMENT
Overall Performance During Reporting Period

RATEE NAME: JAMES, ROBERTA M.

ASSESSMENT	POOR (1)	NEEDS IMPROVEMENT (2)	AVERAGE (3)	ABOVE AVERAGE (4)	TRULY AMONG THE BEST (5)
RATER'S ASSESSMENT	☐	☐	☐	☐	☐
ADDITIONAL RATER'S ASSESSMENT	☐	☐	☐	☐	☐

Last feedback was performed on: 30 Jul 2011   If feedback was not accomplished in accordance with AFI 36-2406, state the reason.

If feedback was not accomplished, list reason why in this area.

VI. ADDITIONAL RATER'S COMMENTS (Limit text to 3 lines)   ☐ CONCUR   ☐ NON-CONCUR

- Use this section to concur/nonconcur and allow additional rater to comment on the ratee's overall performance
- Additional rater must be the rater's rater unless additional rater does not meet grade requirements
- Use bullet statements that describe the action, impact, and result of the ratee's performance

NAME, GRADE, BR OF SVC, ORGN, COMMAND AND LOCATION	DUTY TITLE		DATE
JIMMIE A. PARKER, Lt Col, USAF AF Specialized Equipment Squadron (AETC) Randolph AFB, TX	Commander		
	SSN 5678	SIGNATURE Click here to sign	

VII. REVIEWER'S COMMENTS (Limit text to 3 lines)   ☐ CONCUR   ☐ NON-CONCUR

- Use this section to concur/nonconcur & allow reviewer to comment on the ratee's overall performance
- Reviewer must be the rater's rater unless reviewer does not meet grade requirements
- Use bullet statements that describe the action, impact, and result of the ratee's performance

NAME, GRADE, BR OF SVC, ORGN, COMMAND AND LOCATION	DUTY TITLE		DATE
STAN T. WALL, Brig Gen, USAF HQ Air Education and Trng Command (AETC) Randolph AFB, TX	Director of Equipment, and Info Ops		
	SSN 9999	SIGNATURE Click here to sign	

VIII. FINAL EVALUATORS POSITION
☐ SENIOR RATER
☐ SENIOR RATER'S DEPUTY
☐ INTERMEDIATE LEVEL
☐ LOWER LEVEL

IX. TIME-IN-GRADE ELIGIBLE
N/A for CMSgt or CMSgt Selectee
☐ N/A
☐ YES
☐ NO

X. FUNCTIONAL EXAMINER/AIR FORCE ADVISOR
(Indicate applicable review by marking the appropriate box)   ☐ FUNCTIONAL EXAMINER   ☐ AIR FORCE ADVISOR

NAME, GRADE, BR OF SVC, ORGN, COMMAND AND LOCATION	DUTY TITLE		DATE
See AFI 36-2406 for applicability.			
	SSN	SIGNATURE Click here to sign	

XI. UNIT COMMANDER/CIVILIAN DIRECTOR/OTHER AUTHORIZED REVIEWER   ☐ CONCUR   ☐ NON-CONCUR

NAME, GRADE, BR OF SVC, ORGN, COMMAND AND LOCATION	DUTY TITLE		DATE
JIMMIE A. PARKER, Lt Col, USAF AF Specialized Equipment Squadron (AETC) Randolph AFB, TX	Commander		
	SSN 5678	SIGNATURE Click here to sign	

XII. RATEE'S ACKNOWLEDGEMENT

I understand my signature does not constitute agreement or disagreement. I acknowledge all required feedback was accomplished during the reporting period and upon receipt of this report.   ☐ Yes   ☐ No

SIGNATURE	DATE
Click here to sign	

PRIVACY ACT STATEMENT
AUTHORITY: Title 10, United States Code, Section 8013 and Executive Order 9397, 22 November 1943.
PURPOSE: Information is needed for verification of the individual's name and Social Security Number (SSN) as captured on the form at the time of the rating.
ROUTINE USES: None. RATIONALE: This information will not be disclosed outside DoD channels.
DISCLOSURE: Disclosure is mandatory; SSN is used for positive identification.

AF FORM 911, 20070625   PREVIOUS EDITIONS ARE OBSOLETE   PRIVACY ACT INFORMATION: The information in this form is FOR OFFICIAL USE ONLY. Protect IAW the Privacy Act of 1974.

Chapter 12
Training and Education

Overview

Where can you find information about financial assistance and commissioning programs?
Base Education Office
Pg 275, 12.1

Training Management

What must supervisors explain to trainees regarding their training?
The relationship of training to career progression
Pg 275, 12.5

What does the overall success of the training program depend on?
The supervisor's ability to advise and assist Airmen to reach long-range career objectives
Pg 275, 12.5

How many components does the Air Force On-the-Job-Training (OJT) program consist of?
Three
Pg 275, 12.6

Which training component is developed through Career Development Courses (CDCs)?
Job knowledge
Pg 275, 12.6.1

Which training component includes hands-on training?
Job proficiency
Pg 275, 12.6.2

Which training component is gained during and after upgrade training?
Job experience
Pg 275, 12.6.3

What is the key to the Total Force training program?
Upgrade Training
Pg 275, 12.7

When an Airman completes the initial skills course, what skill level will be obtained?
3-skill level
Pg 276, 12.7.1

When an Airman completes Career Development Courses (CDCs), applicable mandatory skills, 12 months in Upgrade Training (UGT), and mandatory requirements listed in the Air Force Enlisted Classification Directory (AFECD), what skill level is obtained?
5-skill level
Pg 276, 12.7.2

What is a 7-skill level Airman called?
A Craftsman
Pg 276, 12.7.3

What is a 9-skill level Airman called?
A Superintendent
Pg 276, 12.7.4

Who serves as training consultant to all unit members?
The Unit Training Manager (UTM)
Pg 276, 12.9.1

How soon after the assignment of a new person does the supervisor conduct a comprehensive trainee orientation?
Within 60 days
Pg 276, 12.9.1.2

Who provides third party certification and evaluation on tasks identified by the Air Force Career Field Manager (AFCFM)?
The Task Certifier
Pg 277, 12.9.4

What is the focal point of the Air Force training program?
The trainee
Pg 277, 12.9.5

What form is used to reflect past and current qualifications and determines training requirements?
AF Form 623
Pg 278, 12.10.1

What do evaluators use AF IMT 803 for?
To conduct and document completion of task evaluations
Pg 278, 12.10.6

What do supervisors use AF IMT 1098 to document?
Selected tasks that require recurring training or evaluation
Pg 278, 12.10.7

What is the strategy to ensure completion of all work center job requirements?
The Master Training Plan (MTP)
Pg 278, 12.10.8

Who is responsible for ensuring trainees are enrolled and receive required CDC material within 45 days of in-processing?
The Unit Training Manager (UTM)
Pg 279, 12.11.2.3

How long does a trainee have to complete each Career Development Course (CDC) volume?
Within 30 days
Pg 279, 12.11.2.5

How does a trainee answer the unit review exercise (URE) questions?
In an open book style
Pg 279, 12.11.2.6

Who notifies the Unit Training Manager (UTM) the trainee is ready to test?
The supervisor
Pg 279, 12.11.2.7

If the trainee receives an unsatisfactory result on the (CDC) exam, how long after notification is corrective action required?
30 days
Pg 279, 12.11.2.9

Which one of the following is not an option if a trainee receives a second unsatisfactory result on the CDC exam?
Place the trainee in supervised review training
Pg 279, 12.11.2.10

Community College of the Air Force (CCAF)

The Community College of the Air Force (CCAF) provides enlisted members of the active duty Air Force, Air National Guard, and Air Force Reserve Command an Associate of Applied Science degree. True or false?
True
Pg 280, 12.12.1

The Community College of the Air Force (CCAF) is the largest community college in the world. True or false?
True
Pg 280, 12.12.2

Where is the Community College of the Air Force (CCAF) located?
Maxwell-Gunter AFB, Alabama
Pg 280, 12.12.2

Enlisted personnel are automatically registered into a degree program during basic military training (BMT). True or false?
True
Pg 280, 12.12.4

The Community College of the Air Force (CCAF) is a nationally recognized credentialing program. True or false?
True
Pg 281, 12.13.3

Education

How many programs does the Air Force offer for enlisted personnel to help defray the cost of obtaining off-duty education?
Three
Pg 283, 12.17

Military tuition assistance funds are taxed. True or false?
False
Pg 283, 12.17.1

Military tuition assistance funds can be used to purchase textbooks. True or false?
False
Pg 283, 12.17.1

Table 12.1 CCAF Degree Program Structure (pg 274)

Item	Degree Requirements	Semester Hours Needed
1	Physical Education	4
2	Technical Education	24
3	Leadership, Management, and Military Studies (LMMS)	6
4	Program Electives	15
	General Education Requirements	
5	Oral Communication	3
6	Written Communication	3
7	Math	3
8	Social Science	3
9	Humanities	3
	Total	64

In addition to entering the service for the first time on or after 1 July 1985, what else must participants in the Montgomery GI Bill (MGIB) do to be eligible?
They must have their pay reduced by $100 a month for the first 12 months
Pg 283, 12.17.2

When can the Montgomery GI Bill (MGIB) be used while in service?
After two years of continuous active duty
Pg 283, 12.17.2

When do Montgomery GI Bill (MGIB) benefits expire?
10 years after separation or retirement
Pg 283, 12.17.2

Which educational financial assistance is available to those serving on or after September 11, 2001?
The Post 9-11 GI Bill
Pg 283, 12.17.3

How many college credits can a military member earn at no financial cost?
Up to 60 semester hours
Pg 283, 12.18

Which standardized tests are essentially course achievement tests?
The DANTES subject standardized tests (DSST)
Pg 284, 12.18.1

The College-Level Examination Program (CLEP) measures college-level achievement in five basic areas that are required for college freshmen and sophomores. True or false?
True
Pg 284, 12.18.2

Where is the resident campus for the Enlisted-to-Air Force Institute of Technology (AFIT) Program?
Wright-Patterson AFB, OH
Pg 284, 12.19.1

Enlisted members can obtain a commission while on active duty. True or false?
True
Pg 284, 12.21

Do active duty Airmen selected for the Airman Education and Commissioning Program (AECP) attend civilian educational institutions part time? True or false?
False, they attend full time
Pg 284, 12.21.1

A military member has to possess an associate or higher degree from an accredited college or university to be eligible for a commission through the Officer Training School (OTS) program. True or false?
False, it must be a baccalaureate
Pg 285, 12.21.2

What program offers world-class education and a guaranteed career right out of college with no financial cost?
The United States Air Force Academy (USAFA)
Pg 285, 12.21.3

Who is eligible for acceptance to the United States Air Force Academy (USAFA)?
An applicant must be a citizen of the United States, unmarried with no dependents, of good moral character, and at least 17, but less than 22 years of age, by July 1 of the year he or she would enter.
Pg 285, 12.21.3

Which program allows an individual to become a full time college student and receive a tuition of up to $15,000 per year?
The Scholarship for Outstanding Airmen to ROTC (SOAR) Program
Pg 285, 12.21.4

After graduating, being commissioned as a Second Lieutenant and returning to active duty under the Scholarships for Outstanding Airmen to ROTC (SOAR) Program, how many years must the individual serve?
At least 4 years
Pg 285, 12.21.4

If selected for the Airman Scholarship and Commissioning Program (ASCP), a member has to be discharged from active duty and enlist into the Air Force Inactive Obligated Reserve. True or false?
True
Pg 285, 12.21.5

Chapter 13
Resource Management

Managing Organizational Change

Which of the three-stages of change is the most neglected?
Unfreezing
Pg 287, 13.3.2

What is the first reaction to change?
Usually resistance
Pg 287, 13.3.3

What is one of the most essential elements of a successful change?
A good plan
Pg 287, 13.3.3

How many common forms of resistance are there?
Four
Pg 287, 13.3.3

What can help reduce the resistance of change?
Educating and communicating with the employees
Pg 288, 13.3.4.1

What can a leader expect to see by having employees participate and be involved in the change process?
The resistance should reduce
Pg 288, 13.3.4.2

Why should coercion be the last technique a leader uses to force people to accept change?
Because it will negatively affect attitudes and have long-term negative consequences
Pg 288, 13.3.4.5

How can leaders who are implementing a change improve the chances of success?
By breaking the changes into sequential steps
Pg 288, 13.3.5

Which stage of change involves modifying technology, tasks or distribution of people?
Changing
Pg 288, 13.4

What is the final stage of change called?
Refreezing
Pg 289, 13.5

Traits of a Healthy Team

What influences every stage of team development and can ultimately determine whether mission goals are met?
The spirit in which a team operates
Pg 289, 13.6

Responding with alienation, ignoring inputs, and withholding vital information indicate a lack of what between team members?
Trust
Pg 290, 13.7.2

What type of behavior can cause us to lose trust in people?
Unethical
Pg 290, 13.8

What types of behaviors are considered unethical?
Those that do not conform to accepted principles of right and wrong that govern our profession
Pg 290, 13.8

Sharing information can help a team succeed. True or false?
True
Pg 290, 13.9.1

How can teams redirect their focus and energy and correct problems quickly rather than letting them intensify?
By using critical feedback
Pg 290, 13.10

What is at the heart of any healthy team interaction?
Trust
Pg 291, 13.12

Problem Solving

What does CPI mean in the area of problem solving?
Continuous process improvement
Pg 291, 13.13

What will the 8-step Air Force continuous process improvement (CPI) model provide if it is rigorously applied?
It will help root out waste in the day-to-day work
Pg 291, 13.14

There are four decision making loop phases (called the OODA loop) outlined in the AFSO21. What is phase number one?
Observe
Pg 292, Table 13.1

There are four decision making loop phases (called the OODA loop) outlined in the AFSO21. What is phase number three?
Decide
Pg 292, Table 13.1

What is the first step to finding an effective solution to a problem?
A good problem statement
Pg 292, 13.15.3.2

What lean tool is a framework to ensure resources and activities are linked to key enterprise strategies, directives, and goals?
Strategic Alignment and Deployment (SA&D)
Pg 292, 13.15.3.3.1

What problem solving tool shows the difference between the level of performance seen today and the level of performance identified as needed tomorrow
Performance Gap Analysis
Pg 293, 13.15.4.1.2.1

What tool identifies the so-called weakest link or the slowest step?
Bottleneck analysis
Pg 293, 13.15.4.1.2.2

What defines the performance levels required to make a vision a reality?
Improvement targets
Pg 293, 13.15.5.2

What type of analysis is the process of digging as deeply as possible into a problem and finding the deepest point that is still within the team's area of influence?
Root cause analysis
Pg 293, 13.15.6.1

Which of the steps in the OODA 8-Step problem solving process is the most commonly skipped and under completed of the entire process?
Step 8 - standardize successful processes (act) - this is the step that ensures the results of the process stick
Pg 295, 13.15.10.1

8 – Step Problem Solving Process
(Pg 292, Table 13.1)

Observe:
   Step 1 – Clarify and validate the problem
   Step 2 – Break down the problem/identify performance gaps
Orient:
   Step 3 – Set improvement targets
   Step 4 – Determine root causes
Decide:
   Step 5 – Develop countermeasures
Act:
   Step 6 – See countermeasures through
   Step 7 – Confirm results and process
   Step 8 – Standardize successful processes

SMART Targets
(Pg 293, 13.15.5.3)

Specific – have clearly defined, desirable outputs that are applicable to the process improvement activity
Measurable – include time frames and data obtainable from specific sources
Attainable – for a goal to be attainable, resources must be available; a goal can have some risk, but success must be possible
Results focused – link targets to the mission, vision and goals, and ensure they are meaningful to the user
Timely – provide step-by-step views versus giant leaps, and measure at interim milestones

The 5 Whys Analysis Tool
(Pg 287, 13.15.6.2 – 13.15.6.2.6)

5 Whys – when you think you understand a cause of the problem, ask "why" five times, or until you have reached the point that you've got a bottom line response

Brainstorming – a cross-functional team that works in the problem area almost always knows the root cause of the problem, but they do not realize it at the time. Brainstorming is an opportunity to suggesting as many ideas as possible to pull information out of the team member that they, perhaps, did not realize was important

Pareto analysis – a good rule of thumb is that 80 percent of the problem is likely caused by 20 percent of the inputs. Usually, the only inputs anyone can remember are the ones someone else is responsible for. Objectively graphing the data can point to the critical 20 percent

Affinity diagrams – with thousands of inputs, outputs, and measures, finding a way to group like items can simplify a problem enough that it can be more easily understood

Cause and effect diagrams – often called the "fishbone" diagram, it's a quick and simple way to visually depict the relationship between specific categories of process inputs and undesirable outputs

Control charts – objective graphs of process output over time, control charts usually include predefined upper and lower performance level limits

Managing Resources Other than Personnel

Of the following, what is not an element included in the RMS (Resource Management System)?
Inventory of seized property
Pg 296, 13.16.2

What do Resource Management System (RMS) duties include?
The stewardship of money, manpower, and equipment
Pg 296, 13.16.2

What do commanders need to do to ensure successful financial management?
Review, validate, and balance the financial plan
Pg 296, 13.16.2.1

What do comptrollers provide that supports the organization's mission and the Air Force?
Sound financial management and advice to the commander and staff
Pg 296, 13.16.2.2

What are the duties of the cost center managers (CCMs)?
They monitor the consumption of work hours, supplies, equipment, and services
Pg 296, 13.16.2.4

Who establishes the financial management board (FMB) at each base?
The senior or host Commander
Pg 297, 13.16.3

What is the financial management board (FMB) responsible for?
Determines program priorities and effective allocation of resources
Pg 297, 13.16.3

What does the financial working group (FWG) manage?
Commodities and resources of the base or unit
Pg 297, 13.16.4

Who is responsible for the prudent management, control, storage, and cost-effective use of Government property under their control?
Commanders and supervisors at all levels
Pg 297, 13.17.1

What is the title of the person responsible for Government property in their possession?
Property Custodian
Pg 297, 13.17.3

A property custodian can be held liable for the loss, destruction, or damage of property or resources under their control. True or false?
True
Pg 297, 13.17.3

What types of costs does the operating budget cover?
Costs associated with the operation of all Air Force organizations
Pg 298, 13.18.3

Does the budget program operate on an annual or fiscal year basis?
Fiscal
Pg 298, 13.18.3

How much money does the Air Force lose every year due to individuals abusing the system by wasting precious resources, and committing acts of fraud?
Millions of dollars in money and resources
Pg 298, 13.19.1

What is the extravagant, careless, or needless expenditure of Air Force funds or the consumption of Air Force property that results from deficient practices, systems controls, or decisions?
Waste
Pg 298, 13.19.1.2

At what level should Air Force members try to resolve Fraud, Waste, and Abuse (FWA) issues?
At the lowest possible level
Pg 298, 13.19.3.1

What should an individual understand about submitting a report dealing with Fraud, Waste, and Abuse (FWA)? True or false?
They are subject to punitive action (or adverse administration action) if they knowingly make false statements and if they submit other unlawful communications
Pg 299, 13.16.3.1.2 (Note)

Who has the responsibility to safeguard the personal identity and complaints of individuals seeking assistance or participating in an IG process such as an investigation?
The Inspector General (IG)
Pg 299, 13.19.3.2

Can information be disclosed concerning Fraud, Waste, and Abuse (FWA)? True or false?
True, only if required by law or regulation
Pg 299, 13.19.3.3

Chapter 13 ends here for those testing to SSgt, TSgt, or MSgt. If testing to SMSgt or CMSgt, continue studying this chapter

Planning, Programming, Budgeting, and Execution (PPBE)

What does FYDP stand for?
Future Years Defense Program
Pg 302, 13.22.1

What part of the Planning, Programming, Budgeting, and Execution (PPBE) process provides the means to anticipate changes and understand the long-term implications of near-term choices and decisions?
The planning process
Pg 302, 13.22.1

What part of the Planning, Programming, Budgeting, and Execution (PPBE) process matches available resources against validated requirements to achieve the strategic plan and submit program proposals?
The programming process
Pg 302, 13.22.2

What part of the Planning, Programming, Budgeting, and Execution (PPBE) process has the key objective to develop a balanced, capabilities-based Air Force program in the form of the Air Force program objective memorandum (POM)?
The programming process
Pg 302, 13.22.2

What occurs concurrently with the programming phase of the Planning, Programming, Budgeting, and Execution (PPBE) process?
The budgeting phase
Pg 302, 13.22.3

What part of the Planning, Programming, Budgeting, and Execution (PPBE) process focuses on running the Air Force day to day?
Execution
Pg 303, 13.22.4

It is likely the budget will change during the execution phase. True or false?
True
Pg 303, 13.22.4

Congress allows some flexibility to move resources within the operating budget without requesting permission. True or false?
True
Pg 303, 13.22.4

Who helps establish and forecast a budget to ensure sufficient funds are available to accomplish the mission?
All SNCOs
Pg 303, 13.23

Government Property and Equipment

Who is responsible for ensuring all personnel are taught proper care and safeguarding principles of public property?
All Commanders and supervisors
Pg 303, 13.27.2

What is the name of the standard equipment management system applicable to all Air Force activities?
Air Force Equipment Management System (AFEMS)
Pg 304, 13.27.3

What has worldwide visibility of all in-use and warehoused equipment assets?
Air Force Equipment Management System (AFEMS)
Pg 304, 13.27.3

Who designates a property custodian for Government property used by the unit?
The organization commander or equivalent
Pg 304, 13.28

How often must the property custodian perform an inventory?
Upon assuming responsibility and at least annually
Pg 304, 13.28

When is the property custodian relieved of their responsibility?
Only when the account is transferred to another custodian
Pg 304, 13.28

What is used to research and investigate the cause of loss, damage, destruction, or theft of Government property and determine if it was attributable to an individual's negligence or abuse?
A Report of Survey (ROS)
Pg 304, 13.29

The organization possessing the lost or damaged property is responsible for initiating a Report of Survey (ROS). True or false?
True
Pg 304, 13.29.2.1

Who can be appointed as an investigating official for a Report of Survey (ROS)?
Any impartial officer, SNCO, or civilian (GS-7 or above)
Pg 304, 13.29.2.2

Who must an investigator interview during a Report of Survey (ROS)?
Any person with knowledge of the case
Pg 305, 13.29.3.1

An individual charged in the ROS may appeal to the next level in the chain of command above the person who assigned the financial liability assessment. True or false?
True
Pg 305, 13.29.5.3

Facility Management

Who can the unit Commander designate (in writing) as the primary and an alternate facility manager for each facility that is assigned to the organization?
An E-4 and above, or civilian equivalent
Pg 306, 13.31.2

If a facility is multi-purpose, who should be assigned as the primary facility manager?
The major user should be assigned as the primary facility manager
Pg 306, 13.31.2

In a multi-purpose facility, can any other organization appoint an alternate facility manager? True or false?
True
Pg 306, 13.31.2

The facility manager is responsible for submitting work requirements (verbally or in writing) to the base civil engineer facility maintenance unit. True or false?
True
Pg 306, 13.31.3

Who serves as the single point of contact for all maintenance, repair, alterations, and new construction?
The base civil engineer operations flight
Pg 306, 13.32.1

Would fixing a leaky faucet be considered as planned or scheduled work?
Scheduled
Pg 306, 13.32.2

Would moving a doorway from one wall to another be considered as planned or scheduled work?
Planned
Pg 306, 13.32.2

When is the authority and resources necessary to accomplish planned work acquired?
During the budget programming phase
Pg 306, 13.33.2

What is the dollar limit that O&M appropriation-funded unspecified minor military construction projects may not exceed (not including special exception)?
750,000
Pg 306, 13.33.2

Projects that are solely to correct a life, health, or safety threatening deficiency that costs more than $750,000 have to have congressional notification. True or false?
True
Pg 306, 13.33.2

The facility manager is responsible for updating real property records. True or false?
False
Pg 306, 13.34.1

Energy Conservation Program

Who is the Nation's largest energy consumer?
The Federal government
Pg 306, 13.35

What percent does the Government have to annually increase their use of alternative (non-petroleum-based) fuel by?
10 percent annually
Pg 307, 13.35.3

What percentage of compliance with Electronic Product Environmental Assessment Tool standards do newly procured electronic products have to meet?
95 percent
Pg 307, 13.35.6

What type of facilities will be excluded from the utility reduction policy?
Privatized housing and facilities that meet the Department of Energy exclusion requirements
Pg 308, 13.36.2

Chapter 14
Communicating in Today's Air Force

Overview

What types of communication are used the most in the Air Force?
Speaking and writing
Pg 309, 14.1.1

What must happen in order for communication to take place?
The audience must get the message and interpret the message in the way the sender intended
Pg 309, 14.1.1

Communication Basics

There are _____ core principles of good communication.
Five
Pg 309, 14.2

An easy way to remember the five core principles of good communication is by using the acronym FOCUS. What does FOCUS stand for?
Focused, Organized, Clear, Understanding, and Supported
Pg 309, Figure 14.1

Figure 14.1 FOCUS Principles (Pg 309)

Focused	Address the issue, the whole issue, and nothing but the issue
Organized	Systematically present your information and ideas
Clear	Communicate with clarity and make each word count
Understanding	Understand your audience and its expectations
Supported	Use logic and support to make your point

Seven Steps for Effective Communication

What does good communication require?
Preparation
Pg 310, 14.8

Fig 14.2 Seven Steps for Effective Communication (Pg 310)

1	Analyze purpose and audience
2	Research your topic
3	Support your ideas
4	Organize and outline
5	Prepare a daft
6	Edit the draft
7	Fight for feedback

Step 1 - Analyze, Purpose and Audience

The purposes of most Air Force writing or speaking are: to direct, inform, persuade or inspire. True or false?
True
Pg 310, 14.9.1

What type of communication approach is used when you need to pass on information describing actions you expect to be carried out by your audience?
Direct
Pg 310, Figure 14.3

What type of communication approach is used when you need to pass on information?
Inform
Pg 310, Figure 14.3

If you are trying to sell your audience on a new idea or new policy, what type of communication approach would you be using?
Persuade
Pg 310, Figure 14.3

What communication approach is frequently used in writing or speaking in the military?
Inspire
Pg 310, Figure 14.3

What will help you meet your communication goals?
Realizing your own strengths and weaknesses
Pg 310, 14.9.3

Which audience do you directly communicate with, either verbally or in writing?
Primary receiver
Pg 310, 14.9.5.1

Which audience do you indirectly communicate with through the primary receivers?
Secondary receiver
Pg 311, 14.9.5.2

Who are the most powerful members of the audience, the ones that really make the decisions?
Key decision makers
Pg 311, 14.9.5.3

Who are the individuals that typically review communications before they reach the intended audience?
The gatekeepers
Pg 311, 14.9.5.4

What can be a barrier in military communication?
Rank
Pg 311, 14.9.6.1

Step 2 - Research Your Topic

Once you are clear on your purpose and audience, what is your next step in preparing your communication?
Research your topic to uncover information that will support your communication goals
Pg 311, 14.10

Step 3 - Support Your Ideas

What allows the audience to interpret quantitative information by summarizing data?
Statistics
Pg 312, 14.11.3

What process is used to separate a whole into smaller pieces?
Analysis
Pg 312, 14.11.5.1

Step 4 - Organize and Outline

What allows for the organization of data in a time-based sequence (past to present or present to future)?
Chronological
Pg 313, 14.12.3

Figure 14.4. Approaches to Researching.

Approach 1
Review purpose and scope of the overall project. Sometimes your purpose and scope will evolve as you learn more about the topic, and you may need to do some preliminary research just to get smart enough to scope out the effort.

Approach 2
Assign a deadline. It is easy to get lost in the research process. Don't do an outstanding job of data retrieval, then marginal job on the presentation because you ran out of time.

Approach 3
Ask the boss. Even if you can eventually find the answer on your own, save some time by asking your supervisor for suggestions on where to start.

Approach 4
Determine what is known. Before you look for answers outside yourself, look in the mirror first. You may have valuable knowledge about an assigned research project, but you need to acknowledge and guard against your own biases in working a research problem.

Approach 5
Determine where to look for information. Coworkers and base personnel are easy because you can meet with them face-to-face. Office files and references in paper form and on your computer network may be valuable sources of information. Finally, the Internet and library offer an unlimited supply of information.

What allows for the organization of data using directions?
Spatial or geographical
Pg 313, 14.12.5

Step 5 - Draft

A draft is a final product. True or false?
False
Pg 313, 14.13

Which part of effective communication is getting your ideas down on paper?
Preparing a draft
Pg 313, 14.13

What captures the audience's attention in a draft?
The introduction
Pg 313, 14.13.1

What portion of an introduction sets the tone, captures the audience's attention, and encourages the audience to read further?
The stage-setting remarks
Pg 313, 14.13.1.1

What is considered as the heart of your message?
The body
Pg 314, 14.13.2

What part of the draft message is often the most neglected?
The conclusion
Pg 314, 14.13.3

What type of writing reaches out to the reader and gets to the point quickly with fewer words?
The active voice
Pg 314, 14.13.7.1

Fear of rejection is one of the reasons for writers block. True or false?
True
Pg 315, 14.13.8

Step 6 - Edit the Draft

How many times should you read your document in order to edit it efficiently?
At least three times
Pg 315, 14.14

What can help you catch errors in your paper?
Reading it out loud
Pg 316, 14.14.3

Step 7 - Fight for Feedback

What is the last step in preparing effective communication?
Fighting for feedback
Pg 316, 14.15

A co-worker would be a good source of feedback for communication you have prepared. True or false?
True
Pg 316, 14.15

Feedback can be both positive and negative. True or false?
True
Pg 317, Figure 14.6

Writing

It is okay to print an official memorandum on both sides of the paper in order to conserve paper. True or false?
False
Pg 317, 14.16.1.1

Should a personal letter be any longer than one page?
Preferably not
Pg 317, 14.16.2

Figure 14.6 Feedback Philosophies, (Pg 317)

Feedback

Should describe rather than judge

Is both positive and negative. A balanced description of other people's work considers both strong and weak points

Is specific rather than general. Highlight or underline specific items you want to bring to the author's attention

Is directed at behavior the author can control. A suggestion to improve the briefing room's temperature, for example, is probably beyond the author's control

What two items should be included in a personal letter?
A salutation and a complimentary close
Pg 317, 14.16.2

There a set format for a memorandum for record (MR). True or false?
True
Pg 317, 14.16.3

What format of memorandum is used to record information that would not normally be recorded and is considered an "in-house document"?
Separate-page MR
Pg 317, 14.16.3.1

What type of memorandum for record (MR) is usually on the file copy of a correspondence and gives the reader a quick synopsis of the purpose of the correspondence?
Explanatory MR
Pg 319, 14.16.3.2

What is the appropriate position to type or stamp the date on a memorandum?
Right hand side, 10 lines from the top and about one inch from the right margin
Pg 318, Figure 14.7

The word memorandum should not be in all capital letters. True or false?
False
Pg 319, Figure 14.7

Where is the appropriate place to type the signature element on a memorandum?
At least three spaces to the right of page center and five lines below the last line of text
Pg 319, Figure 14.7

There are three phases of effective bullet writing; which phase includes selecting the proper power verb to best describe an action?
Extract the facts
Pg 320, 14.17.1.2

What phase of writing bullet statements includes refining the statements and making them accurate, brief, and specific?
Streamlining
Pg 320, 14.17.3

Face-to-Face: Speaking and Listening

A speaker has control over the audience's reaction. True or false?
False
Pg 321, 14.18.1

What is the correct rate of speaking speed to use when giving speeches?
There is no correct rate
Pg 321, 14.18.1.1

What should you do prior to delivering your speech?
Check out the room you will be speaking in
Pg 321, 14.18.1.2

What refers to using the notes in your voice to speak higher or lower?
Pitch
Pg 321, 14.18.1.3

Why is it important to utilize pausing during a speech?
The pause technique serves the same function as punctuation in writing
Pg 321, 14.18.1.4

What term is used to explain the art of expressing words distinctly?
Articulation
Pg 321, 14.18.1.5

What is one of the most important factors in nonverbal communication?
Eye contact
Pg 321, 14.18.2.1

What lets the listeners know the speaker is interested in them?
Eye contact
Pg 321, 14.18.2.1

What is one of the three common speech delivery formats?
Impromptu
Pg 322, 14.18.3.1 - 14.18.3.3

What type of delivery format normally occurs when someone has to speak without warning or has only a few moments notice?
Impromptu
Pg 322, 14.18.3.1

Figure 14.7. The Official Memorandum.

DEPARTMENT OF THE AIR FORCE
AIR FORCE OCCUPATIONAL MEASUREMENT SQUADRON

1 July 2013

MEMORANDUM FOR SAF/IGI

FROM: AFOMS/PD
     550 D Street East, Suite 2
     Randolph AFB TX 78150-4427

SUBJECT: Sample Memorandum Format

1. Type or stamp the date on the right side of the memorandum 10 lines from the top of the page about 1 inch from the right margin.

2. Type the MEMORANDUM FOR caption in all caps four lines below the date or 14 lines from the top of the page. If you do not use the DoD Seal on your computer-generated letterhead or you are using plain bond paper, begin the caption approximately 11 line spaces from the top of the page.

3. Type the FROM caption in all caps two line spaces below the last line of the MEMORANDUM FOR caption. The FROM caption should contain the full mailing address of the function originating the correspondence.

4. Type the SUBJECT caption in all caps, two line spaces below the last line of the FROM caption.

5. Begin typing the text flush with the left margin two line spaces below the SUBJECT caption. Number and letter each paragraph.

6. Type the signature element at least three spaces to the right of page center, five lines below the last line of text. Type the name in UPPERCASE and include grade and service on the first line, the duty title on the second line, and the name of the office or organization level on a third line (if not announced in the heading).

7. Type "Attachments:" flush with the left margin, 10 lines below the last line of text or three lines below the signature element. Do not number when there is only one attachment; when there are two or more attachments, list each one by number in the order referred to in the memorandum. Describe each attachment briefly. Cite the office of origin, type of communication, date, and number of copies (in parentheses) if more than one.

Loretta W. Gess
LORETTA W. GESS, GS-11, DAF
Human Resources Manager

2 Attachments:
1. HQ USAF/DP Memo, 1 Jul 13 (2)
2. AFOMS/CC Msg, 122300Z Mar 13

Figure 14.8 – Separate-Page MR (Pg 315)

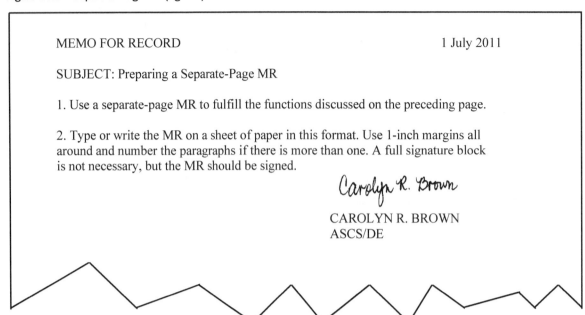

MEMO FOR RECORD   1 July 2011

SUBJECT: Preparing a Separate-Page MR

1. Use a separate-page MR to fulfill the functions discussed on the preceding page.

2. Type or write the MR on a sheet of paper in this format. Use 1-inch margins all around and number the paragraphs if there is more than one. A full signature block is not necessary, but the MR should be signed.

Carolyn R. Brown

CAROLYN R. BROWN
ASCS/DE

Figure 14.9 – Explanatory MR (Ample Spacing) (Pg 315)

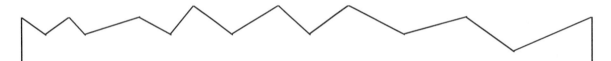

MEMO FOR RECORD   12 Mar 11

Omit the subject when typing the explanatory MR on the record copy. If space permits, type the MR and date two lines below the signature block. When there is not enough space, type "MR ATTACHED" or "MR ON REVERSE" and put the MR on a separate sheet or on the back of the record copy if it can be read clearly. Number the paragraphs when there are more than one. The signature block is not required; merely sign your last name after the last word of the MR.

Brown

Figure 4.10 – Explanatory MR (Minimum Spacing) (Pg 315)

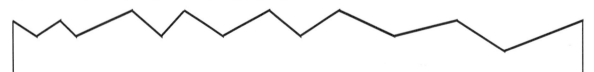

MR: When you have a very brief MR and not enough space on the bottom of your correspondence, use this tighter format. Sign your last name followed by the date.

What type of speech delivery format is used when an individual has ample time to be ready?
Prepared
Pg 322, 14.18.3.2

What type of speech delivery format requires that every word spoken be absolutely perfect?
Manuscript
Pg 322, 14.18.3.3

When a briefer is unsure of the answer to a question, they should attempt an "off the top of the head" answer. True or false?
False
Pg 322, 14.18.4.1

What type of speaking is generally one-way with no verbal participation by the listeners?
Teaching lectures
Pg 322, 14.18.4.2

What type of speaking has three basic purposes?
Formal speaking
Pg 322, 14.18.4.3

The average speaking rate is 120 words per minute, what is the average processing rate?
500 words per minute
Pg 323, 14.19.4.1.5

Electronic Communications and the Internet

All government communications systems are subject to monitoring. True or false?
True
Pg 324, 14.25

Suspected violations of electronic messaging policy are not always reported to your supervisor and/or the information protection office. True or false?
False
Pg 324, 14.25.6

What is e-mail protocol called?
Netiquette
Pg 325, 14.27

Why is using all capital letters in an e-mail considered inappropriate?
It is considered a form of shouting and rude
Pg 325, 14.27.2.3

What is one of the most common mistakes when sending e-mails?
Forgetting to attach the attachment
Pg 326, 14.27.5.2

What is a good way to save time when e-mailing?
Create mailing lists
Pg 326, 14.27.6.2

What should you do if you plan to be away from your e-mail for an extended period of time?
Set up an auto reply message
Pg 326, 14.27.6.5

You can download/install recreational freeware and shareware on your computer. True or false?
False
Pg 326, 14.28.3.13

Conducting an Effective Interview

What are all job interviews designed to do?
Find the right person for a particular job
Pg 328, 14.29.1.1

The interview process is designed only for the employer to ask the prospective employee questions. True or false?
False
Pg 328, 14.29.1.2

What is your job when you go to an interview?
To convince the interviewer you are the perfect match for the job
Pg 328, 14.29.1.3

You should ask questions of the potential employer at an interview. True or false?
True, they expect you to
Pg 329, 14.29.3.1.7

What is an essential part of the interview process?
Your listening skills
Pg 329, 14.29.3.2

What is considered unnecessary during a phone interview?
Filling in pauses with conversation
Pg 330, 14.29.4.1.3

You should NOT send a short thank you note to the organization you interviewed with. True or false?
False
Pg 330, 14.30.1

Chapter 14 ends here for those testing to SSgt, TSgt, or MSgt. If testing to SMSgt or CMSgt, continue studying this chapter

Staff-Level Communication

If you are unable to keep a meeting to under an hour, what should you plan to do?
Schedule time for breaks
Pg 333, 14.32.1.4

How long prior to a meeting should an agenda be sent to the attendees?
No less than 1 or 2 days prior to the meeting
Pg 333, 14.32.1.6

It is recommended to wait approximately 5 minutes after the start time of a meeting to allow for those who may be running late. True or false?
False, the meeting should start on time
Pg 333, 14.32.2.1

What should be in the last paragraph when you prepare meeting minutes?
Information regarding a future meeting
Pg 334, 14.32.3.2

Instruments of Written Communication

What document contains written statements centered on a single idea or a collection of accomplishments with their respective impacts?
A bullet background paper
Pg 335, 14.33

What document describes a temporary duty trip to another location and includes the purpose, travelers, itinerary, discussions, and conclusions or recommendations?
A trip report
Pg 336, 14.36

BULLET BACKGROUND PAPER
ON
THE BULLET BACKGROUND PAPER

An increasingly popular version of the background paper is the "bullet" background paper. The bullet format provides a concise, chronological evolution of a problem, a complete summary of an attached staff package, or main thrust of a paper.

Main ideas follow the introductory paragraph and may be as long as several sentences or as short as one word (such as "Advantages").

- Secondary items follow with a single dash and tertiary items follow with multiple indented dashes. Secondary and tertiary items can be as short as a word or as long as several sentences.
- Format varies.
    -- Center title (all capital letters); use 1-inch margins all around; single-space the text; double-space between items—except double-space title and triple-space to text; use appropriate punctuation in paragraphs and complete thoughts.
    -- Headings such as SUBJECT, PROBLEM, BACKGROUND, DISCUSSION, CONCLUSION, or RECOMMENDATION are optional.

Keys to developing a good backgrounder:

- Write the paper according to the knowledge level of the user; that is, a person who is very knowledgeable on the subject won't require as much detail as one who knows very little.
- Emphasize main points.
- Attach additional support data; refer to it in the backgrounder.
- Require minimum length to achieve brevity with short transitions.
- End with concluding remarks or recommendations.

Include an identification line (author's grade and name, organization, office symbol, telephone number, typist's initials, and date) on the first page 1 inch from the bottom of the page or at least two lines below the last line of text.

MSgt Smith/AFOMS/PD/123-9876/ejs/1 Dec 13

Chapter 15
Personnel Programs

Manpower Management

Who allocates programmed manpower resources to the major commands (MAJCOM)?
HQ USAF Directorate of Manpower and Organization
Pg 337, 15.3

The requesting organization has to provide a reason before manpower allocations can be changed. True or false?
True
Pg 337, 15.4.1

Air Force manpower does not get adjusted to accommodate cyclical or temporary requirements, so how does it provide the resources to perform the workload?
Civilian overtime, temporary full- and part-time civilian positions, temporary duty (TDY) of military or civilian personnel, and the use of contract services
Pg 337, 15.4.2

Manpower standards are established to ensure work center operations are efficient and standardized. True or false?
True
Pg 338, 15.5.2.1

What is the ultimate goal of organizational performance?
Mission accomplishment
Pg 338, 15.5.2.1

What is used to help manage manpower resources?
The Unit Manpower Document
Pg 338, 15.6

What is the primary document that reflects the manpower required to accomplish the unit's mission?
The Unit Manpower Document
Pg 338, 15.6

Enlisted Assignments

Personnel TEMPO (PERSTEMPO) measures quality of life. True or false?
True
Pg 339, 15.7

Why does the Air Force equitably distribute involuntary assignments among similarly qualified personnel?
To minimize family separation and personal hardship
Pg 339, 15.7.2

What is the primary factor in selecting a member for a Permanent Change of Station (PCS)?
Qualifications to perform productively in the position
Pg 339, 15.9.1

How long are CMSgt assignments limited to at MAJCOMs, HQ Air Force, Joint Staff positions, and special duty positions?
3 years
Pg 340, 15.9.6.1

What limitations are set for first-term Airmen (FTA) for assignments in different locations during their first 4-year term?
No more than two assignments
Pg 341, 15.9.7

What policy assists members in resolving short term problems involving family members?
Humanitarian Policy
Pg 341, 15.9.8.1.1

Married military couples are always assigned together. True or false?
False, each member of a military couple serves in his or her own right
Pg 341, 15.9.8.3

What does the Voluntary Stabilized Base Assignment Program (enlisted only) offer an Airman who volunteers for a position at a hard to fill location?
A stabilized tour
Pg 342, 15.9.8.4

What is the maximum TDY period for any one location in a 12-month period?
180 days
Pg 342, 15.9.8.8

How long of a deferment can an individual be authorized following the date an adopted child is officially placed in the member's house?
6 months
Pg 342, 15.9.8.9

How much time on station does a FTA have to have in order to go from CONUS to OS?
At least 12 months
Pg 342, 15.9.9.2

What provides a list of upcoming assignments for enlisted Airmen to align personal preferences to actual AF needs?
The Enlisted Quarterly Assignment Listing (EQUAL)
Pg 343, 15.9.10

Who is responsible for the currency and accuracy of assignment preferences for each Airman?
Each Airman is individually responsible
Pg 343, 15.9.11

Family Care

How long after a discussion with a superior does a member have to produce a family care plan?
60 days
Pg 344, 15.10

If a member fails to produce a family care plan in the allotted time, can disciplinary action and/or administrative separation be administered? True or false?
True
Pg 344, 15.10

Military members are required to have a will. True or false?
False, but it is strongly encouraged
Pg 344, 15.10

A family care plan has to include provisions for short-term and long-term absences and a caregiver for affected family members. True or false?
True
Pg 344, 15.12

Who is responsible for counseling all Airmen with family members upon arrival at a new duty station?
The commander or first sergeant
Pg 344, 15.12.1.1

At what point, after arriving at a new duty station, does family care counseling take place?
During in-processing
Pg 344, 15.12.1.1

Commanders and First Sergeants are allowed to delegate counseling requirements. True or false?
False
Pg 344, 15.12.1.1

How often are Commanders or First Sergeants required to individually brief all military members in their organization on family care responsibilities?
Annually
Pg 344, 15.12.1.2

Reenlistment and Retraining Opportunities

Everyone in the Air Force has the right to reenlist. True or false?
False, reenlistment is a privilege not a right
Pg 345, 15.13.1

The Unit Commander has total Selective Reenlisted Program (SRP) selection and non-selection authority for all Airmen. True or false?
True
Pg 345, 15.13.2.1

Who is responsible for providing the Unit Commanders with recommendations concerning the Airman's career potential?
The immediate supervisor
Pg 345, 15.13.2.2

How long after the Commander advises an Airman of being non-selected for reenlistment does he/she have to make it known of his/her intention to appeal?
3 workdays
Pg 345, 15.13.3.2

What increments are enlistment extensions granted in?
Monthly
Pg 346, 15.14

The majority of Airmen are generally permitted to reenlist or extend their enlistment if their Date of Separation (DOS) exceeds their High Year Tenure (HYT). True or false?
False
Pg 346, 15.15

What is the maximum Selective Reenlistment Bonus (SRB) payable to eligible Airmen per zone?
90,000
Pg 346, 15.16.2

The Selective Reenlistment Bonus (SRB) is paid all at one time. True or false?
False
Pg 346, 15.16.2

Supervisors should encourage Airmen to pursue retraining into a shortage skill if a Career Job Reservation (CJR) is not immediately available. True or false?
True
Pg 347, 15.17.2

What program gives Airmen a choice and/or voice in their career path?
Air Force Retraining Program
Pg 347, 15.18

How many months must a First Term Airman complete (4-year enlistment) before being able to retrain?
35 months
Pg 347, 15.18.1

What happens if the member has not been approved after three consecutive months of consideration for retraining?
The entire retraining application is disapproved
Pg 347, 15.18.1

The annual NCO Retraining Program moves NCOs from AFSCs with significant overages into AFSCs that have shortages. True or false?
True
Pg 347, 15.18.2

What are the two phases of the annual NCO Retraining Program?
Voluntary and involuntary
Pg 347, 15.18.2

Benefits and Services

What is the main purpose of the VA home loan program?
To help veterans finance the purchase of homes with favorable loan terms at a rate of interest competitive with the rate charged on other types of mortgage loans
Pg 348, 15.19.4

How many years of total active federal military service does an enlisted member need to be eligible to retire?
20
Pg 348, 15.20

What is the minimum timeframe a retirement application can be submitted through vMPF before the minimum required service?
120 days
Pg 348, 15.20

A member electing to retire overseas (OS) and live permanently in that country has to comply with command and host government residency rules before the date of retirement. True or false?
True
Pg 349, 15.20.1

What normally determines which retirement pay plan applies to a member?
The date initially entered military service (DIEMS)
Pg 349, 15.20.2

Military pay stops when a member dies. True or false?
True
Pg 350, 15.21.1

Who established the Survivor Benefit Plan (SBP)?
Congress
Pg 350, 15.21.1

How much does the Survivor Benefit Plan (SBP) cost a member while on active duty?
There is no cost
Pg 350, 15.21.1

Table 15.1. Retirement Pay Plans.

LINE	A Plan	B Eligibility (as determined by DIEMS)	C Retired Pay Formula	D Cost-of-Living Adjustment (COLA) (note 1)
1	Final Basic Pay	Entered service before 8 September 1980	2.5 percent multiplied by the years of service plus 1/12 x 2.5 percent for each additional full month, multiplied by final basic pay of the retired grade (10 USC 1406)	Full inflation protection; COLA based on consumer price index (CPI)
2	High-3 (note 2)	Entered service on or after 8 September 1980 and before 1 August 1986	2.5 percent multiplied by the years of service plus 1/12 x 2.5 percent for each additional full month, multiplied by the average of the highest 36 months of basic pay (note 3) (10 USC 1407)	
3	High-3 with Redux/Career Status Bonus (CSB) option* *Instead of retiring under High-3, these members may choose to receive the CSB at 15 years of service in exchange for agreeing to serve to at least 20 years of service and then retiring under the less generous Redux plan. The member may elect a lump sum of $30K, two payments of $15K, three payments of $10K, four payments of $7.5K, or five payments of $6K	Entered service on or after 1 August 1986	High-3: 2.5 percent multiplied by the years of service plus 1/12 x 2.5 percent for each additional full month, multiplied by the average of the highest 36 months of basic pay OR *Redux/CSB option: 2.5 percent multiplied by the years of service plus 1/12 x 2.5 percent for each additional full month, minus one percentage point from the product for each year less than 30 years, multiplied by the average of the highest 36 months of basic pay. At age 62, retired pay is recalculated without deducting the one percentage point for each year less than 30, which allows it to catch up to what it would have been without the Redux penalty.	High-3: Full inflation protection; COLA based on CPI OR *Redux/CSB option: partial inflation protect-tion; COLA based on CPI minus 1 percent. At age 62, retired pay is adjusted to reflect full COLA since retirement. Partial COLA then resumes after age 62.

Notes:
1. COLA is applied annually to retired pay.
2. High-3 is a reference to the average of the high 3 years or, more specifically, the high 36 months of basic pay as used in the formula.
3. If a member is demoted or an officer is retired in a lower grade as a result of an Officer Grade Determination, the retired pay plan is Final Basic Pay of the lower, retired grade (10 USC, Section 1407(f)).

Figure 15.2. Red Cross Services.

Emergency Communication Services

The Red Cross ensures that in times of personal and family crisis the American people can keep in touch with their loved ones serving in the U.S. military. Urgent messages concerning births, deaths, and serious illness are delivered to service members deployed anywhere in the world, including on ships at sea and at embassies and isolated military units.

Delivering emergency communication messages to the troops is provided 24 hours a day, 7 days a week, and 365 days a year through a network of employees and volunteers at Red Cross chapters and offices on military installations around the world and who deploy with U.S. service members in Kuwait, Afghanistan, and Iraq.

Commanders have come to rely on emergency communication messages from the Red Cross when making their decision to grant emergency leave. Emergency communication messages are verified and contain the most current information.

Social Services

The Red Cross also facilitates access to financial assistance in partnership with the military aid societies, counseling, family support at participating chapters, and assistance with representation at the Board of Veterans Appeals. When an emergency arises that requires the presence of the service member or his or her family, the Red Cross may facilitate access to an interest-free loan for travel expenses and other emergency situations through the partnership with the AFAS and other military aid societies.

Funds may be authorized for other emergencies and are disbursed on the basis of need. In addition, Red Cross chapters provide referrals to organizations in local communities that provide financial aid and/or resources.

Red Cross Services to Veterans

Trained Red Cross workers specialize in assisting veterans, their families, and surviving spouses with preparing and filing appeals to the Board of Veterans Appeals. The Red Cross does not charge for this service nor does it ask for membership fees. Also, the Red Cross has certified volunteers who work in VA hospitals.

Red Cross Staff Members Deploy Overseas

Service to the Armed Forces staff members deploy with the troops to Iraq, Kuwait, and Afghanistan to deliver emergency communication messages in conflict areas. In the friendly atmosphere of communication and support centers, soldiers can enjoy coffee and share personal and family concerns in a safe and confidential environment. Talking with Red Cross workers provides an outlet for service members who may not be able to voice their concerns elsewhere. Red Cross teams also visit patients in hospitals and clinics.

Outreach to Members of the National Guard, Reserves, and their Families

Red Cross chapters have been reaching out to community-based service members and their families since 2000 through the Get to Know Us Before You Need Us Program.

Offered in communities across the United States, the program provides National Guard members, Reserve units, military recruiters, and members of ROTC units with information relating to Red Cross programs and services. Get to Know Us teaches military personnel and their families how to access Red Cross services, which includes reaching deployed loved ones in an emergency, counseling, access to financial assistance, and coping with separation issues.

Volunteer Opportunities for Military Families

The Red Cross also offers a host of volunteer opportunities to military and veteran communities. Volunteer programs on military installations and in military and veterans hospitals involve community service, education, enhancement of job skills, and personal development. Volunteers are important assets to the installation command and to military medical facilities.

Volunteers are placed based on their areas of interest. If they do not have a specific request or area of interest, they may be placed in an area where the need is the greatest. Volunteers may serve as greeters, hospital guides, wheelchair escorts, patient chaperones, and pharmacy aides.

What is the Airman and Family Readiness Center (A&FRC) services designed to assist commanders in doing?
To assist in assessing and supporting the welfare of the military community and building a strong sense of community and support within the Air Force
Pg 350, 15.22.1

The Airman and Family Readiness Center (A&FRC) provides crisis assistance. True or false?
True
Pg 351, 15.22.1.10

What is the core service provided by the American Red Cross?
Emergency communication messages
Pg 352, 15.23

American Red Cross services are available to inactive service members. True or false?
True
Pg 352, 15.23

Personnel Records and Individual Rights

How often can an individual review their Personal Information File (PIF)?
At any time
Pg 354, 15.24.2

What is the maximum wait time to receive a reply for records requested under the Freedom of Information Act (FOIA)?
20 workdays
Pg 354, 15.26

What is the highest level of administrative review for correcting military records?
The Air Force Board for Correction of Military Records (AFBCMR)
Pg 355, 15.27.1

What does an individual have to do before applying to the Air Force Board for Correction of Military Records (AFBCMR) to have their records corrected?
Exhaust other administrative remedies for relief first
Pg 355, 15.27.3

What did the Air Force Discharge Review Board (AFDRB) begin doing in November 1975?
They added a traveling board that travels throughout the United States
Pg 355, 15.28.2

An individual has the right to personally appear before the Air Force Discharge Review Board (AFDRB). True or false?
True
Pg 355, 15.28.2

Awards and Decorations

What is one of the most common service awards worn by Air Force members today?
Global War on Terrorism Service Medal
Pg 356, 15.31.1.1

What is the Gallant Unit Citation (GUC) awarded for?
For extraordinary heroism against an armed enemy
Pg 357, 15.31.2.1

Who can recommend an individual for a decoration?
Any person (other than the individual being recommended) having firsthand knowledge of the act or service
Pg 358, 15.32.2

Airman Promotion System

The objective of the enlisted promotion system is to provide a visible, relatively stable career progression opportunity over the long term. True or false?
True
Pg 359, 15.33

What percentage of Airmen may serve in the Regular Air Force in the grades of SMSgt and CMSgt
3.5 percent
Pg 359, 15.34

What is promotion eligibility based on for members?
Proper skill level, sufficient time in grade (TIG), sufficient time in service (TIS), and a recommendation by the immediate commander
Pg 359, 15.35

Table 15.2. TIS and TIG Requirements, Promotion Eligibility Cutoff Dates (PECD), and Test Cycles for Promotion to Airman (Amn) through CMSgt.

RULE	A For Promotion To	B TIS	C TIG	D PECD	E Test Cycle
1	Amn	---	6 months	NA	NA
2	A1C	---	10 months	NA	NA
3	SrA	36 months	20 months or 28 months	NA	NA
4	SSgt	3 years	6 months	31 March	May - June
5	TSgt	5 years	23 months	31 December	February - March
6	MSgt	8 years	24 months	31 December	February - March
7	SMSgt	11 years	20 months	30 September	December
8	CMSgt	14 years	21 months	31 July	September

What are some of the reasons an Airman may be considered ineligible for promotion?
Approved retirement, declination for extension or reenlistment, court-martial conviction, control roster action, not recommended by the commander, failure to appear for scheduled testing without a valid reason, absent without leave, etc
Pg 359, 15.36

If an individual is ineligible for promotion, has already tested and has a projected promotion, will it be cancelled? True or false?
True
Pg 359, 15.36

What length of service retainability must selectees for MSgt and SMSgt with 18 years of Total Active Federal Military Service (TAFMS) sign?
2 years
Pg 359, 15.38

What length of service retainability must selectees for CMSgt with 18 years of Total Active Federal Military Service (TAFMS) sign?
3 years
Pg 359, 15.38

Airmen selected for promotion to SSgt, MSgt, or SMSgt have to complete in-resident PME prior to assuming their grade. True or false?
True
Pg 360, 15.40

If those selected for promotion to SSgt, MSgt, or SMSgt do not complete their PME prior to the promotion effective date are they still promoted or is it withheld?
Withheld
Pg 360, 15.40

How much Time in Grade (TIG) does an Airman Basic (AB) have to have to be eligible for promotion to Airman?
6 months
Pg 360, 15.41.1

How much Time in Grade (TIG) does an Airman have to have to be eligible for promotion to A1C?
10 months
Pg 360, 15.41.1

What skill level does an A1C promoting to SrA have to possess?
3-skill level
Pg 360, 15.41.2

The two programs that SSgt through MSgt can be promoted under are the WAPS and STEP. True or false?
True
Pg 361, 15.41.3

What is the highest possible score a member can receive on the Weighted Airman Promotion System (WAPS)?
460 points
Pg 361, 15.41.3.1

How many points are the promotion fitness exam (PFE) and specialty knowledge test (SKT) combined worth on the WAPS?
200 points
Pg 361, 15.41.3.1

The advantage of the Air Force making promotions under WAPS and within each AFSC is that eligible members compete for promotion only with those currently in the same AFSC. True or false?
True
Pg 361, 15.41.3.1

Table 15.3. Minimum Eligibility Requirements for Promotion. (Note 1)

RULE	A If promotion is to (note 2)	B and PAFSC as of PECD is	C and TIG the first day of the month before the month promotions are normally made is	D and TAFMS the first day of the last month of the cycle is (note 3)	E and the member has	F then
1	SrA	3 level (note 4)	Not applicable	1 year		the Airman is eligible for promotion if recommended in writing by the promotion authority. He/she must be Regular Air Force in enlisted status as of the PECD, serve continuously until the effective date of promotion, and not be in a condition listed in AFI 36-2502, Table 1.1, on or after the PECD; must be in promotion eligibility status code X on effective date of promotion. (note 6)
2	SSgt	5 level (note 4)	6 months	3 years		
3	TSgt	7 level (note 4)	23 months	5 years		
4	MSgt	7 level	24 months	8 years		
5	SMSgt	7 level (note 4)	20 months	11 years	8 years of cumulative enlisted service (TEMSD) creditable for basic pay (note 5)	
6	CMSgt	9 level (note 4)	21 months	14 years	10 years cumulative enlisted service (TEMSD) creditable for basic pay (note 5)	

Notes:

1. Use this table to determine standard minimum eligibility requirements for promotion consideration. HQ USAF may announce additional eligibility requirements. The individual must serve in the Regular Air Force and have continuous active duty as of PECD.

2. The HYT policy applicable as of PECD may affect promotion eligibility in grades SrA and above.

3. Use years of satisfactory service for retirement in place of the TAFMSD to determine promotion eligibility for ANG and AFR Airmen ordered to Regular Air Force. (**Exception:** Active Guard or Reserve or statutory tours.) AFR or ANG Airmen are eligible for promotion if extended active duty is on or after PECD.

4. Airmen must meet skill-level requirements by the effective date of promotion for SrA and by the PECD for SSgt. SSgts test and compete for promotion to TSgt if they have a 5-skill level as of PECD; however, they must have a 7-skill level before promotion. MSgts and SMSgts must meet minimum skill-level requirements listed above. In some cases, commanders may waive this to allow them to compete for promotion. Airmen demoted to SrA and who are past their HYT for that grade will have their HYT adjusted based on TIG requirements only. The HYT is adjusted regardless of whether or not they are eligible to compete for promotion. The HYT date will be the fourth month after selections are made for the first SSgt promotion cycle the Airman is TIG eligible. It is not mandatory that an Airman be considered for promotion if ineligible according to AFI 36-2502, Table 1.1.

5. Service in a commissioned, warrant, or flight officer status is creditable for pay. Such service does not count for this requirement (38 Comptroller General 598). You may consider a promotion for Airmen who meet this requirement on the first day of the last month promotions are normally made in the cycle. Actual promotion does not occur earlier than the first day of the month following the month the Airman completes the required enlisted service. This applies if the selectee had a sequence number in an earlier promotion increment; however, if the Airman meets the required enlisted service on the first day of the month, the DOR and effective date is that date.

6. If a TDY student meets the requirements of this table but does not maintain satisfactory proficiency, the MPS that services the Airman's TDY unit notifies the MPS servicing the Airman's unit of assignment.

Table 15.4. Calculating Points and Factors for Promotion to SSgt through MSgt.

RULE	A If the factor is	B then the maximum score is
1	SKT	100 points. Base individual score on percentage correct (two decimal places). (note 1)
2	PFE	100 points. Base individual score on percentage correct (two decimal places). (note 1)
3	TIS	40 points. Award 2 points for each year of TAFMS up to 20 years, as of the last day of the last month of the promotion cycle. Credit 1/6 point for each month of TAFMS (15 days or more = 1/6 point; drop periods less than 15 days). Example: The last day of the last month of the cycle (31 Jul 03 minus TAFMS date (18 Jul 96) equals 7 years 14 days (inclusive dates considered equals 7 x 2 = 14 points). (note 1)
4	TIG	60 points. Award 1/2 point for each month in grade up to 10 years, as of the first day of the last month of the promotion cycle (count 15 days or more as 1/2 point; drop periods less than 15 days). Example: The first day of the last month of the promotion cycle (1 Jul 03) minus current DOR (1 Jan 00) equals 3 years 6 months 1 day (inclusive dates considered) equals 42 x .5 = 21 points. (note 1)
5	Decorations	25 points. Assign each decoration a point value based on its order of precedence. (note 2) Medal of Honor: 15 Air Force, Navy, or Distinguished Service Cross: 11 Defense Distinguished Service Medal, Distinguished Service Medal, Silver Star: 9 Legion of Merit, Defense Superior Service Medal, Distinguished Flying Cross: 7 Airman, Soldier, Navy-Marine Corps, Coast Guard Bronze Star, Defense/Meritorious Service Medals, Purple Heart: 5 Air, Aerial Achievement, Air Force Commendation, Army Commendation, Navy-Marine Corps Commendation, Joint Services, or Coast Guard Commendation Medal: 3 Navy-Marine Corps, Coast Guard, Air Force, Army, or Joint Service Achievement Medal: 1
6	EPRs	135 points. Multiply each EPR rating that closed out within 5 years immediately preceding the PECD, not to exceed 10 reports, by the time-weighted factor for that specific report. The time-weighted factor begins with 50 for the most recent report and decreases in increments of five (50-45-40-35-30-25-20-15-10-5) for each report on file. Multiply that product by the EPR conversion factor of 27. Repeat this step for each report. After calculating each report, add the total value of each report for a sum. Divide that sum by the sum of the time-weighted factors added together for the promotion performance factor (126.60). (notes 1 and 3) **Example:** EPR string (most recent to oldest): 5B-4B-5B-5B-5B-4B 5 x 50 = 250 x 27 = 6,750 4 x 45 = 180 x 27 = 4,860 5 x 40 = 200 x 27 = 5,400 28,485 ÷ 225 = 126.60 5 x 35 = 175 x 27 = 4,725 5 x 30 = 150 x 27 = 4,050 4 x 25 = 100 x 27 = 2,700 225 28,485

NOTES:
1. Cutoff scores after the second decimal place. Do not use the third decimal place to round up or down.
2. The decoration closeout date must be on or before the PECD. The "prepared" date of the DECOR 6 recommendation for decoration printout must be before the date HQ AFPC made the selections for promotion. Fully document resubmitted decorations (downgraded, lost, etc.) and verify they were placed into official channels before the selection date.
3. Do not count nonevaluated periods of performance, such as break in service, report removed through appeal process, etc., in the computation. For example, compute an EPR string of 4B, XB, 5B, 4B the same as 4B, 5B, 4B EPR string.

15.42.2.7. Ensure they receive at least 60 days' access to study materials prior to testing.

15.42.2.8. (For SMSgt and CMSgt eligibles) Ensure their selection folder at HQ AFPC is accurate and complete.

What happens if more than one individual has the same score for promotion at the cutoff point of the quota?
The Air Force promotes everyone with that score
Pg 361, 15.41.3.1

How many points are Phase I and Phase II of the promotion process to the grades of SMSgt and CMSgt worth?
795 points
Pg 363, 15.41.4

What is the best way to prepare for the Weighted Airman Promotion System (WAPS) test?
It is an individual responsibility
Pg 363, 15.42.1

What must a member do if he/she will not be available during the entire testing cycle due to TDY?
Be prepared to test prior to TDY departure
Pg 363, 15.42.2.6

Who is responsible for ensuring selection folders (for SMSgt and CMSgt) at HQ AFPC are accurate and complete prior to WAPS testing?
Each individual
Pg 363, 14.42.2.8

What is the study reference material for all Promotion Fitness Examines (PFEs) and US Air Force Supervisory Examinations (USAFSE)?
AFPAM 36-2241, Professional Development Guide
Pg 364, 15.43.1

Who develops test questions for all Air Force promotion tests?
SNCOs from field units
Pg 364, 15.44.1

How often are all the Air Force promotion tests revised?
Annually
Pg 364, 15.44.1

All questions on the PFE, SKT, and the USAFSE are located in publications from the reference list. True or false?
True
Pg 365, 15.44.2

How do promotion tests get scored?
Electronically
Pg 365, 15.45

Are group studies for promotion tests permitted or prohibited?
Strictly prohibited
Pg 365, 15.46

Commercial study guides may be used to prepare for promotion testing. True or false?
True
Pg 365, 15.46.3

A member can use commercially prepared study guides on a government computer. True or false?
False, it would imply Air Force sanctioning of the guide
Pg 365, 15.46.3

Chapter 15 ends here for those testing to SSgt, TSgt, or MSgt. If testing to SMSgt or CMSgt, continue studying this chapter

SNCO Promotion Program

What are individuals eligible for promotion responsible for?
Those eligible should have the current study reference materials, know when the testing cycle starts, ensure the information in their selection folder at AFPC is accurate and complete, study as needed, and test when scheduled
Pg 368, 15.49.1

What Enlisted Performance Reports (EPRs) will be used to compute the EPR weighted factor score?
The last 5 years
Pg 368, 15.50.4

What portion of your total score does the evaluation board portion account for?
Over 50%
Pg 368, 15.51

How many members are on each panel of the evaluation board?
Three
Pg 368, 15.51.1

What areas of a members' record does the evaluation board look at?
Performance, education, breadth of experience, job responsibility, professional competence, specific achievements, and leadership
Pg 368, 15.51.2

Individuals have no control over the information the evaluation board reviews. True or false?
False
Pg 368, 15.51.2

How many Enlisted Performance Reviews (EPRs) does the evaluation board review?
10 years preceding the cutoff date
Pg 371, 15.51.2.1

What does breadth of experience mean?
The individual's overall professional background, experience, and knowledge gained during his or her career to the present
Pg 371, 15.51.2.3

How might professional competence be measured by the evaluation board?
What rating and endorsing officials say about the individual's expertise, how much the individual knows about the job, and how well he or she accomplishes it
Pg 371, 15.51.2.5

The evaluation board looks at only awards and decorations when they look for specific achievements. True or false?
False
Pg 371, 15.51.2.6

What scores can an individual receive from the evaluation board panel?
18-30
Pg 371, 15.52.2.1

If there is more than one point difference in the scores of each promotion evaluation panel member, how is it resolved?
It gets returned to the panel for resolution
Pg 371, 15.52.2.2

What happens if a promotion evaluation board panel cannot agree on a resolution of a split score?
The board president resolves it
Pg 371, 15.52.2.2

How can promotion evaluation board scores change (sometimes significantly) from one year to the next?
New panel members with different thought processes, previous eligibles with changed or improved records, and a large pool of new eligibles
Pg 372, 15.52.2.4

If an individual is determined as not fully qualified (NFQ) by the evaluation board members, how is the individual notified?
In writing
Pg 372, 15.52.3

Promotion panel scores and weighted scores are combined after the board is finished. True or false?
True
Pg 372, 15.52.4

Work center supervisors should periodically review their Unit Manning Document (UMD) to ensure it accurately reflects unit requirements. True or false?
True
Pg 375, 15.54

What does a Unit Manning Document (UMD) display?
Current and projected requirements
Pg 375, 15.54

What are the two types of manpower requirements?
Funded and unfunded
Pg 375, 15.55.1

Funded manpower requirements are validated and allocated. True or false?
True
Pg 375, 15.55.1

Unfunded manpower requirements are needs that are deferred because of budgetary constraints. True or false?
True
Pg 375, 15.55.1

What percent of the total enlisted force does Congress normally limit to the grade of CMSgt?
Normally 1 percent
Pg 375, 15.55.2

An authorization change request (ACR) is used to request a change to an existing requirement of the Unit Manning Document (UMD). True or false?
True
Pg 375, 15.56.1

Figure 15.3. Sample Senior NCO Promotion DVR.

Enlisted Data Verification Record (DVR)

The following data is reflected in your Weighted Airman Promotion System (WAPS) Record. The data reflected is AS OF the Promotion Eligibility Cutoff Date (PECD) and may not be the same as what is in the Military Personnel Data System (MILPDS).

The information reflected on this DVR will be used in the promotion process for the cycle indicated. Review this data in detail, especially your CAFSC, decorations, PME and education data and retain for your personal records. Information reflected is as of Promotion Eligibility Cutoff Date (PECD), except a projected retirement date will continue to be updated until the actual promotion brief is produced (about 30-45 days prior to the board). For the weighted portion of your score, only performance reports for 5 years (max of 10) that closeout on or before the PECD are used. The evaluation board reviews all reports closing out up to 10 years prior to PECD. Any additional reports are listed for your information only. If you have recently retrained or entered a Special Duty Identifier, your CAFSC effective date is the date you departed for training. If you detect any errors or have any questions, contact your customer service center or personnel representative immediately. Your personal involvement is a must—it's your promotion

This is considered an official document and it is your responsibility to verify your promotion information.

GENERAL INFORMATION   AS OF: 03 DEC 2010

NAME: SMITH, JOHN A. **RANK:** SMSG **SSAN:** XXX-XX-4321
UNIT: DET DPSO AF PERSONNEL CTR FO, **DATE OF RANK:** 01 NOV 2002 **PROMOTION CYCLE:** 10E9
RANDOLPH AFB, TX 78150-0000

PROMOTION ELIGIBILITY CUTOFF DATE (PECD): 31 JUL 2010
PROMOTION ELIGIBILITY STATUS: ELIGIBLE - PENDING TEST(S)

DUTY INFORMATION

PECD UNIT: 0007 MISSION SUPT SQ **DUTY TITLE:** SUPT, MISSION SUPPORT SQ
DYESS AFB, TX 78150-0000 **DUTY LEVEL:** W/B

AIR FORCE SPECIALTY CODE (AFSC) INFORMATION:
PRIMARY AFSC: 3S091   **CONTROL AFSC:** 3S0X0   **DUTY AFSC:** 3S091   **PROMOTION AFSC:** 3S0X0

CAREER INFORMATION

TOTAL ACTIVE FEDERAL MILITARY SERVICE DATE: 01 MAY 1987   **PROJECTED RETIREMENT SEPARATION DATE:**
HIGH YEAR TENURE DATE: MAY   **RETIREMENT REASON:**

PROFESSIONAL MILITARY EDUCATION

COURSE	DATE COMPLETED
USAF SENIOR NCO ACADEMY	DEC 2002
NCO ACADEMY	JUL 2000
AIRMAN LEADERSHIP SCHOOL	MAY 1994

ACADEMIC EDUCATION

LEVEL	SPECIALTY	DATE
AA ASSOCIATE DEGREE	HUM RES MGT/PERS ADM	MAY 2005

DECORATIONS   EPR

DECORATIONS	TOTAL AWARDED	CLOSING DATE	REASON	RATING	CLOSEOUT DATE
MERIT SVC MED	1	10 AUG 2006	PCS	5B	21 DEC 2006
AF COMM MED	4	01 OCT 2000	PCS	5B	21 DEC 2005
AF ACHIEV MED	1	01 AUG 1989	ACH	5B	21 DEC 2004
NAVY ACH MED	2	19 JUN 1997	ACH	5B	15 NOV 2003
				5B	15 NOV 2002

ASSIGNMENT HISTORY

EFF DATE	DAFSC	DUTY TITLE	COM LV	ORGANIZATION
05 May 2005	3S091	MPF SUPERINTENDENT	WB	0008 MISSION SUPPORT SQ
19 Nov 2004	3S071	NCOIC, ACFT MXS/NUM CEM MATTER	H2	AF WIDE SPT
20 Nov 2002	3S071	NCOIC, GENERAL INTEL ASGNS	H2	AF PERSONNEL CTR
31 Dec 2000	3S071	NCOIC COMMANDER'S SUPPORT STAFF	2E	AF LEGAL SER AG
31 Dec 1999	3S051	NCOIC, AFLSA ORDERLY ROOM	2E	AF LEGAL SER AG
01 Apr 1999	3S071	ASGNS NCO, MEDICAL SPT ASGNS	H2	AF PERSONNEL CTR

Figure 15.5. Calculating Points and Factors for SMSgt and CMSgt Promotions

R U L E	A	B
	If the factor is	then the maximum score is
1	USAFSE	100 points. Base individual score on percentage correct (note 1).
2	TIS	25 points. Credit one-twelfth point for each month of TAFMS, up to 25 years, computed as of the last day of the cycle (note 1).
3	TIG	60 points. Credit one-half point for each month in current grade based on DOR up to 10 years, computed as of the first day of the last month of the cycle (note 1).
4	Decorations/ Awards	25 points. Assign each decoration a point value based on its order of precedence as follows (note 2): Medal of Honor: 15 Air Force, Navy, or Distinguished Service Cross: 11 Defense Distinguished Service Medal, Distinguished Service Medal, Silver Star: 9 Legion of Merit, Defense Superior Service Medal, Distinguished Flying Cross: 7 Airman, Soldier, Navy-Marine Corps, or Coast Guard Bronze Star, Defense/Meritorious Service Medals, Purple Heart: 5 Air, Aerial Achievement, Air Force Commendation, Army Commendation, Navy-Marine Corps Commendation, Joint Services Commendation, or Coast Guard Commendation Medal: 3 Navy - Marine Corps Achievement, Coast Guard Achievement, Air Force Achievement, Army Achievement, or Joint Service Achievement Medal: 1
5	EPRs	135 points. Multiply each EPR rating that closed out within 5 years immediately preceding the PECD (not to exceed 10 reports) by the time-weighted factor for that specific report. The time- weighted factor begins with 50 for the most recent report and decreases in increments of 5 (50-45-40-35-30-25-20-15-10-5) for each report on file. Multiply that product by the EPR conversion factor of 27. Repeat this step for each report. After calculating each report, add the total value of each report for a sum. Divide that sum by the sum of the time-weighted factors added together for the promotion performance factor; for example, 126.60 (notes 1 and 3). **Example:** EPR string (most recent to oldest): 5B-4B-5B-5B-5B-4B 5 x 50 = 250 x 27 = 6,750 4 x 45 = 180 x 27 = 4,860 5 x 40 = 200 x 27 = 5,400 28,485 ÷ 225 = 126.60 5 x 35 = 175 x 27 = 4,725 5 x 30 = 150 x 27 = 4,050 4 x 25 = 100 x 27 = 2,700 225 28,485

Notes:

1. Cut off scores after the second decimal place. Do not use the third decimal place to round up or down.

2. The decoration closeout date must be on or before the PECD. The "prepared" date of the DECOR 6, Recommendation for Decoration Printout, must be before the date AFPC made the selections for promotion. Fully document resubmitted decorations (downgraded, lost, etc.) and verify they were placed into official channels before the selection date.

3. Do not count nonevaluated periods of performance (break in service, report removed through appeal process, etc.) in the computation. For example, compute an EPR string of 4B, XB, 5B, 4B the same as an EPR string of 4B, 5B, 4B.

What are some of the most frequent Authorization Change Requests (ACRs) made to the Unit Manning Document (UMD)?
AFSC changes, position realignments, redistribution of funding from a funded requirement to an unfunded requirement, and grade conversions
Pg 375, 15.56.2

Commercial Services Management (CSM)

A competitive sourcing study compares the total cost of in-house government operation to that of a private sector source. True or false?
True
Pg 376, 15.59.1

What are adversely affected personnel provided if the government is unable to place them in other Federal positions?
The right of first refusal for contractor jobs for which they are qualified
Pg 377, 15.59.2.1

In-sourcing is the conversion of a contracted function to DoD civilian or military performance or any combination of the two. True or false?
True
Pg 377, 15.60.1.1

Civilian Personnel Management and Programs

What can be established when funds are available for short-notice requirements that cannot be met through normal manpower requirements?
Civilian overhire positions
Pg 378, 15.65.3

Civilian overhire positions are normally filled by using temporary appointments or appointments not to exceed one year. True or false?
True
Pg 378, 15.65.3

How long can a term appointment last?
Up to 6 years
Pg 378, 15.65.3

Employees adversely affected by reduction in force (RIF) normally have mandatory selection or priority referral rights. True or false?
True
Pg 379, 15.67.1

Supervisors always have an opportunity to select an employee from a list of applicants even if there are mandatory selections or priority referrals on it. True or false?
False
Pg 379, 15.67.1

What type of recruitment sources can supervisors choose from?
External and internal
Pg 379, 15.67.3

What types of employees are considered as internal candidates?
Current permanent DoD employees
Pg 379, 15.67.3

What options are available for external recruitment?
U.S. citizens, transfers from other non-DOD agencies, reinstatement of former career and/or career-conditional employees, and various veterans' preference applicants
Pg 379, 15.67.3

If a selecting official chooses to interview qualified candidates, the same questions should be asked to each candidate. True or false?
True
Pg 379, 15.67.4

Selection officials should interview each candidate for approximately the same length of time? True or false?
True
Pg 379, 15.67.4

Who is responsible for determining civilian training requirements?
Supervisors
Pg 379, 15.68

The purpose of the annual training-needs survey is to provide an opportunity for supervisors to project training requirements for the upcoming fiscal year. True or false?
True
Pg 380, 15.68.1.1

What are the three primary training sources for civilians?
Agency (Air Force), interagency, and nongovernment
Pg 380, 15.68.2.1

How often do civilian employees receive an appraisal?
Annually
Pg 380, 15.69.1

Performance awards are a management option. True or false?
True
Pg 380, 15.69.1

Supervisors for each civilian employee are responsible for setting the performance elements (duties and tasks). True or false?
True
Pg 380, 15.69.1.1

What performance awards can be used as tools to motivate GS and FWS employees to perform above an acceptable level?
Cash, time-off, and quality step increase
Pg 381, 15.69.1.4

Civilian employees can grieve a management decision regarding performance awards. True or false?
False
Pg 381, 15.69.1.4

What happens if a civilian employee fails one or more of their performance elements?
They are given an opportunity to improve
Pg 381, 15.69.1.5

What can happen if the performance of a civilian employee does not improve to a satisfactory level after given the opportunity to do so?
Removal from the position, placement in another position at the same or lower grade, or separation from civilian employment
Pg 381, 15.69.1.5

The goal of the Air Force regarding civilian discipline is to maintain a constructive work environment. True or false?
True
Pg 381, 15.69.3.2

When can action be taken for a civilian employee based on their inability to perform because of a physical or mental disability?
When the disability cannot be reasonably accommodated
Pg 381, 15.69.3.2

What is a chief concern of the labor organizations representing Air Force employees?
Proper administration of discipline
Pg 381, 15.69.3.4

Is an oral or written admonishment the least severe disciplinary action for a civilian employee?
Oral
Pg 382, 15.69.3.5

What may be an appropriate penalty for a civilian for significant misconduct or repeated infractions?
A written reprimand
Pg 382, 15.69.3.5

A suspension places a civilian employee in a non-pay and non-duty status. True or false?
True
Pg 382, 15.69.3.6

How often are civilian employees paid?
Every two weeks
Pg 382, 15.70.1.1

Civilian employees are compensated differently if they live in a high cost area. True or false?
True
Pg 382, 15.70.1.1

Are pay rates overseas higher or lower compared to those in the United States?
Lower
Pg 382, 15.70.1.1

How often are the General Schedule (GS) pay scales increased?
Normally each year in January
Pg 382, 15.70.1.1

The Federal Wage System (FWS) pay is based on an area-by-area basis. True or false?
True
Pg 382, 15.70.1.2

How do civilian employees progress through the steps within their pay grade?
Through longevity in the pay grade
Pg 382, 15.70.1.3

How many steps does the General Schedule (GS) pay grade have?
10
Pg 382, 15.70.1.3

How many steps are in the Federal Wage System (FWS) pay grades?
5
Pg 382, 15.70.1.3

Who is responsible for establishing daily work hours including designated rest and lunch periods for civilian employees?
The installation and tenant commanders
Pg 382, 15.70.2.2

There are two types of alternate work schedules for civilian employees. True or false?
True
Pg 382, 15.70.2.2

A flexible work schedule allows a civilian employee to start/end the day at different times. True or false?
True
Pg 382, 15.70.2.2

A compressed work schedule allows a civilian employee to work 80 hours in a pay period of fewer than 10 workdays. True or false?
True
Pg 382, 15.70.2.2

How much sick leave does a civilian employee earn each year?
13 days
Pg 383, 15.70.3.1

What is the cap of how much leave a civilian employee can accumulate working in the United States?
30 days
Pg 383, 15.70.3.1

What is the cap for sick leave?
There is no cap
Pg 383, 15.70.3.1

When should a civilian employee report to his/her supervisor that they will be out sick due to an illness or injury?
Within the first two hours of the duty day
Pg 383, 15.70.3.2

What types of absence are not charged to annual leave for a civilian employee?
Jury duty, dismissals for extreme weather conditions, or absences excused by the installation commander
Pg 383, 15.70.3.3

Approximately what percent of Air Force civilian employees are covered by labor agreements between unions and installations or MAJCOMs?
Approximately 70 percent
Pg 383, 15.71.1

Who is responsible for raising employee concerns in the early stages of policy formulation and to resolve employee complaints?
Union officials
Pg 383, 15.71.3

What items are not covered in union contracts?
Pay, benefits, or other matters governed by Federal laws and government-wide regulations
Pg 383, 15.71.4

How are costs paid for formal grievances when an outside arbitrator is called in?
Usually it is equally shared by the union and management
Pg 383, 15.72.1

What issues do the Merit System Protection Board (MSPB) hear?
Appeals of suspensions without pay of more than 14 days, demotions (change to lower grade), and removals
Pg 383, 15.72.3

If management is found guilty of an Unfair Labor Practice (ULP), they can be required to post an apology on employee bulletin boards. True or false?
True
Pg 384, 15.72.4

Chapter 16
Wing Support

Air Force Portal

What provides access to online information, services and combat support applications?
Air Force Portal
Pg 385, 16.2.1

Military Pay, Allowances, and Entitlements

What is linked to increases in private sector wages measured by the employment cost index?
Annual military pay raises
Pg 385, 16.3.1.1

What determines the actual rate of military basic pay?
Grade and length of military service
Pg 385, 16.3.1.2

What are military allowances provided for?
For specific needs such as food or housing
Pg 386, 16.4

Most military allowances are not taxable. True or false?
True
Pg 386, 16.4

Which is a non-taxed allowance to offset the cost of meals?
BAS
Pg 386, 16.4.1

Which is the allowance based on housing costs in local markets?
BAH
Pg 386, 16.4.2.1

When is BAH payable?
When government quarters are not provided
Pg 386, 16.4.2.1

At what rate is the overseas housing allowance (OHA) paid?
Actual rental costs
Pg 386, 16.4.2.2

Which is the allowance to help maintain, repair and replace uniforms?
CRA
Pg 387, 16.4.3

Which acronym is the allowance for compensation due to enforced family separation
FSA
Pg 387, 16.4.4

What are the two general categories of payroll deductions?
Voluntary and involuntary
Pg 387, 16.6

Is the Armed Forces Retirement Home (AFRH) payroll deduction voluntary or involuntary?
Involuntary
Pg 388, 16.6

What is the maximum deduction allowed for the AFRH?
$1.00 a month
Pg 388, 16.6.1.5

What is the limit for the number of voluntary deduction allotments a member may have come out of their pay?
Six
Pg 388, 16.6.2.1

How far in advance should a pay allotment be requested?
30 days before the desired month it is to take effect
Pg 388, 16.6.2.2

What is the maximum amount of Service members' Group Life Insurance (SGLI)?
400,000
Pg 388, 16.6.2.3

A member pays for spousal coverage under Service members' Group Life Insurance (SGLI). True or false?
True
Pg 388, 16.6.2.3

A member pays for SGLI coverage for a child. True or false?
False, it is provided at no cost
Pg 382, 16.6.2.3

Military service members have a choice of how often they are paid. True or false?
True, they can be paid either once or twice a month
Pg 388, 16.7.1

How much of a PCS advance can be given?
Up to 3 months of basic pay
Pg 389, 16.7.3

What office does all official transportation requirements have to be made through?
The Commercial Travel Office (CTO)
Pg 389, 16.8.1.3

When the AF restricts travel of dependents overseas, dependents can move CONUS at government expense. True or false?
True
Pg 389, 16.8.2

What can defray living expenses while in temporary lodging?
Temporary Lodging Expenses (TLE)
Pg 390, 16.8.4

The government pays for household items to be shipped when a member has a PCS move. True or false?
True
Pg 390, 16.8.5

What can be shipped separately from the bulk of HHG, not to exceed 1,000 pounds net?
Unaccompanied baggage
Pg 390, 16.8.6

How are per diem rates determined?
By location
Pg 390, 16.9.1

Miscellaneous reimbursable expenses can be used for tips, passports, etc. True or false?
True
Pg 390, 16.9.3

Who is responsible for preparing the travel voucher to claim reimbursement for TDY?
The traveler
Pg 391, 16.9.4.1

The traveler is responsible for errors if someone else completes the travel voucher. True or false?
True, they are still responsible for the truth and accuracy of the information
Pg 391, 16.9.4.1

Travel claims are settled by mandated electronic funds transfer. True or false?
True
Pg 391, 16.9.4.2

If you are TDY for 45 days or more, how often do you need to file an interim voucher?
Every 30 days
Pg 391, 16.9.4.2

Who is responsible for program execution and management of their component's DoD travel card program?
Agency Program Coordinators (APC)
Pg 391, 16.10.2

How does an individual receive cash advances on the Government Travel Card?
From an ATM
Pg 391, 16.10.3.1

How long prior to travel can the ATM advance be obtained?
3 working days
Pg 391, 16.10.3.2

ATM fees and foreign currency conversion fees are reimbursable. True or false?
True
Pg 391, 16.10.3.2

Is split disbursement mandatory or optional when you go TDY and use a government charge card?
Mandatory
Pg 392, 16.10.5

The card contractor can initiate pay garnishment proceedings through the judicial system against cardholder accounts that are over how many days of delinquency?
126 days
Pg 392, 16.10.7.1

Are TSP contributions taken out before or after taxes?
Before
Pg 393, 16.11.1

Is there a limit to how much can be contributed to the Thrift Savings Plan (TSP)?
$17,000 in 2012
Pg 393, 16.11.2

Leave Management

Members can be paid for unused leave. True or false?
True
Pg 393, 16.13.2

What is the maximum unused leave a member can be paid for during their military career?
60 days
Pg 393, 16.13.2

How long can Special Leave Accrual (SLA) be kept if earned in combat zones?
4 fiscal years
Pg 393, 16.14

A member is charged leave if hospitalized or on quarters status. True or false?
False
Pg 394, 16.15.2

A member can be recalled from leave by the unit Commander. True or false?
True
Pg 394, 16.17

When granting advance leave, there should be a reasonable expectation the member will accrue more leave. True or false?
True
Pg 395, 16.18.2

What leave enables members to resolve emergencies or urgent situations?
Advanced leave
Pg 395, 16.18.2

What leave can be used to meet the medical needs for recuperation?
Convalescent leave
Pg 395, 16.18.3

What leave is granted for family emergencies for immediate family?
Emergency leave
Pg 395, 16.18.4

The Unit Commander can delegate leave approval. True or false?
True, but no lower than the First Sergeant for enlisted personnel
Pg 395, 16.18.4

Is there a limit to the amount of emergency leave that can be approved?
30 days with a possible 30 day extension
Pg 395, 16.18.4

If emergency leave is required for more than 60 days, what should the Unit Commander advise a member to do?
Apply for a humanitarian or exceptional family member reassignment or a hardship discharge
Pg 395, 16.18.4

What leave is taken in conjunction with retirement or separation?
Terminal leave
Pg 395, 16.18.6

When a member cannot request advanced leave, what can they use?
Excess leave
Pg 396, 16.18.7

You can use a DoD-owned or -controlled aircraft plus travel time to travel for Environmental and Morale leave. True or false?
True
Pg 396, 16.18.8

A regular pass includes non-duty days Saturday, Sunday, and a holiday. True or false?
True
Pg 396, 16.19.1

What type of pass can a Unit Commander award 3 or 4 days for special occasions or circumstances?
A special pass
Pg 396, 16.19.2

What is the new category of administrative absence to recognize members who mobilize or deploy?
Post-Deployment/Mobilization Respite Absence (PDMRA)
Pg 397, 16.21.2

What must supervisors ensure members provide prior to approving leave?
A valid address and emergency telephone number where they can be reached
Pg 397, 16.22.2

What is the Air Force automated system used to request and process leave instead of using a hard copy?
LeaveWeb
Pg 398, 16.22.4

Equal Opportunity (EO)

What is the primary objective of the Equal Opportunity (EO) program?
To eradicate unlawful discrimination
Pg 398, 16.24.1

Is unlawful discrimination normally written or verbal?
It can be either or both
Pg 398, 16.25.1

Behavior is still considered unlawful discrimination even if it occurs off base. True or false?
True
Pg 398, 16.25.1

Commanders can require personnel to use English when it is necessary for the performance of their duties. True or false?
True
Pg 383, 16.25.4

Sexual harassment can be verbal. True or false?
True
Pg 399, 16.26.1

The Military Equal Opportunity (MEO) complaint process is strictly for military personnel. True or false?
False
Pg 399, 16.27.1

Can a Commander, supervisor, or a co-worker file a military equal opportunity (MEO) complaint on behalf of another individual? True or false?
False, they will be referred to their respective chain of command
Pg 399, 16.27.1

A preponderance of evidence is to be gathered before the MEO complaint clarification process. True or false?
False
Pg 399, 16.27.3.1.1

How many days can the military equal opportunity (MEO) complaint clarification process take?
It must be complete within 20 duty days
Pg 400, 16.27.3.1.3

How many duty days are allowed for the military equal opportunity (MEO) complaint clarification process for sexual harassment complaints?
It must be complete within 14 duty days
Pg 400, 16.27.3.1.4

How many calendar days after an the alleged offense does a military formal complaint have to be filed?
Within 60 calendar days
Pg 400, 16.27.3.2

What age does someone have to be to file an EEO complaint based on age?
40 or older
Pg 400, 16.28

How long does the civilian equal opportunity office have to complete the informal complaint process?
30 calendar days
Pg 400, 16.28.1.2

Can a civilian formal complaint be filed at any installation or only where the alleged discrimination occurred?
Only at the installation where it occurred
Pg 400, 16.28.2.1

Legal Services

If a member believes they have been wronged by their commanding officer, what article can they request a redress under?
138
Pg 401, 16.33

If a member receives a Commander's denial of redress, how long does the member have to submit the complaint?
90 days
Pg 402, 16.33.3

Ground Safety

What is an unplanned event or series of events resulting in death, injury, occupational illness, or damage, to or loss of, equipment or property?
An Air Force mishap
Pg 402, 16.34.2

Who is responsible for ensuring job safety training is provided?
The Commander
Pg 403, 16.34.3.2

Each individual is responsible for complying with safety standards. True or false?
True
Pg 403, 16.34.3.4

Which safety root cause can stem from failure to correct known problems?
Supervisory Influence
Pg 404, 16.35.2.1.2

If a worker is required to work outside without proper clothing, which safety root cause would this be considered as?
Preconditions for unsafe acts
Pg 404, 16.35.2.1.3

Which safety root cause is when an individual actively violates guidance?
Unsafe Acts
Pg 404, 16.35.2.1.4

A member can lose benefits if injured due to his own misconduct while not on duty. True or false?
True
Pg 405, 16.36.1

Who is in the best position to identify hazards?
Supervisors
Pg 405, 16.37.1

Job safety analysis will have to be used to evaluate each work task that is not governed by a technical order or other guidance. True or false?
True
Pg 405, 16.37.3

What causes the highest number of Air Force injury-related deaths each year?
Traffic mishaps
Pg 406, 16.39.1

What has become an issue in recent years in traffic safety?
Using a navigation device
Pg 406, 16.39.2

Risk Management (RM)

What do all Air Force missions and daily routines involve?
Risk
Pg 407, 16.40.1.1

What is the level of risk management that is used when there is little or no time to conduct formal RM?
Real-Time
Pg 408, 16.40.2.2

Who normally has the greatest insight, past experiences and are invaluable in identifying hazards?
Subject Matter Experts (SMEs)
Pg 408, 16.40.3.1

Which risk management process involves the application of quantitative and/or qualitative measures?
Assess hazards
Pg 409, 16.40.3.2

Which risk management process involves the development and selection of the specific strategies to reduce hazards?
Make risk decisions
Pg 409, 16.40.3.3

Which RM step occurs when a planned activity is already underway or has a low risk?
Assess the situation
Pg 411, 16.40.4.1

Which RM step is tied to making risk control decisions?
Balance control
Pg 411, 16.40.4.2

Sexual Assault

Who implements and manages the sexual assault prevention programs?
The Sexual Assault Response Coordinator (SARC)
Pg 413, 16.42

Who serves as the single point of contact for a sexual assault victim from beginning to end?
The Sexual Assault Response Coordinator (SARC)
Pg 413, 16.42.1

How long does a victim advocate provide services?
Until the victim states support is no longer needed
Pg 413, 16.43

When does the SARC assign a victim advocate to the victim?
Upon notification
Pg 413, 16.44

What is the most underreported violent crime in the military and American society?
Sexual assault
Pg 413, 16.45.1

A sexual assault restricted report gives the victim time to make an informed decision. True or false?
True
Pg 413, 16.45.4

Who is able to make a restricted report concerning sexual assault?
Only military personnel
Pg 414, 16.46

How long after a sexual assault restricted report has been made is it reported to the wing vice commander?
Within 24 hours
Pg 414, 16.48.1

What do deploying members receive before departing for deployment?
Sexual assault training
Pg 415, 16.52.1

Figure 16.4. Risk Assessment Matrix.

Risk Assessment Matrix				PROBABILITY				
				Frequency of Occurrence Over Time				
				A Frequent	B Likely	C Occasional	D Seldom	E Unlikely
S E V E R I T Y	E F F E C T O F H A Z A R D	**Catastrophic** Loss of Mission Capability, Unit Readiness or asset; death.	I	1	1	2	2	3
		Critical Significantly degraded mission capability or unit readiness; severe injury or damage.	II	1	2	2	3	4
		Moderate Degraded mission capability or readiness; minor injury or damage.	III	2	3	3	4	4
		Negligible Little or no impact to mission capability or unit readiness; minimal injury or damage.	IV	3	4	4	4	4
				Risk Levels				
				1—Extremely High 2—High 3—Medium 4—Low				

Chapter 17
Dress and Appearance

NOTE – this chapter is applicable only to personnel testing for promotion to SSgt or TSgt

Dress and Appearance

Why must all members adhere to standards of neatness, cleanliness, safety, and military image when wearing the uniform?
To provide the appearance of a disciplined Service member
Pg 417, 17.2

When can a member put their hands in the pockets of their uniform?
Members will not stand or walk with hands in pockets of any uniform combination unless to insert or remove items
Pg 417, 17.2

What is the exception for a member in uniform using a personal electronic media device?
Ear pieces are authorized during physical training (PT) when wearing the PT uniform
Pg 417, 17.2

Enlisted members have to pay for required organizational and/or functional items they are directed to wear. True or false?
False
Pg 417, 17.3.1

Wearing the uniform is mandatory when departing from a military airfield or US Government commercial contracted flight. True or false?
False
Pg 417, 17.3.2

Men are authorized to have shaved heads True or false?
True
Pg 418, 17.5.1.1

Women are permitted to wear hair scrunchies. True or false?
False
Pg 418, 17.5.1.2

Women are able to have shaven heads, military high-and-tight, or flat-top haircuts. True or false?
False
Pg 418, 17.5.1.2

Who are restricted from wearing wigs or hairpieces?
Personnel engaged in aircraft flight line or in-flight operations
Pg 418, 17.5.1.3

Under special conditions, beards are authorized for men. True or false?
True
Pg 418, 17.5.2.1

Women can wear makeup in field conditions. True or false?
False
Pg 418, 17.5.3

There is a limit placed on the length of fingernails. True or false?
True, they cannot exceed ¼ inch in length past the tip of the finger
Pg 418, 17.5.4

Fingernail polish is permitted. True or false?
True, but it will be a single color (except bright red, orange, purple, black or other extreme colors)
Pg 418, 17.5.5

Define what excessive is for a tattoo on an exposed body part.
Exceeding ¼ of exposed body part
Pg 418, 17.6.2

If a member fails to remove unauthorized tattoos in a timely manner, they can be subject to involuntary separation. True or false?
True
Pg 419, 17.6.3.1

Which uniform is equivalent to the civilian tuxedo or evening gown?
Mess Dress
Pg 419, 17.8.1

Saluting is required when in a mess dress uniform. True or false?
False
Pg 419, 17.8.1

What is the length of women's mess dress skirt?
Ankle
Pg 420, 17.8.4

Is a tie or inverted-V tie tab mandatory or optional with the mess dress uniform?
Mandatory
Pg 420, 17.8.6

Which gender are cufflinks optional for when wearing the mess dress uniform?
Women
Pg 420, 17.8.7

What is the difference in the US lapel insignia worn by officers and enlisted members?
The enlisted insignia have circles around the US and the officer insignias do not
Pg 420, 17.9.1.1

What side of the service dress uniform is the name tag worn on?
The right side
Pg 420, 17.9.1.2

What is the maximum number of devices that can be worn on each ribbon of the service dress uniform?
Four
Pg 420, 17.9.1.3

What is the maximum number of earned badges that can be worn on the blue service uniform?
Four
Pg 421, 17.9.2.1

The tie (men) and the inverted-V tie tab (women) is optional on the service dress uniform. True or false?
False, they are mandatory
Pg 421, 19.9.2.1

Aeronautical, Space, Cyber, and Chaplain badges are mandatory. True or false?
True
Pg 421, 17.10.4

What type of fit will the long-sleeved shirt/blouse for the women's service uniform have?
A tapered fit
Pg 422, 17.10.5.5

Men are able to wear pre-tied ties with the service uniform. True or false?
True, it is optional
Pg 422, 17.5.6.1

When the flight cap is not worn by a female, where should it be stored?
Tuck the cap under the belt on either side
Pg 422, 17.11

Women are not required to wear hose with their skirt. True or false?
False
Pg 422, 17.12

Women are permitted to wear patterned hose. True or false?
False
Pg 422, 17.12

The ABU can be starched and hot pressed. True or false?
False, it is prohibited
Pg 423, 17.14

What type of socks can be worn with the physical fitness (PT) gear?
They must be white, any length and may have small conservative trademark logos
Pg 424, 17.15

What is the maximum width a bracelet can be?
1/2 inch
Pg 424, 17.16.1

What is the maximum number of rings that can be worn on both hands combined?
Three, they must be worn at the base of the finger
Pg 424, 17.16.1

Thumb rings are authorized. True or false?
False
Pg 424, 17.16.1

Mirrored lenses are not permitted on sunglasses. True or false?
True
Pg 424, 17.16.2

Sunglasses can be worn while in formation. True or false?
False
Pg 424, 17.16.2

How many Personal Digital Assistants (PDAs), pagers, or cellular phones can be worn on the uniform belt?
One
Pg 424, 17.16.3

What are the restrictions on umbrellas?
They must be plain, black, and carried in the left hand
Pg 424, 17.16.3.2

Chapter 18
Fit Force

Overview

What is the goal of the fitness program?
To motivate members to participate in year-round physical conditioning that emphasizes total fitness
Pg 425, 18.1

How does a Commander know the overall fitness of their personnel?
From the annual fitness assessment
Pg 425, 18.1

Physical Fitness and Fitness Components

In addition to the five major components of fitness, what other two items are essential?
Warm up and cool down
Pg 425, 18.3

What component of fitness is the maximum force generated by a specific muscle or muscle group?
Muscular strength
Pg 425, 18.3.3

What component of fitness is the ability of a muscle group to execute repeated contractions over a period of time to cause muscular fatigue?
Muscular endurance
Pg 425, 18.3.4

What component of fitness is the ability to move a joint freely, without pain, through the full range of motion?
Flexibility
Pg 425, 18.3.5

What is the best way to condition the cardio respiratory system?
Three adequately intense workouts per week on alternate days
Pg 425, 18.4.1

What danger should leaders be aware of during cardiovascular training?
Overtraining
Pg 425, 18.4.1

What does a low intensity exercise require to achieve cardiovascular improvements?
A longer duration of the exercise
Pg 426, 18.4.3

What type of exercise will improve cardiovascular fitness?
Only sustained activities that require a large volume of exercise and use of large muscle groups
Pg 426, 18.4.4

What can exercising sporadically do to an individual?
It can do more harm than good
Pg 426, 18.5.2

Table 18.1. Scoring Chart.

ITEM	A	B	C
	Fitness Levels	**Scores**	**Currency of Fitness Testing**
1	Excellent (all 4 components)	Composite score ≥ 90, all component minimums met	Within 12 months
2	Excellent (3 or less components)	Composite score ≥ 90, all component minimums met	Within 6 months
3	Satisfactory	Composite score ≥ 75-89.99, all component minimums met	Within 6 months
4	Unsatisfactory	Composite score < 75, and/or one component minimum not met	Within 90 days

How long of a timeframe should be allowed between workouts for the same muscle groups?
At least 48 hours
Pg 426, 18.5.3

It is best to follow a pushing exercise with another pushing exercise that results in movement at the same joints. True or false?
False
Pg 427, 18.5.4

What is a major challenge for all fitness training programs?
Maintaining enthusiasm and interest
Pg 427, 18.5.5

What is the root to many activity-related injuries?
Lack of flexibility
Pg 427, 18.6.1

What will help prevent injury and reduce muscle soreness?
Conducting a good warm-up and a cool down
Pg 427, 18.6.1

What are the two largest factors that contribute to maintaining a positive body composition?
Exercise and diet
Pg 427, 18.7

What is a realistic weight loss goal?
Losing 1-2 pounds a week
Pg 427, 18.7.1

What daily caloric intake should a male Airman (not under medical supervision) consume when dieting?
At least 1,500 calories
Pg 428, 18.7.2

What daily caloric intake should a female Airman (not under medical supervision) consume when dieting?
At least 1,200 calories
Pg 428, 18.7.2

What is the best way fat can be burned during exercise?
If oxygen is used
Pg 428, 18.7.4

How many calories are in 1 pound of fat?
3500
Pg 428, 18.7.5

What increases the flow of blood to the muscles and tendons helping to reduce the risk of injury?
Performing a warm up
Pg 428, 18.8.1

What can happen if you suddenly stop after vigorously exercising?
It can cause blood to pool in the muscles reducing blood flow to the heart and brain
Pg 428, 18.8.2.1

What is the composite fitness score used by the Air Force based on?
Aerobic fitness, muscular strength, and body composition
Pg 429, 18.10.1

What is the minimum acceptable composite score for health, fitness, and readiness levels?
75
Pg 429, 18.10.1

What is the numeric composite score scale?
0 to 100
Pg 429, 18.10.2

How long are pregnant service members required to engage in physical activities?
Throughout the pregnancy and postpartum period according to medical provider recommendations
Pg 430, 18.11.4

When are pregnant members exempt from fitness testing?
During pregnancy and for 180 days after the delivery date
Pg 430, 18.11.4

During what timeframe do the components (body composition, aerobic and muscular fitness assessments) have to be completed?
Within a 3-hour window on the same day
Pg 430, 18.12

How long should the rest period be between fitness assessment components?
A minimum of 3 minutes
Pg 430, 18.12

If medically exempted from the 1.5 mile walk in the aerobic assessment, how far does a member have to walk?
1 mile
Pg 431, 18.12.2

How is upper body muscular strength and endurance measured in the physical fitness assessment?
With a 1 minute timed pushup test
Pg 431, 18.12.3

What program is mandatory for all members with an unsatisfactory fitness score?
The Balanced Eating, Work Out Effectively, Living Longer (BE WELL) Program
Pg 431, 18.13.1

Who oversees the administration of the fitness program for the unit?
The Unit Fitness Program Manager (UFPM)
Pg 431, 18.14.2

Nutrition

What are essential calorie-containing nutrients that are needed in relatively large amounts?
Macronutrients
Pg 432, 18.15.1

Nutrients

What are known as the energy powerhouse?
Carbohydrates
Pg 432, 18.15.1.1

What portion of your calorie intake need to be carbohydrates?
One half to two thirds
Pg 432, 18.15.1.1

The human body stores proteins. True or false?
False
Pg 432, 18.15.1.2

Where can the healthier mono- and poly-unsaturated fats be found?
Fatty fish such as tuna and salmon and plant foods such as olive oil, canola oil, peanut oil, avocados, and most nuts.
Pg 432, 18.15.1.3

Which macronutrient is essential for life?
Water
Pg 432, 18.15.1.4

What is the key to a long healthy life?
A healthy weight
Pg 433, 18.15.3

What is considered a healthy and safe weight loss goal?
1-2 pounds per week
Pg 433, 18.15.3

What provides enough fluid to maintain hydration and enough carbohydrates to maintain proper blood sugar during activities?
Pre exercise snack or meal
Pg 434, 18.5.5

Substance Abuse

What will individuals experiencing problems relating to substance abuse (SA) receive?
Counseling and treatment
Pg 434, 18.16.1

The Air Force provides comprehensive clinical assistance to eligible beneficiaries seeking help for an alcohol problem. True or false?
True
Pg 435, 18.18

How long will your license be suspended if you drive or are in physical control of a motor vehicle with a 0.10 percent or greater alcohol level?
1 year
Pg 435, 18.18.2

If a state uses a lower blood alcohol percentage than the Air Force, which standard will be used?
The lower standard
Pg 435, 18.18.2

Does the Air Force provide punitive or non-punitive assistance to members who seek help for an alcohol problem?
Non-punitive
Pg 435, 18.19.1.1

Why is a Commander directed drug testing used as a last resort?
Results cannot be used in actions under the UCMJ
Pg 436, 18.19.2.3

What is the most common method of drug testing?
Inspection testing
Pg 436, 18.19.2.3.1

Will Commanders grant any protection to a member who voluntarily discloses evidence of personal drug use or possession?
They will grant limited protection
Pg 437, 18.19.2.5.1

The Commander can use voluntarily disclosed information against a member in an action under the UCMJ or when weighing characterization of service in a separation. True or false?
False
Pg 437, 18.19.2.5.1

What must Commanders provide to members seeking help for alcohol problems?
Sufficient incentive without fear of negative consequences
Pg 437, 18.19.2.5.2

What is the critical first step to help someone with substance abuse?
Identifying individuals who need treatment
Pg 437, 18.20

How soon after notification does the alcohol and drug abuse prevention and treatment (ADAPT) staff members conduct the substance abuse (SA) assessment?
Within 7 calendar days
Pg 437, 18.21

What two types of services do substance abuse treatments get divided into?
Non-clinical and clinical
Pg 438, 18.22

Who will be referred for SA treatment if they are involved in alcohol related misconduct?
All active duty members
Pg 438, 18.22.1

What should be anticipated during the aftercare treatment of an alcoholic?
Relapses
Pg 438, 18.22.2.3

What type of consequence shall be considered by their commander for an individual who has failed the alcohol and drug abuse prevention and treatment (ADAPT) program?
Administrative separation
Pg 439, 18.24.2.1

A Line of Duty (LOD) determination can impact disability retirement and severance pay, forfeiture of pay, period of enlistment, as well as veteran benefits. True or false?
True
Pg 439, 18.26

Tobacco Use

What is the Air Force's goal concerning tobacco?
To have a tobacco-free force
Pg 439, 18.27

Tobacco decreases night vision, fine motor coordination, increases the risk of injuries and impairs or slows healing when injuries occur. True or false?
True
Pg 439, 18.28.1

What is the addictive chemical substance found in tobacco products?
Nicotine
Pg 439, 18.28.3

What does tobacco usage cost the Air Force each year?
Over $1.6 billion
Pg 440, 18.29

Medical Care

What is the DoD health care program for active duty and retired members of the uniformed services, their families, survivors, and certain former spouses?
TRICARE
Pg 441, 18.32.1

TRICARE is available in most areas. True or false?
True, TRICARE is available worldwide
Pg 441, 18.32.1

Figure 18.3. Signs and Symptoms of Substance Abuse.

Arrests or legal problems	Failed attempts to stop or cut down	Memory loss
Concerns expressed by family, friends	Financial irresponsibility	Morning drinking and hangovers
Denial or dishonesty about use	Frequent errors in judgment	Suicidal thoughts or behaviors
Deteriorating duty performance	Health problems related to drinking	Unexplained or frequent absences
Dramatic mood swings	Increased use of alcohol	Violent behavior

What are the three choices of TRICARE?
Prime, Standard, and Extra
Pg 441, 18.35

What is the cost of coverage under TRICARE for active duty members?
There is no cost
Pg 441, 18.35.1

What type of options are TRICARE Standard and TRICARE Extra?
Fee-for-service
Pg 442, 18.35.2

Suicide Prevention

What is the third leading cause of death amongst Regular Air Force personnel?
Suicide
Pg 443, 18.38

Two personal perceptions that place someone at risk for suicide are (1) a lack of belongingness with or connectedness to others, and (2) a sense they are a burden to those around them. True or false?
True
Pg 443, 18.40

What percent of Air Force suicide victims (CY 2009 - 2011) were receiving treatment for mental health concerns?
More than 50 percent
Pg 444, 18.43

Since CY09 what percent of Air Force suicide victims were involved in legal difficulties of one kind or another at the time of their deaths?
34 percent
Pg 444, 18.44

Since CY09 what percent of Air Force suicide victims were suffering from relationship problems?
54 percent
Pg 445, 18.46

Most suicides are impulsive. True or false?
False
Pg 445, 18.48.1

Many suicide victims communicate their intention to kill themselves. True or false?
True
Pg 445, 18.48.2

Figure 18.4. Active Duty Service Member Costs. (Note)

TRICARE	PRIME	EXTRA	STANDARD
Annual Deductible	None	**SSgt and above:** $150 Individual/$300 Family **SrA and below:** $50 Individual/$100 family	**SSgt and above:** $150 Individual/$300 Family **SrA and below:** $50 Individual/$100 family
Annual Enrollment Fee	None	None	None
Civilian Outpatient Visit	No cost	15 percent of negotiated fee	20 percent of allowed charges for covered service
Civilian Inpatient Admission	No cost	*Greater of $25 or $15.65/day	*Greater of $25 or $15.65/day
Civilian Inpatient Mental Health	No cost	Greater of $20/day or $25/admission	Greater of $20/day or $25/admission
Civilian Inpatient-Skilled Nursing Facility Care	$0 per diem charge per admission	$15.65/day ($25 minimum) Charge per admission	$15.65/day ($25 minimum) Charge per admission
*Fiscal Year 2009 costs			
Note: Rates effective 1 October 2009. Co-pays/deductibles change annually. TRICARE catastrophic cap on out-of-pocket expenses for TRICARE covered services is $1,000 per active duty family per fiscal year (deductibles, cost shares, copayments, etc.).			

Statistics show a definite increase in suicides during the holidays. True or false?
False
Pg 446, 18.48.4

How do many victims act once they make up their minds they are going to commit suicide?
They often become tranquil
Pg 446, 18.49

Most suicide victims want to die. True or false?
False
Pg 446, 18.50

How can suicides be stopped?
By addressing quality of life issues on a daily basis
Pg 446, 18.51.1

Who is in a position to identify changes in behavior or performance that may signal a problem for an individual?
A supervisor (and immediate associates)
Pg 446, 18.51.3

Who is responsible for suicide prevention?
The entire Air Force community
Pg 447, 18.52.1

A Commander is always contacted when an Airman visits a mental health provider. True or false?
False
Pg 447, 18.52.3

What was determined about suicide as a result of the integrated product team (IPT) commissioned by General Thomas S. Moorman in 1996?
It is not a medical problem but a community problem
Pg 447, 18.54.1

What is the acronym developed by the Air Force to facilitate personal engagement in suicide prevention?
ACE - Ask, Care, and Escort
Pg 450, 18.55.1

Is it suggested to send an individual to a chaplain or mental health clinic alone?
No, they may change their mind on the way
Pg 450, 18.55.1.3

How can a member enhance their psychological resilience if they have a moderate or high chance of being exposed to a traumatic event as part of their duties?
Engage in realistic training or strengthen perceived ability to cope
Pg 451, 18.58.6.1 and 18.58.2

What is used to train a member to realistic events such as body handling, survival training, and mock captivity?
Realistic training
Pg 451, 18.58.6.1

Stress Management

According to the endocrinologist Hans Selye, the body's reaction to stress is the same regardless of whether the source is good or bad, positive or negative. True or false?
True
Pg 451, 18.60.1

Figure 18.5. Signs of Distress.

Agitation	Difficulty coping	Increased appetite	Poor work performance
Alcohol misuse	Disciplinary problems	Indecisiveness	Relationship difficulties
Anxiety	Excessive sleeping	Insomnia	Restlessness
Apathy	Feeling "blah"	Irritability	Sadness
Avoiding recreation	Feeling guilty	Loss of interest	Social isolation
Constant fatigue	Feeling overwhelmed	Low energy	Social withdrawal
Decreased appetite	Feeling worthless	Low self-esteem	Suicidal ideation
Decreased libido	Financial problems	Poor concentration	Weight gain
Depression	Hopelessness	Poor personal hygiene	Weight loss

As a supervisor, how can your management approach help reduce your subordinates' stress levels?
You can identify potential stressors and develop strategies to remove or reduce them.
Pg 453, 18.62.2

What are some factors in the work environment you may be able to improve, as a supervisor, to help reduce stress levels for your subordinates?
Temperature, noise, and light levels
Pg 453, 18.62.2

Redeployment Support Process

Who is responsible for establishing and publishing personnel recovery (leave, passes, attribution and retention) policies for returning combat forces?
The MAJCOM
Pg 454, 18.64

Childcare providers receive training on caring for children who are experiencing family separation and reintegration. True or false?
True
Pg 454, 18.68.4

Chapter 19
Security

Information Assurance

Information assurance is the responsibility of the Commander. True or false?
False, it is everyone's responsibility
Pg 457, 19.2.1

The Air Force implements and maintains the information assurance program to secure its information and information technology (IT) assets through the effective employment of what core information assurance disciplines?
Communications security (COMSEC), computer security (COMPUSEC), and emissions security (EMSEC)
Pg 457, 19.2.3

Which information assurance discipline consists of measures and controls that ensure confidentially, integrity and availability of information systems assets?
COMPUSEC
Pg 457, 19.3.1

What is an action, device, procedure, technique, or other measure that reduces the vulnerability of an information system to an acceptable and manageable level?
A countermeasure
Pg 457, 19.3.3

Information Operations (IO) and Information Warfare (IW) activities pose the greatest threats to communications and information systems. True or false?
True
Pg 457, 19.3.4

What two-factor authentication can be used to secure access to systems and networks?
Common Access Card (CAC) and a personal identification number (PIN)
Pg 458, 19.3.4.2.1

What should an individual do when their workstation will be unattended?
Remove the CAC from the reader
Pg 458, 19.3.4.2.2

It is considered safe to use removable media devices as long as you use your Common Access Card (CAC). True or false?
False
Pg 458, 19.3.4.3

Portable Electronic Devices (PEDs) have the capability of recording, storing, transmitting, and/or processing information. True or false?
True
Pg 459, 19.3.4.4

An individual can use their own Portable Electronic Device (PED) to connect to the Air Force network. True or false?
False, the Air Force prohibits it
Pg 459, 19.3.4.4.5

It is permissible to open email attachments from an unknown source. True or false?
False
Pg 460, 19.3.4.7.2

What are the measures and controls taken to deny access by unauthorized persons to information derived from US Government information systems?
Communications Security (COMSEC)
Pg 460, 19.4

What is the objective of Emissions Security (EMSEC)?
To deny access to valuable information by unauthorized users
Pg 461, 19.5

Installation Security

What do OPSEC analysts provide decision makers with?
A means of weighing a risk level
Pg 461, 19.6.3

At what times are OPSEC principles used?
Day-to-day activities
Pg 461, 19.6.4

As original classification authorities (OCA), who has the authority to determine the original classification of an item?
The Secretary of Defense, the secretaries of the military departments, and other officials who are specifically delegated this authority in writing
Pg 462, 19.7.1.1

What guide contains specific items of information to be protected, the applicable classification levels, the reason for classifying, any special-handling caveats, the downgrading and declassification instructions, declassification exemptions, the original authority, and a point of contact?
Security Classification Guide (SCG)
Pg 462, 19.7.1.1.1

What is the primary means of informing holders of classified information about specific protection requirements for the information they have been given?
The classification markings on the document
Pg 462, 19.7.1.3

Are the classification markings on information applied in a specific place?
Classification markings should be conspicuous
Pg 462, 19.7.1.3

When should information be declassified?
As soon as it no longer meets the standards for classification
Pg 463, 19.7.1.5

Who is responsible for taking proper precautions to ensure unauthorized persons do not gain access to classified information?
Everyone granted access with classified information is personally responsible
Pg 463, 19.7.2.1

An integral part of the security check system is to secure all vaults, rooms and containers used to store classified material. True or false?
True
Pg 463, 19.7.2.3

How must all transactions for Top Secret materials be conducted?
Through the Top Secret Control Officer (TSCO)
Pg 463, 19.7.2.4.1

What should an individual do when finding classified material out of the proper control?
Take custody of it and safeguard the material, if possible, and immediately notify the appropriate security authorities
Pg 464, 19.7.2.5

DoD military and civilian personnel are subject to sanctions if they knowingly, willfully, or negligently disclose classified information to unauthorized persons. True or false?
True
Pg 464, 19.7.3

If security clearance eligibility is denied or revoked, individuals are granted due process and may appeal the decision. True or false?
True
Pg 464, 19.8.2

The base boundary can extend beyond the fenced perimeter, property lines, and legal boundaries. True or false?
True
Pg 464, 19.10.5

The Base Security Zone (BSZ) is the area inside the base perimeter from which the base may be vulnerable from standoff threats (mortars, rockets, man portable aerial defense systems, etc.). True or false?
False
Pg 465, 19.10.6

What is the four-part process that defines the operating environment, describes the operating environments effect, evaluates the enemy and determines the enemy course of action (ECOA)?
Intelligence Preparation of the Operational Environment (IPOE)
Pg 467, 19.11.6

What provides Installation Commanders, Integrated Defense Working Groups (IDWG), Defense Force Commanders and defense planners the ability to produce effects-based, Integrated Defense Plans (IDP) by using a standardized model to identify risks and develop risk management strategies?
Integrated Defense Risk Management Process (IDRMP)
Pg 467, 19.12

What does a Criticality Assessment (CA) of assets identify?
What assets are worthy of protection and whose loss or damage would have a negative impact on the mission
Pg 468, 19.12.1.1

Vulnerability is defined as the weaknesses that can be exploited by an adversary because of inadequate security, lax or complacent personnel trends, vulnerable software or hardware, and insufficient security policies or procedures. True or false?
True
Pg 468, 19.12.1.2

What is the most important step in the Integrated Defense Risk Management Process (IDRMP)?
Decision and implementation
Pg 468, 19.12.1.6

What protection level is assigned to those resources for which the loss, theft, destruction, misuse, or compromise would result in great harm to the strategic capability of the United States?
Protection Level 1 (PL1)
Pg 469, 19.13.1

What protection level is assigned to those resources which the loss, theft, destruction, misuse, or compromise would cause significant harm to the war-fighting capability of the United Stated?
Protection Level 2 (PL2)
Pg 469, 19.13.2

What protection level is assigned to those resources for which the loss, theft, destruction, misuse, or compromise would damage United States war-fighting ability?
Protection Level 3 (PL3)
Pg 469, 19.13.3

Antiterrorism (AT) Program

How often are Commanders to conduct field and staff training to exercise Antiterrorism Training (AT) plans?
At least annually
Pg 469, 19.15

The first step in developing an effective Antiterrorism Training program is what?
Identifying the potential terrorism threat to DoD personnel and assets.
Pg 470, 19.16.2

The intent of the Random Antiterrorism Measures (RAM) Program is to provide random, multiple security measures that consistently change the look of an installation's anti-terrorism program. True or false?
True
Pg 470, 19.17

What is an individual's most predictable habit?
The route he/she travels from home to their place of duty or to commonly frequented local facilities
Pg 471, 19.23

What is the act of obtaining, delivering, transmitting, communicating, or receiving information about the national defense with intent or reason to believe the information may be used to the injury of the United States or to the advantage of any foreign nation?
Espionage
Pg 471, 19.25.1.1

The process of debriefing normally involves an individual who is in custody. True or false?
False
Pg 472, 19.25.2.3

AFI 71-101, Volume 4, "Counterintelligence" requires individuals who have reportable contacts, or if they acquire reportable information, to immediately report the contact/information to the AFOSI. What is defined as immediately?
Within 30 days of the contact
Pg 472, 19.25.3

Abbreviations & Acronyms

A1C—Airman first class
A&FRC—Airman and Family Readiness Center
A&P—airframe and powerplant
AADC—area air defense coordinator
AAS—associate of applied science
AB—Airman basic; air base
ABU—Airman battle uniform
AC—abdominal circumference
ACC—Air Combat Command
ACM—Afghanistan Campaign Medal
ACN—authorization change notice
ACO—Allied Command Operations
ACR—authorization change request
AD—active duty
ADAPT—alcohol and drug abuse prevention and treatment
ADAPTPM—ADAPT program manager
ADC—Area Defense Counsel; Air Defense Command
ADCON—administrative control
ADFM—active duty family member
AEA--actual expense allowance
AECP—Airman Education and Commissioning Program
AED—automated external defibrillator
AEF—American expeditionary force; air and space expeditionary force
AEFI—air and space expeditionary force indicator
AEG—air and space expeditionary group
AEP—Affirmative Employment Program
AES—air and space expeditionary squadron
AETC—Air Education and Training Command
AETF—air and space expeditionary task force
AEW—aerospace expeditionary wing
AF—Air Force
AFB—Air Force Base
AFBCMR—Air Force Board for Correction of Military Records

AFCCA—Air Force Court of Criminal Appeals
AFCFM—Air Force career field manager
AFCYBER—Air Force Cyber Command
AFDD—Air Force Doctrine Document
AFDRB—Air Force Discharge Review Board
AFELA—Air Force educational leave of absence
AFEM—Armed Forces Expeditionary Medal
AFEMS—Air Force Equipment Management System
AFFOR—Air Force forces
AFHRA—Air Force Historical Research Agency
AFIA—Air Force Inspection Agency
AFIADL—Air Force Institute of Advanced Distributed Learning
AFIMS—Air Force Incident Management System
AFIT—Air Force Institute of Technology
AFJQS—Air Force job qualification standard
AFLSA—Air Force Longevity Service Award
AFMA—Air Force Manpower Agency
AFMC—Air Force Materiel Command
AFOEA—Air Force Organizational Excellence Award
AFOMS—Air Force Occupational Measurement Squadron
AFOSI—Air Force Office of Special Investigations
AFOUA—Air Force Outstanding Unit Award
AFPC—Air Force Personnel Center
AFR—Air Force Reserve
AFRC—Air Force Reserve Command
AFRH—Armed Forces Retirement Home
AFROTC—Air Force Reserve Officer Training Corps
AFS—Air Force specialty
AFSC—Air Force specialty code
AFSM—Armed Forces Service Medal; active duty service members
AFSNCOA—Air Force Senior Noncommissioned Officer Academy
AFSO—Air Force Smart Operations
AFSOC—Air Force Special Operations Command

AFSOF—Air Force special operations forces

AFSPC—Air Force Space Command

AFSP—Air Force Strategic Plan

AFSPP—Air Force Suicide Prevention Program

AFVEC—Air Force Virtual Education Center

AI—air interdiction

ALS—Airman Leadership School

AMA—American Medical Association

AMC—Air Mobility Command

Amn—Airman

ANG—Air National Guard

AO—areas of operation

AOC—air operations center

AOR—area of responsibility

APC—agency program coordinator

APR—airman performance report

ARC—air reserve component; American (National) Red Cross

ARMS—Automated Records Management System

ASBC—Air and Space Basic Course

ASCP—Airman Scholarship and Commissioning Program

AT—antiterrorism

ATM—automated teller machine

ATO—antiterrorism officer

AU-ABC—Air University Associate-to-Baccalaureate Cooperative Program

AWACS—Airborne Warning and Control System

AWOL—absent without official leave

BAH—basic allowance for housing

BAH-DIFF—basic allowance for housing differential

BAQ—basic allowance for quarters

BAS—basic allowance for subsistence

BBP—bullet background paper

BCEE—Thomas N. Barnes Center for Enlisted Education

BDU—battle dress uniform

BES—budget estimate submission

BMI—body mass index

BMT—basic military training

BOP—base of preference

BSZ—base security zone

Btu—British thermal units

BTZ—below the zone

C2—command and control

C3—command, control, and communications

CA/CRL—custodian authorization/custody receipt listing

CAC—common access card

CAFSC—control Air Force specialty code

CAIB—community action information board

CAN—authorization change notice

CAREERS—Career Airman Reenlistment Reservation System

CAS—close air support

CAT—combat application tourniquet

CBRN—chemical, biological, radiological, and nuclear

CBRNE—chemical, biological, radiological, nuclear and high-yield explosive

CCAF—Community College of the Air Force

CCCA—common core compliance area

CCDR—combatant commander

CCM—command chief master sergeant

CCRC—common core readiness criteria

CDC—career development course

CD—compact disk

CE—course examination

CEM—chief enlisted manager

CEMP—comprehensive emergency management plan

CEPME—College for Enlisted Professional Military Education

CERT—credentialing and education research tool

CFACC—combined force air and space component commander

CFC—Combined Forces Command Korea

CFETP—career field education and training plan

CGO—company grade officer

CI—compliance inspection; counterintelligence

CIA—Central Intelligence Agency

CINC—commander in chief

CJCS—Chairman, Joint Chiefs of Staff

CJR—career job reservation

CLEP—College-Level Examination Program

CMC—Commandant of the Marine Corps

CMS—Case Management System

CMSAF—Chief Master Sergeant of the Air Force

CMSgt—chief master sergeant

CNAF—Air Force component numbered air forces

CNO—Chief of Naval Operations

CO—commanding officer

COCOM—combatant command

COLA—cost-of-living adjustment
COMAFFOR—Commander, Air Force Forces
comp—compensatory
COMPUSEC—computer security
COMSEC—communications security
CONUS—continental United States
CPD—core personnel document
CPF—civilian personnel flight
CPG—career progression group
CPI—consumer price index
Cpl—corporal
CPR—cardiopulmonary resuscitation
CRA—clothing replacement allowance
CRO—change of reporting official
CS—competitive sourcing; chief of staff
CSA—Chief of Staff, US Army
CSAF—Chief of Staff, United States Air Force
CSAR—combat search and rescue
CSB—career status bonus
CSS—commander support staff
CTO—commercial travel office
CUI—controlled unclassified information
CV—vice commander
DAF—Department of the Air Force
DAFSC—duty Air Force specialty code
DANTES—Defense Activity for Nontraditional Education Support
DCA—defensive counterair
DCAPES—deliberate and crisis action planning and execution segments
DCS—defensive counterspace, deputy chief of staff
DE—developmental education
DEERS—Defense Enrollment Eligibility Reporting System
DEROS—date eligible for return from overseas
DFAS—Defense Finance and Accounting Service
DFC—defense force commander
DHS—Department of Homeland Security
DIEMS—date initially entered military service
DL—distance learning
DLA—Defense Logistics Agency
DMS—defense message system
DOB—date of birth
DoD—Department of Defense
DOR—date of rank

DOS—date of separation
DR—demand reduction
DRF—disaster response force
DRU—direct reporting unit
DSM—Diagnostic Statistical Manual
DSST—DANTES subject standardized test
DTRA—Defense Threat Reduction Agency
DV—distinguished visitor
DVR—data verification record
DWI—driving while intoxicated
E&T—education and training
EAS—Electronic Access Sytem
ECAMP—Environmental Compliance Assessment and Management Program
ECI—employment cost index
ECS—expeditionary combat support
EDS—employee development specialist
EEO—equal employment opportunity
EEOC—Equal Employment Opportunity Commission
EES—Enlisted Evaluation System
EFACC—Emergency Family Assistance Control Center
EFMP—Exceptional Family Member Program
EFT—electronic funds transfer
EM—Emergency Management
e-mail—electronic mail
EML—environmental and morale leave
EMSEC—emissions security
EO—equal opportunity; executive order
EOC—emergency operations center; end of cycle
EOT—equal opportunity and treatment
EPC—environmental protection committee; Educational Programs Cadre
EPME—Enlisted Professional Military Education
EPR—enlisted performance report
EPTS—existed prior to service
EQUAL—Enlisted Quarterly Assignments Listing
ESF—emergency support functions
ESS—electronic staff summary
ETCA—education and training course announcement
ETS—expiration of term of service
EWO—electronic warfare officer
FA—fitness assessment
FAC—functional account code
FBI—Federal Bureau of Investigations

FICA—Federal Insurance Contributions Act
FITW—Federal income tax withholding
FOA—field operating agency
FOCUS—Focused, Organized, Clear, Understanding, Supported
FOE—follow-on element
FOIA—Freedom of Information Act
FOUO—for official use only
FPCON—force protection condition
FSA—family separation allowance
FSA-R—FSA reassignment
FSA-S—FSA serving on a ship
FSA-T—FSA temporary
FSH—family separation, basic allowance for housing
FSO—financial services office
FSSA—family subsistence supplemental allowance
FSSP—First Sergeant Selection Program
FTA—first-term Airmen
FWA—fraud, waste, and abuse
FWS—Federal Wage System
FY—fiscal year
FYDP—Future Years Defense Program
GCC—geographic combatant commander
GCE—ground crew ensemble
GCM—general court-martial
GCMA—general court-martial authority
GCSS-AF—Global Combat Support System
GEOLOC—geographical location
GFM—global force management
GHQ—general headquarters
GPS—global positioning system
GS—General Schedule
GUC—Gallant Unit Citation
GWOTEM—Global War on Terrorism Expeditionary Medal
GWOTSM—Global War on Terrorism Service Medal
HAF—Headquarters Air Force
HAWC—Health and Wellness Center
HAZMAT—hazardous material
HGS—high grade service
HHG—household goods
HQ—headquarters
HR—hazard report
HS—homeland security
HSC—Homeland Security Council

HSI—health services inspection
HSM—Humanitarian Service Medal
HUMINT—human intelligence
HYT—high year of tenure
IAO—information assurance officer
IC—incident commander
ICBM—intercontinental ballistic missile
ICC—installation control center
ICM—Iraq Campaign Medal
ID—Integrated Defense
IDS—Integrated Delivery System
IFAK—individual first aid kit
IG—Inspector General
IGO—intergovernmental organization
IO—information operations
IPE—individual protection equipment
IPT—integrated product team
IRA—individual retirement account
IRS—internal revenue service
ISD—instructional systems development
ISR—intelligence, surveillance, reconnaissance
IT—information technology
IW—information warfare
JCS—Joint Chiefs of Staff
JFACC—joint forces air component commander
JFC—joint force commander
JFTR—Joint Federal Travel Regulation
JIACG—joint interagency coordination group
JMUA—Joint Meritorious Unit Medal
JOPES—Joint Operations Planning and Execution System
JPAS—Joint Personnel Adjudication System
JTF—joint task force
KDSM—Korea Defense Service Medal
kg—kilogram
KSA—knowledge, skills, abilities
KX—knowledge exchange
LES—leave and earnings statement
LOA—letter of admonishment
LOAC—law of armed conflict
LOC—letter of counseling
LOD—line of duty
LOE—letter of evaluation
LOR—letter of reprimand

LRO—labor relations officer
LRS—logistics readiness squadron
Lt Col—lieutenant colonel
MAAG—Military Assistance Advisory Group
MAC—Military Airlift Command
MAJCOM—major command
MATS—Military Air Transport Service
MCM—Manual for Courts-Martial
MCP—mobile command post
MEO—most efficient organization; military equal opportunity
MEOC—mobile emergency operations center
MFM—MAJCOM functional manager
MGIB—Montgomery GI Bill
MHR—maximum heart rate
MHS—Military Health System
MIA—missing in action
MIHA—move-in housing allowance
MilPDS—Military Personnel Data System
MKTS—Military Knowledge and Testing System
MNF—multinational force
MOF—manpower and organization flight
MOPP—mission-oriented protective posture
MPES—Manpower and Execution System
MPS—military personnel section
MR—memorandum for record
MRE—military rule of evidence
MSgt—master sergeant
MSO—military service obligation
MSPB—Merit System Protection Board
MTF—military treatment facility; medical treatment facility
MTP—master training plan
MUA—Meritorious Unit Award
MyEDP—my enlisted development plan
NAF—nonappropriated fund; numbered Air Force
NATO—North Atlantic Treaty Organization
NBC—nuclear, biological, and chemical
NBCC—nuclear, biological, chemical, and conventional
NCO—noncommissioned officer
NCOA—noncommissioned officer academy
NCOIC—noncommissioned officer in charge
NDAA—National Defense Authorization Act
NDSM—National Defense Service Medal

NFQ—not fully qualified
NGO—nongovernmental organization
NIMS—National Incident Management System
NJP—nonjudicial punishment
NORAD—North American Aerospace Defense Command
NRP—National Response Plan
NSC—National Security Council
NSI—nuclear surety inspection
NSPS—National Security Personnel System
O&M—operation and maintenance
OCA—offensive counterair
OCS—offensive counterspace
OHA—overseas housing allowance
OIC—occupational instructor certification
OJT—on-the-job training
OODA—observe, orient, decide, act
OPCON—operational control
OPLAN—operations plan
OPM—Office of Personnel Management
OPR—office of primary responsibility
OPSEC—operations security
OPSTEMPO—operations tempo
ORI—operational readiness inspection
ORM—operational risk management
OS—overseas
OSC—on-scene commander
OSD—Office of the Secretary of Defense
OTS—Officer Training School
P2—pollution prevention
PA—Privacy Act
PACAF—Pacific Air Forces
PAFSC—permanent Air Force specialty code
PCA—permanent change of assignment
PCS—permanent change of station
PD—position description
PDA—personal digital assistant
PDMRA—post-deployment; mobilization respite absence
PDS—permanent duty station; personnel data system
PECD—promotion eligibility cutoff date
PED—personal electronic device
PERSTEMPO—personnel tempo
PES—promotion eligibility status
PFMP—Personal Financial Management Program
PFW—performance feedback worksheet

PHA—preventive health assessment
PIF—personnel information file
PII—personally identifiable information
PIN—personal identification number
PKI—public key infrastructure
PL—protection level
PL1—Protection Level 1
PL2—Protection Level 2
PL3—Protection Level 3
PL4—Protection Level 4
PME—professional military education
POC—point of contact; privately owned conveyance
POM—program objective memorandum
POV—privately owned vehicle
POW—prisoner of war
PPBE—planning, programming, and budgeting and execution
PPO—preferred provider option
PR—program review
PSN—promotion sequence number
PT—physical training
PTDY—permissive TDY
PTSD—posttraumatic stress disorder
R&R—rest and relaxation
RA—resource advisor
RAM—random antiterrorism measure
RAP—recruiters assistance program
RCM—Rules for Court Martial; responsibility center manager
RIC—record of individual counseling
RIF—reduction in force
RIP—report on individual personnel
RMS—resource management system
RNLTD—report not later than date
ROE—rules of engagement
ROS—report of survey
ROTC—Reserve Officer Training Corps
SA—substance abuse
SAC—Strategic Air Command
SAM—surface-to-air missile
SARC—Sexual Assault Response Coordinator
SAV—staff assistance visit
SBP—survivor benefit plan
SCG—security classification guide

SCM—summary court-martial
SCPD—standard core personnel document
SEA—senior enlisted advisor
SECAF—Secretary of the Air Force
SECDEF—Secretary of Defense
SEI—special experience identifier
SEJPME—Senior Enlisted Joint Professional Military Education
SEL—senior enlisted leader
SF—standard form
SGLI—Servicemembers Group Life Insurance
SII—special interest item
SITW—state income tax withholding
SJA—staff judge advocate
SKT—specialty knowledge test
SLA—special leave accrual
SMSgt—senior master sergeant
SMTP—simple mail transfer protocol
SNCO—senior noncommissioned officer
SNCOA—SNCO Academy
SOAR—Scholarships for Outstanding Airmen to ROTC
SOF—special operations force
SPCM—special court-martial
SPD—standard position description
SQR3—survey, question, read, recall, and review
SrA—senior Airman
SRB—selective reenlistment bonus
SRC—survival recovery center
SRID—senior rater identification
SROE—standing rules of engagement
SRP—Selective Reenlistment Program
SSB—Special Separation Bonus
SSgt—staff sergeant
SSN—social security number
SSS—staff summary sheet
STEP—Stripes for Exceptional Performers
TA—tuition assistance
TAC—Tactical Air Command
TACON—tactical control
TAFMS—total active federal military service
TAFMSD—total active federal military service date
TA—tuition assistance
TDP—TRICARE Dental Program
TDY—temporary duty

TEMSD—total enlisted military service date
THC—tetrahydrocannabinol
THR—target heart rate
TI—training instructor
TIC—toxic industrial chemicals
TIG—time in grade; *The Inspector General*
TIM—toxic industrial material
TIS—time in service
TJAG—The Judge Advocate General
TLA—temporary lodging allowance
TLE—temporary lodging expense
TOS—time on station
TPR—TRICARE Prime Remote
TSCO—top secret control officer
TSgt—technical sergeant
TSP—Thrift Savings Plan
TT—treatment team
TTM—treatment team meeting
TTP—tactics, techniques and procedures
UCC—unit control center
UCCI—United Concordia Companies, Inc
UCMJ—Uniform Code of Military Justice
UFPM—unit fitness program manager
UGT—upgrade training
UIF—unfavorable information file
ULP—unfair labor practice
UMD—unit manning document
UN—United Nations
UPRG—unit personnel record group
URE—unit review exercise
US—United States
USAAF—United States Army Air Forces
USAF—United States Air Force
USAFA—United States Air Force Academy
USAFE—United States Air Forces in Europe
USAFSE—United States Air Force supervisory examination
USC—United States Code
USCAAF—US Court of Appeals for the Armed Forces
USCENTCOM—United States Central Command
USEUCOM—United States European Command
USG—US Government
USJFCOM—United States Joint Forces Command
USNORTHCOM—US Northern Command

USPACOM—US Pacific Command
USSOCOM—US Special Operations Command
USSOUTHCOM—US Southern Command
USSR—Union of Soviet Socialist Republic
USSTRATCOM—United States Strategic Command
USTRANSCOM—United States Transportation Command
UTC—unit type code
UTM—unit training manager
UXO—unexploded ordnance
VA—Veterans Affairs; victim advocate
VCJCS—Vice Chairman, Joint Chief of Staff
VEAP—Veterans Education Assistance Program
vMPF—virtual military personnel flight
VO2—volume of oxygen
VSBAP—voluntary stabilized base assignment program
VSI—voluntary separation incentive
WAAC—Women's Army Auxiliary Corps
WAC—Women's Army Corps
WAPS—Weighted Airman Promotion System
WEAR—we are all recruiters
WG—wage grade
WL—wage leader
WMD—weapons of mass destruction
WMP—war and mobilization plan
WOC—wing operations center
WR—war reserve
WS—wage supervisor
WWI—World War I

Terms

Abuse: The intentional, wrongful, or improper use of government resources. Abuse typically involves misuse of rank, position, or authority.

Aerospace Power: The synergistic application of air, space, and information systems to project global strategic military power.

Air Force Members: All active duty officers and enlisted personnel serving in the United States Air Force.

Air Force Personnel: All civilian employees, including government employees, in the Department of the Air Force (including non-appropriated fund activities), and all active duty officers and enlisted members of the Air Force.

Alignment: Dress and cover.

Attrition: The reduction of the effectiveness of a force by loss of personnel and materiel.

Capital Case: An offense for which death is an authorized punishment under the Uniform Code of Military Justice.

Chain of Command: The succession of commanding officers from a superior to a subordinate through which command is exercised.

Coalition: An ad hoc arrangement between two or more nations for common action.

Coalition Force: A force composed of military elements of nations that have formed a temporary alliance for some specific purpose.

Coherent: Sticking together; a logical relationship of parts. Paramilitary and military measures, short of overt armed conflict, involving regular forces are employed to achieve national objectives.

Cohesion: The act, process, or condition of cohering: *exhibited strong cohesion in the family unit.*

Command and Control (C2): The exercise of authority and direction by a properly designated commander over assigned and attached forces in the accomplishment of the mission.

Compromise: The known or suspected exposure of clandestine personnel, installations, or other assets or of classified information or material to an unauthorized person.

Conflict: A fight; a battle; struggle.

Contingency: An emergency involving military forces caused by natural disasters, terrorists, subversives, or by required military operations. Due to the uncertainty of the situation, contingencies require plans, rapid response, and special procedures to ensure the safety and readiness of personnel, facilities, and equipment.

Continuum: A continuous extent, succession, or whole, no part of which can be distinguished from neighboring parts except by arbitrary division.

Convening Authority: Commanders, usually above the squadron level, who have the authority to order a court-martial be conducted. The convening authorities consult with the staff judge advocate, determine if trial by court-martial is appropriate, and refer the case to a court-martial which they have created and for which they appoint the judge, court members, as well as the trial and defense counsels.

Correctional Custody: The physical restraint of a person during duty or non-duty hours, or both, imposed as a punishment under Article 15, Uniform Code of Military Justice, which may include extra duties, fatigue duties, or hard labor.

Counterair: A US Air Force term for air operations conducted to attain and maintain a desired degree of air superiority by the destruction or neutralization of enemy forces. Both air offensive and air defensive actions are involved. The former range throughout enemy territory and are generally conducted at the initiative of the friendly forces. The latter are conducted near or over friendly territory and are generally reactive to the initiative of the enemy air forces.

Cover: Individuals align themselves directly behind the person to their immediate front.

Dereliction of Duty: The willful neglect of your job or assigned duties.

Deterrence: The prevention from action by fear of the consequences. Deterrence is a state of mind brought about by the existence of a credible threat of unacceptable counteraction.

Distance: The prescribed space from front to rear between units. The distance between individuals in formation is 40 inches as measured from their chests to the backs of the persons in front of them.

Doctrine: Fundamental principles by which the military forces or elements thereof guide their actions in support of national objectives. It is authoritative but requires judgment in application.

Dress: Alignment of elements side by side or in line maintaining proper interval.

Echelon: A subdivision of a headquarters.

Element: The basic formation; the smallest drill unit, comprised of at least 3 individuals, but usually 8 to 12 persons, one of whom is designated as the element leader.

Endorser: The evaluator in the rating chain designated to close out the EPR. The minimum grade requirements vary depending upon the ratee's grade.

Espionage: The act of obtaining, delivering, transmitting, communicating, or receiving information about the national defense with an intent, or reason to believe, that the information may be used to the injury of the United States or to the advantage of any foreign nation.

Esprit de Corps: Devotion and enthusiasm among members of a group for one another.

Evaluator: A general reference to any individual who signs an evaluation report in a rating capacity. Each evaluator must be serving in a grade or position equal to or higher than the previous evaluators and the ratee. **Note:** A commander who is junior in grade to the rater will still review the enlisted performance report (see AFI 36-2403).

Exploitation: Taking full advantage of success in battle and following up initial gains, or taking full advantage of any information that has come to hand for tactical, operational, or strategic purposes.

File: A single column of individuals placed one behind the other.

Fiscal Year: A 12-month period for which an organization plans to use its funds. The fiscal year starts on 1 October and ends on 30 September.

Forensic: Relating to, used in, or appropriate for courts of law or for public discussion or argumentation. Of, relating to, or used in debate or argument; rhetorical. Relating to the use of science or technology in the investigation and establishment of facts or evidence in a court of law: *a forensic laboratory*.

Forfeiture of Pay: A type of punishment where people lose their entitlements to pay for a specified period of time.

Fraud: The intentional misleading or deceitful conduct that deprives the government of its resources or rights.

Functional Area: Duties or activities related to and dependent upon one another.

Grievance: A personal complaint, by a civilian employee, related to the job or working environment and subject to the control of management. This term also includes any complaint or protest based on either actual or supposed circumstances.

Guide: The Airman designated to regulate the direction and rate of march.

Half staff: The position of the flag when it is one-half the distance between the top and bottom of the staff.

Hardware: The generic term dealing with physical items as distinguished from its capability or function, such as equipment, tools, implements, instruments, devices, sets, fittings, trimmings, assemblies, subassemblies, components, and parts.

Hyper-vigilance: The condition of maintaining an abnormal awareness of environmental stimuli, post-traumatic stress syndrome, marked by symptoms like frequent nightmares and repetitive anxiety dreams, insomnia, intrusive disturbing thoughts, *hypervigilance*, and being easily startled.

Information Superiority: The capability to collect, process, analyze, and disseminate information while denying an adversary's ability to do the same.

Information Warfare (IW): Any action taken to deny, exploit, corrupt, or destroy an adversary's information and information functions while protecting friendly forces against similar actions and exploiting our own military information functions.

Infrastructure: A term generally applicable to all fixed and permanent installations, fabrications, or facilities for the support and control of military forces.

Installation Commander: The individual responsible for all operations performed by an installation.

Intelligence: The product resulting from the collection, processing, integration, analysis, evaluation, and interpretation of available information concerning foreign countries or areas.

Interdiction: An action to divert, disrupt, delay, or destroy the enemy's surface military potential before it can be used effectively against friendly forces.

Internet: An informal collection of government, military, commercial, and educational computer networks using the transmission control protocol/internet protocol (TCP/IP) to transmit information. The global collection of interconnected local, mid-level, and wide area networks that use IP as the network layer protocol.

Interrogation: Systematic effort to procure information by direct questioning of a person under the control of the questioner.

Interval: Space between individuals standing side by side. Normal interval is one arm's length. Close interval is 4 inches.

Joint Force: A general term applied to a force composed of significant elements, assigned or attached, of two or more military departments, operating under a single joint force commander. See also joint force commander.

Joint Force Air Component Commander (JFACC): The joint force air component commander derives authority from the joint force commander who has the authority to exercise operational control, assign missions, direct coordination among subordinate commanders, redirect and organize forces to ensure unity of effort in the accomplishment of the overall mission. The joint force commander will normally designate a joint force air component commander. The joint force air component commander's responsibilities will be assigned by the joint force commander (normally these would include, but not be limited to, planning, coordination, allocation, and tasking based on the joint force commander's apportionment decision). Using the joint force commander's guidance and authority, and in coordination with other service component commanders and other assigned or supporting commanders, the joint force air component commander will recommend to the joint force commander apportionment of air sorties to various missions or geographic areas.

Joint Force Commander (JFC): A general term applied to a combatant commander, subunified commander, or joint task force commander authorized to exercise combatant command (command authority) or operational control over a joint force. See also joint force.

Joint Operations: A general term to describe military actions conducted by joint forces, or by service forces in relationships (such as support, coordinating authority), which, of themselves, do not create joint forces.

Joint Task Force (JTF): A joint force that is constituted and so designated by the Secretary of Defense, a combatant commander, a subunified commander, or an existing joint force commander.

Logistics: The science of planning and carrying out the movement and maintenance of forces. In its most comprehensive sense, those aspects of military operations that deal with design and development, acquisition, storage, movement, distribution, maintenance, evacuation, and disposition of materiel; movement, evacuation, and hospitalization of personnel; acquisition or construction, maintenance, operation, and disposition of facilities; and acquisition or furnishing of services.

Military Operations Other Than War: Operations that encompass the use of military capabilities across the range of military operations short of war. These military actions can be applied to complement any combination of the other instruments of national power and occur before, during, and after war.

Military Strategy: The art and science of employing the armed forces of a nation to secure the objectives of national policy by the application of force or the threat of force.

Mitigation (of offense): To lessen or attempt to lessen the magnitude of an offense.

Multinational Operations: A collective term to describe military actions conducted by forces of two or more nations, typically organized within the structure of a coalition or alliance. See also alliance, coalition, and coalition force.

National Strategy: The art and science of developing and using the political, economic, and psychological powers of a nation, together with its armed forces, during peace and war, to secure national objectives.

Non-appropriated Activity: An activity associated with the government, but whose operation is not directly funded by the government; that is, the NCO open mess, officers open mess, and child care center.

Non-appropriated Funds: Funds generated by Department of Defense military and civilian personnel and their dependents and used to augment funds appropriated by the Congress to provide a comprehensive, morale-building welfare, religious, educational, and recreational program, designed to improve the well-being of military and civilian personnel and their dependents.

Operational Chain of Command: The chain of command established for a particular operation or series of continuing operations.

Operational Control (OPCON): The transferable command authority that may be exercised by commanders at any echelon at or below the level of combatant command. Operational control is inherent in combatant command (command authority). Operational control may be delegated and is the authority to perform those functions of command over subordinate forces involving organizing and employing commands and forces, assigning tasks, designating objectives, and giving authoritative direction necessary to accomplish the mission. Operational control includes authoritative direction over all aspects of military operations and joint training necessary to accomplish missions assigned to the command. Operational control should be exercised through the commanders of subordinate organizations. Normally this authority is exercised through subordinate joint force commanders and service and/or functional component commanders. Operational control normally provides full authority to organize commands and forces and to employ those forces as the commander in operational control considers necessary to accomplish assigned missions. Operational control does not, in and of itself, include authoritative direction for logistics or matters of administration, discipline, internal organization, or unit training.

Period of Supervision: The number of calendar days during the reporting period that the ratee was supervised by the rater.

Permissive Reassignment: A permanent change of station at no expense to the government where an individual is given consideration because of personal reasons. Individuals bear all costs and travel in leave status.

Personnel Reliability (PR): A commander's determination of an individual's trustworthiness to perform duties related to nuclear weapons.

Physiological: Having to do with the physical or biological state of being.

Precedence: Priority, order, or rank; relative order of mission or operational importance.

Qualification Training: Actual "hands-on" task performance training designed to qualify an individual in a specific duty position. This portion of the dual channel OJT program occurs both during and after the upgrade training process. It is designed to provide the performance skills required to do the job.

Rank: A single line of Airmen standing side by side.

Rater: The person designated to provide performance feedback and prepare an enlisted performance report (EPR) when required. The rater is usually the ratee's immediate supervisor.

Rations in Kind: The actual food or meal.

Reconnaissance: A mission undertaken to obtain, by visual observation or other detection methods, information about the activities and resources of an enemy or potential enemy; or to secure data concerning the meteorological, hydrographic, or geographic characteristics of a particular area.

Repatriation: The procedure whereby American citizens and their families are officially processed back into the United States subsequent to an evacuation.

Sensitive Information: Data requiring special protection from disclosure that could cause embarrassment, compromise, or threat to the security of the sponsoring power. It may be applied to an agency, installation, person, position, document, materiel, or activity.

Software: A set of computer programs, procedures, and associated documentation concerned with the operation of data processing system, such as compilers, library routines, manuals, and circuit diagrams.

Special Operations (SO): Operations conducted by specially organized, trained, and equipped military and paramilitary forces to achieve military, political, economic, or psychological objectives by unconventional military means in hostile, denied, or politically sensitive areas. These operations are conducted during peacetime competition, conflict, and war, independently or in coordination with operations of conventional, non-special operations forces. Political-military considerations frequently shape special operations, requiring clandestine, covert, or low-visibility techniques, and oversight at the national level. Special operations differ from conventional operations in degree of physical and political risk, operational techniques, mode of employment, independence from friendly support, and dependence on detailed operational intelligence and indigenous assets.

Staff Judge Advocate (SJA): The senior legal advisor on the commander's staff.

Strategy: The art and science of developing and using political, economic, psychological, and military forces as necessary during peace and war, to afford the maximum support to policies, in order to increase the probabilities and favorable consequences of victory and to lessen the chances of defeat.

Subversive: Anyone lending aid, comfort, and moral support to individuals, groups, or organizations that advocate the overthrow of incumbent governments by force and violence is subversive and is engaged in subversive activity. All willful acts that are intended to be detrimental to the best interests of the government and that do not fall into the categories of treason, sedition, sabotage, or espionage will be placed in the category of subversive activity.

Tactical Control (TACON): Command authority over assigned or attached forces or commands, or military capability or forces made available for tasking, that is limited to the detailed and, usually, local direction and control of movements or maneuvers necessary to accomplish missions or tasks assigned. Tactical control is inherent in operational control. Tactical control may be delegated to, and exercised at any level at or below, the level of combatant command.

Tactics: The employment of units in combat; the ordered arrangement and maneuver of units in relation to each other and or to the enemy in order to use their full potentials.

Terrorist: An individual who uses violence, terror, and intimidation to achieve a result.

Theater: The geographical area outside the continental United States for which a commander of a combatant command has been assigned responsibility.

Under Arms: Bearing arms.

Unmanned Aerial Vehicle: A powered, aerial vehicle that does not carry a human operator, uses aerodynamic forces to provide vehicle lift, can fly autonomously or be piloted remotely, can be expendable or recoverable, and can carry a lethal or nonlethal payload. Ballistic or semiballistic vehicles, cruise missiles, or artillery projectiles are not considered unmanned aerial vehicles.

War: Open and often prolonged conflict between nations (or organized groups within nations) to achieve national objectives.

World Wide Web (WWW): Uses the Internet as its transport media and is a collection of protocols and standards that allow the user to find information available on the internet by using hypertext and/or hypermedia documents

Find more professional military reading at
GIPubs.com

We have been producing & selling leadership tools and working with the largest distributor of professional military books and digital media for 10 years. Our products are a great fit for your unit library. The titles we carry can be used to enrich professional development classes, grow Soldiers into Leaders, and help you complete your mission as efficiently as possible. Don't forget those special gift occasions such as; promotions, NCO induction ceremonies, and NCO/Soldier of the Quarter.

Much of this information cannot be found in regulations and what is available in the regs is often difficult to find. Use our years of counseling and leadership experience to your advantage!

The GiPubs Advantage:

- Years of experience working with and shipping directly to military units and individuals
- Most orders ship within 1 business day
- We proudly ship Priority Mail to APO/FPOs
- Our business is strictly focused on military products, and we know our stuff
- Courteous and knowledgeable customer support

Air Force Uniform Tool

From the creators of the Wear It Right! guidebooks, comes the greatest thing to happen to your next inspection. Everyone wants to look sharp in their dress uniforms. Unfortunately, even the shiniest insignias won't impress your commander if they're in the wrong spot. That's why we created this wallet-sized tool to help you position your insignias, medals, and ribbons as accurately and neatly as possible.

Wear it Right!
U.S. Air Force Quick Reference Book

Tired of looking through AFI 36-2903 for answers to uniform and dress questions? Here's your solution! No more searching through a bulky AFI just to get the basics. A great pocket guide for Airmen and Leaders.

A quick reference for: Service Dress, Mess Dress, Formal Dress, Semi-Formal, Battle Dress, Maternity Uniforms, and Physical Fitness Uniforms

Tongue and Quill

Tongue and Quill was produced by the Air Force to improve writing and speaking skills. Although there are many reference to the Air Force in this publication that does not mean the information conveyed only applies to those in the Air Force. This publication is also a helpful resource for those in the Army, Navy, Marines, Coast Guard, educators and students, and civilian corporations around the United States.

Find other great Air Force titles here: **GIPubs.com/air-force.html**

available at www.GIPubs.com

PDG
★ ULTIMATE ★

Ready for more?

4 different study modes

1,700 Questions

Includes quizzes *and* flashcards

Page references for each question

Effective and affordable

Learn more at AirForceCounseling.com/PDG-Ultimate